The Practical

to

Social Welfare Research

Douglas Robertson

and

Alan Dearling

RHP

Russell House Publishing

First published in 2004 by:
Russell House Publishing Ltd.
4 St. George's House
Uplyme Road
Lyme Regis
Dorset DT7 3LS

Tel: 01297-443948
Fax: 01297-442722
e-mail: help@russellhouse.co.uk
www.russellhouse.co.uk

© Douglas Robertson and Alan Dearling

British Library Cataloguing-in-publication Data:
A catalogue record for this book is available from the British Library.

ISBN: 1-898924-93-7

Typeset by TW Typesetting, Plymouth, Devon
'Pink Pills' cover artwork by Hannah Lise Robertson
Printed by Arrowsmith, Bristol

About Russell House Publishing

RHP is a group of social work, probation, education and youth and community work practitioners and academics working in collaboration with a professional publishing team.
Our aim is to work closely with the field to produce innovative and valuable materials to help managers, trainers, practitioners and students.
We are keen to receive feedback on publications and new ideas for future projects.
For details of our other publications please visit our website or ask us for a catalogue. Contact details are on this page.

Contents

List of Diagrams, Figures and Tables

Acknowlegements

In drawing together the material for this book we are indebted to a number of people who gave generously of their time to ensure that we were properly informed of good research within their specialist areas. Colleagues in the Department of Applied Social Science, at the University of Stirling provided information on social work, housing, criminology, dementia, disability, young people, drugs and health matters. To have all these areas covered, within one University Department, is truly unique, and helps explain why the University of Stirling is at the forefront of social welfare research. So thanks to Isobel Anderson, Johnston Birchill, Julie Brownlie, Alison Bowes, Jochen Clasen, Susan Eley, Ruth Emond, Angus Erskine, Vernon Gayle, Christine Hallett, Nicola Illingworth, Ian McIntosh, Gill McIvor, Cathie Murray, Laura Piacentini, Sam Punch, Fiona Russell, Duncan Sim, Kristine Stalker, Mary Taylor, Jim Valentine, Reece Walters and Rowdy Yates. Alan, during the gestation of the book, worked with colleagues at universities including Brunel, Luton, Goldsmiths and the LSE and is grateful for ideas and material provided by colleagues. He is particularly grateful to Phil Bayliss at the University of Plymouth for generous friendship and support.

Finally, we would both like to thank John Perry and the Chartered Institute of Housing for their support of this publication, and Martin Jones, at Russell House Publishing, for his patience.

Douglas Robertson and Alan Dearling
May 2004

Preface: How This Book Came About

Knowing where a piece of research, or the researchers themselves are 'coming from' is a crucial consideration in evaluating the worth of any study. As authors our primary contention is that there is no such thing as 'value free' research, and this is especially true within the broad range which encompasses social welfare research. All research carries with it the 'bag and baggage' of either the author's or the commissioner's values. Research is not generated in a vacuum, but rather is the consequence of a variety of pressures, some of which can be competing. Instead research can either happen as a result of considered planning, chance, or through responding to challenges or opportunities. It is typically more than a matter of 'problem solving' or 'solution finding'. To understand a particular piece of research requires a thorough and careful consideration of the contexts in which it has been generated, then undertaken and finally acted upon. Research can be generated in response to a specific problem. It can also be used to delay the demand for action on a particular problem or issue. Research can be used to inform and explain, but equally it can also distort and manipulate. Further, the results of any research can be open to a variety of interpretations, some of which will receive more attention than others.

This book has its origins in a previous text – *Looking into Housing: A Practical Guide to Housing Research* (Robertson and McLaughlin, 1996) – which was specifically designed to assist housing practitioners undertake or commission research. Douglas Robertson, co-authored that book, with Alan Dearling acting as production editor on behalf of the Chartered Institute of Housing. As such Alan offered ideas and advice for some of the sections, as well as commenting on the overall structure and purpose of the book. As a result of extensive editing and re-writing, plus drawing on the particular backgrounds and perspectives of the two authors, this book evolved. So, although a significant amount of the core information on research techniques is common to both books, the context is entirely different. While the previous focus was solely on housing research, from a management perspective, this book adopts a people and welfare services focus.

Douglas Robertson is Director of the Housing Policy and Practice Unit, at the University of Stirling. Prior to coming to Stirling he worked as a Senior Housing Plan Officer with the City of Glasgow District Council and previously as a Research Fellow at the University of Glasgow, where he completed his PhD thesis on the city's extensive tenement improvement programme. His teaching responsibilities cover housing finance, housing renewal and research methods. Douglas also has extensive research experience carrying out commissions for a wide variety of organisations including the Office of the Deputy Prime Minister, Department of Environment Transport and the Regions, the Joseph

Rowntree Foundation, Scottish Homes and various local authorities and housing associations. As Director, Douglas has responsibility for managing the Unit's overall research strategy. His current research interests include the reform of flat ownership laws, through comparing the practices adopted in other countries; reform of the English housing buying system; accessing the impact of local strategies for housing renewal; and tracing the recent history of the Scottish planning system. In relation to comparative research he recently co-ordinated the European Network of Housing Researchers' Working Group on Urban Renewal in Older Housing.

His most recent publications reflect these research interests. The work on flats, carried out with Katherine Rosenberry, resulted in the report *Home Ownership with Responsibility*; the work on planning policies produced an article for *Planning Perspectives*, entitled 'Pulling in opposite directions: the failure of post war planning to regenerate Glasgow', and another for *Scottish Affairs* on Community Planning; while a commission for Scottish Homes, again with Nick Bailey, resulted in a research report entitled *Review of the impact of Housing Action Areas* and an article for *Urban Studies* entitled 'Housing renewal, urban policy and gentrification'. Douglas has also produced an audio housing field trip around Glasgow for SHARE, the Scottish housing association's training organisation, and an exhibition tracing the history and achievements of Glasgow's community based housing association entitled *'People's Palaces'*. Both these ventures were funded as part of Glasgow 1999: Year of Architecture and Design.

Alan Dearling's background has been in youth and community work, youth justice, youth social work and housing. His publications and training work span most sectors of the voluntary and statutory social services sector. He worked for nearly ten years for the Scottish Office, at the Intermediate Treatment Resource Centre, as a publications and training officer. Since 1988 he has been a commissioning editor, researcher and publisher working for Longman, Pitman, the Chartered Institute of Housing, the Joseph Rowntree Foundation and Russell House Publishing. His work primarily focuses on the field of youth and community work; social work; housing and health. From 1991 to the present, he has also worked as a part-time research fellow and consultant for the University of Wales College at Cardiff, Brunel University, Luton, Goldsmiths University and the London School of Economics. His twenty-plus publications are eclectic, ranging from *Effective Use of Teambuilding*; *The Social Welfare Wordbook* and *Making a Difference: young people and community safety*; through to *Youth Action and the Environment*, *No Boundaries: New Travellers on the Road (Outside of England)* and *Another Kind of Space: creating ecological dwellings and environments*.

The contents of this book, therefore, represent a synthesis of the two authors' distinct backgrounds and professional careers. As a result, the book utilises a diverse range of selected research examples, which cover most of what could be termed 'people services'. The book aims to engage and involve the reader in the range of research processes which they may need to employ in carrying out their day-to-day work. There is also a challenging discussion on the politics and ethos of research and its potential for damage and delay, as well as the contribution research can make to progressing or understanding the various elements contained within any social welfare topic. Finally, the authors have sought to present a selection of relatively new social research techniques and processes, many of which focus on methods to involve and empower members of the communities being researched. Overall, it is hoped this approach will be both helpful and appropriate for those undertaking or commissioning research within the rapidly evolving worlds of social welfare.

Research Issues

What is research, and why do we do it?

All of us engage with research, in one way or another. Have you not taken part in a consumer research study, answering questions posed by an interviewer in the street, or filled in your Census form once every 10 years? Research also impinges on our work, via audit, restructuring or a performance review, typically conducted by, or commissioned for senior management. The basic statistics we compile in carrying out our job are often collected and used to provide insight into how a service or agency is performing. And every day we are exposed to the results of the latest public attitude survey detailing the popularity or otherwise of policies, personalities or products.

Yet, just how many of us feel confident enough to challenge the basis of how these 'facts' have been constructed?

- What exactly was the question that was asked?
- How many people were interviewed?
- How was the sample draw up?
- Who exactly carried out the work?
- What did those funding the study want to get from it?

Given that we all engage with, and are affected by the consequences of the many research studies undertaken, it is crucial we properly understand what goes into the research process. This is even more critical when you work in an area like social welfare and the 'people-services', in general, which are constantly subject to a wide range of different types of research study. The aim of this book is to ensure you gain that expertise, and appreciate the process of research, as well as the climate in which it is produced.

The book is designed to encourage you and your colleagues not to simply accept that research is *per se*, a good thing, but rather to provide you with the means to question the thinking that formulated particular research questions and then enable you to critically assess the methods adopted to answer these questions. In essence, we are providing the means for you to be a stakeholder in social welfare research. In order to do this you need to understand how research questions get framed, what methods can be employed to address specific questions and then, how the research process is managed to ensure it generates the information necessary to answer these particular questions. Careful consideration of the assumptions and theories that are employed when devising questions, deciding upon the information to be collected and how that data will be subsequently analysed are all equally relevant. Research is, after all, defined as being the systematic collection and subsequent interpretation of information through the application of a particular hypothesis or theory. So what exactly does this mean?

Information is the crucial building block in any research exercise. Yet, merely amassing good quality information will never, in itself, produce a coherent and rigorous piece of research. Information or data needs to be systematically collected and subject to robust analysis and interpretation. To do this properly the researcher's conception and understanding of the issues involved is as important as their understanding the range of research tools and methods. This understanding, in turn, influences both the data collected and its subsequent analysis and interpretation. Those conducting research and those responding to it, therefore, both need to have a range of appropriate skills. For instance, a grasp of the environment and community(ies) in which particular issues exist, is often vital, especially in the field of social welfare. Just as important is a solid understanding of how research should be formulated, then executed. This book provides suggestions on how to appreciate both objectives.

In an ideal world, research should be conducted to enhance and improve our understanding of a particular issue or event. Yet, if research is badly designed, or poorly undertaken it can diminish that understanding and even disempower the people being researched. There are also occasions when research is specifically employed to obscure or divert understanding because of the political or personal motivations of funding or commissioning bodies. Appreciating the motivation behind a specific piece of research is also an important consideration when judging the worth and value of the subsequent published work.

To help you understand and appreciate the various dimensions of the research process this book helps you consider:

- The raison d'être behind the planning of new research.
- The various mechanisms that help determine the type of research questions posed.
- How the specific focus of a research study is decided.
- How and why specific methods and approaches are adopted.
- How to develop research tools that involve and empower users.
- How models can be employed for testing and comparison purposes.
- How and why the belief systems and backgrounds of researchers can influence research findings.
- What checks and fail safe procedures need to be built into a specific programme of research work.
- What skills are required to properly examine and analyse the collected research data.
- How both the dissemination and use of research work is controlled.

To guide you through this range of issues the book is divided into three distinct, but related sections. The first of these, **Planning the project** takes you through the entire research planning stage. Whether undertaking the study yourself, or commissioning the work from someone else, it is crucial that you understand and appreciate the issues that arise at the various planning stages. **Putting a project together** provides a comprehensive review of the different methods that can be applied to answer your particular research questions. The final section, **Finishing off the project** covers the critical data evaluation and analysis stages, stressing the importance of theorising. The section concludes by looking at the various ways the resulting study can be presented.

Throughout this book we have provided relevant practical examples of research projects to illustrate the range of particular research issues. Some of this material is cited in the traditional way, with a reference provided to the source of the research. Others have been paraphrased or anonomised because not all the work referred to provides an example of 'best' practice. Certain examples are used to illustrate just how easily things can and do go wrong. Learning from others' mistakes always proves insightful. Helping you to understand what is necessary in order to undertake a robust piece of research is our ambition. Letting you appreciate the implications of not achieving this goal is also illustrated. Hopefully this book will improve your ability to both undertake and evaluate research in whatever area of social research you work in.

What is social welfare?

Before going any further it would be helpful to provide some understanding of what we consider to constitute *social welfare*. Essentially this is a catch all term which embraces the broad provision of what used to be known as the *personal social services*. As such it covers all the statutory and voluntary services provided for families and children; care in the community provision; education; employment; the law and legal services; housing; immigration and nationality, as well as benefits and welfare advice. From its foundations in the Christian voluntary movements of the nineteenth century, welfare provision was gradually augmented through the emergence of a substantial statutory sector in the first half of the twentieth century, during the birth years of the so-called 'welfare state'. From the 1960s onwards a new type of specialist services, often in the volunteering sector, pioneered work with marginalised groups such as the homeless, mentally ill, drug takers and single parents. More recently, with the creation of a purchaser provider split in the delivery of many social welfare services, private business concerns have also become significant providers.

Together it constitutes a big list and the professional groups which are encompassed range from youth and community workers, social workers, teachers, housing professionals, care workers, doctors, nurses, psychologists, community health workers, social security staff and employment benefits staff, through to probation officers, prison staff, police and the court officials. Within this spectrum, and around the margins, there are many specialist workers whose specific job remits are often defined by the problems they are employed to tackle: drugs workers, child protection workers, community relations staff and benefits advisors, to name but a few. Then there are the significant numbers of volunteers, often unqualified, who work in areas such as after-school clubs, youth work, tenants' associations, charity shops and ancillary services.

Added to this list are all the higher and further education establishments who are responsible for much of the pre- and post-qualification training for staff working in the social welfare field. Then there are the senior administrators, whether from central or local government, or the voluntary sector, who are often engaged in policy evaluation and future service development. At times this, and other operational aspects of social welfare provision also involve elected representatives in local and central government, and committee members who manage the wide variety of voluntary projects. While the above represents an exhausting list, it is certainly not exhaustive!

What is social welfare research?

Given the above, social welfare research would best be described as a broad church, which draws on a number of distinct intellectual disciplines. Social welfare research is a real world activity that involves the various professionals working in the innumerable activities embraced by social welfare provision. Given this context, research should not be viewed as a discrete professional activity, but rather as part of the everyday work carried out by all these professions. While there is clearly a role for professional researchers, it is also important to enhance the skills of workers who, as part of their day-to-day work, will take responsibility for some aspect of research within their organisation. It is particularly important in the social welfare field, that research is an inclusive, rather than an exclusive activity, and one that embraces those receiving the various services as well as those doing the providing.

More often than not social welfare research is characterised as being 'applied' rather than 'pure'. This means that typical, everyday types of research:

- Evaluate the quality, quantity and efficiency of the service provided.
- Develop a policy case for strategic interventions at an international, national, regional, local, organisational, departmental or project level.
- Detail organisational needs, often in a funding and resources context.
- Identify specific needs by calculating possible numbers of service users.
- Assess the range of needs exhibited by these potential service consumers.
- Offer a description of a particular project, or agency, established to address a specific need, or needs.
- Assess the particular behaviour and attitudes displayed by clients.
- Identify and plan for possible responses to 'problems' which may be exhibited in systems, groups, geographical localities or by individuals.
- Monitor performance against defined targets, plans and corporate statements.

- Attempt to determine the 'costs' and 'value' of that service, or services.
- Propose revisions in priority setting, decision-making and established aims through amending mission statements, strategic goals and measured objectives within a business plan or operational review context.
- Involves and empowers the consumers of the services to engage with the future policy, management and practice of welfare service provision.

Looking at the typical research undertaken in another way, we can see how specific types of applied research focus on different parts of the social welfare operation. Using Bulmer's (1984) categorisation of research types, social welfare research focuses primarily on specific problem-orientated studies, action research, plus intelligence and monitoring rather than basic social science or strategic social science. That is not to say that some of the applied work undertaken does not contribute to the further development of these broader research types. Also some research undertaken within the social welfare context can merit such a categorisation. However, problem-orientated studies are the mainstay of social welfare research.

Priority setting, problem solving, evaluation and appraisal of the work carried out by a range of different organisations have always been core activities for social welfare services. In each of the examples, noted in the table below, the basic building blocks to conduct each of these research tasks relies heavily upon data derived from case work notes or the day-to-day operational information collected by staff in organisations such as the police, health, housing or social services. In this context, the research produced is almost invariably problem-centred, or applied, but that's not to say it is not influenced to some degree by theory.

Practice and theory

What is termed 'pure' research relates directly to a limited number of academic disciplines. Sociology, anthropology, economics, psychology, social and political theory are perhaps the most pertinent and important in the field of social welfare. Within each of these fields there is a plethora of relevant theoretical and methodological approaches, for instance, positivism, Marxism, structuralism, symbolic interactionism, feminism, critical theory, social action and post-modernism. As a result, there are competing 'theories', 'models' and 'perspectives' that exist within each theoretical tradition, all of which can significantly influence the nature and focus of the final research product. In academic circles this is often termed as the construction of competing paradigms.

Those commissioning a particular piece of research may demand the adoption of one such perspective, or another, when constructing and then subsequently analysing and interpreting the study results. Positivism, for example, would demand that an empirical study should generate numbers so that the instances of certain occurrences or observations can be measured to reveal cause and effect relationships. It is also the case

Typical Examples of Social Research Activity

Why we do it, and what do we want to achieve?	What are the possible consequences?	What are the Pros?	What are the Cons?
Establish partnerships, e.g. crime and disorder partnerships	'Top down' action with organisations monitoring effectiveness – focus on process	Effective change of management in service delivery	Possibly disempowering for both staff and users
Look for ways to achieve behaviour change amongst potentially problematic consumers of services e.g. refugees, drug takers, alcoholics	Finding solutions and successful praxis to social problems	May alleviate or prevent social problems occurring	Can provide a 'quick fix' without lasting impact
User groups, e.g. tenants, young people, mental health clients, ethnic minorities in specific special needs groups	Assessment of needs and risks acts as a means to make and maintain contact with clients	Identifies individual needs and may help to prioritise overall services delivery	May cause stereotyping or labelling. There may also be problems of cultural and personal sensitivity as well as confidentiality issues
Data analysis of clients and actions taken with them, e.g. community-based sentencing and care orders	Helps informs policy	May enhance both professional practice and service delivery	Can lead to mechanistic decisions and actions
Identification of means of empowerment of special needs groups, e.g. disabled, single mothers, older people	'Bottom up' if appropriately organised can provide an assessment of what is a need, or desire (so called wants list)	Can mix and match a personal welfare service delivery tailored to individual needs	May actually lead to confusion over what constitutes needs and wants
Profiling of local areas to highlight services and the gaps	To gain resources for local areas, or organisations or departments	Can provide a springboard for funding applications such as through SRB or SIPs bids	May divert precious staff time away from core tasks
Examining the long term future of existing projects to assess their effectiveness and value	Can provide a test of effectiveness and best value through the application of instruments such as performance indicators	Can highlight the value of a project and improve staff and user morale, as well as identifying and justifying the need for new initiatives	May be used as a legitimising tool to close down short-term funded projects

that professional training often imbues people with distinct theoretical perspectives and these, in turn, can colour and delimit their understanding and appreciation of the issue under question. By adopting a structuralist perspective on childcare Parsons and Bales (1955) argued that societies needs demanded that women should remain at home in order to carry out child rearing. Researchers adopting a feminist perspective are likely to argue a different perspective. Being aware of the implications of adopting one theoretical or methodological perspective or another is always an important consideration in assessing the value of any research.

Theory has much value in a research context. For example, in adopting a sight analogy, when a blind person has their sight restored they are initially unable to comprehend what they see. It takes time for them to build up an understanding of the relevance of different visual stimuli. In the very same way, theory and methodologies provide a framework of relevance and understanding to those undertaking research work. At the same time, the adoption of one theoretical framework will necessarily both help and hinder understanding. While certain patterns and relationships might be revealed, we have to ask, are these of relevance and value? Other theories will place the emphasis elsewhere. Taken together, overall understanding may also be enhanced, or may be obscured. Social research, for Ravn (1991, 112), is '*an activity recognized by many as not just unveiling the facts but as constructing them*'. Theory plays an important role in this process.

While this is not a book about theoretical models of social research, it is important to reach some basic level of understanding as to how theory and practice interact. Some approaches to research adopt an explicitly theoretical perspective, in that they take on a specific theory and then test it against evidence drawn from the 'real' world. Studies of suicide often adopt a theory to explain national patterns and then set about collecting data to test the robustness of the theory. Others opt to start from observations and data collection, then use this material to construct a theory. The recent work of McColgin et al. (2002) in conducting in-depth interviews with people with dementia in order to construct a theory of their social competence provides a classic example. This is often referred to as *grounded theory* and is the common approach in social welfare studies (Glasser and Strauss, 1967; Strauss and Corbin, 1997). Appreciating the significance and usefulness of a theory, or hypothesis is critical to research, as it is this which distinguishes research from mere data collection.

Research is often employed to evaluate the various dimensions of a particular problem and then provide options to remedy or ameliorate the impact of that problem. As all research is conducted within a politicised environment, it is also important to understand the influence of social, economic and political processes in the framing, execution and reporting of research. This is the climate in which research is produced: research is never conducted within a cultural vacuum. Properly conducted research should, as a result, detail and where necessary challenge existing belief structures, rather than accept them as the norm. If such challenges do not occur, then the existing social structures within society will merely become enshrined within the research undertaken, and be considered the norm (Young, 1991). For social welfare research, such extreme forms of 'ethnocenticism' are to be avoided. This is the practice whereby other groups or cultures are measured against a personal, social or cultural 'yardstick'. In social welfare research this has often helped to reinforce the notion of the 'deserving' and 'undeserving' poor within our society. Comparative research, the examination of how similar issues and behaviours are tackled in another location, jurisdiction or country can be a useful tool in identifying differences and similarities, and thus help us to better understand the prevalent social climate as well as the power of cultural and ethnic influences.

Research and managerialism

As will be evident from the research examples provided previously there has long been a link between applied research and the management of social welfare services. Internal or external monitoring, outcome evaluation studies of the day-to-day work of specific services or projects are the standard means of assessing whether such services are meeting the goals set down for them. Such work utilises both quantitative data (numeric information detailing the numbers using the services, or the time taken to process a particular claim) or qualitative data (information which provides insight as to how individuals themselves view the quality of the service provided). In recent years, with the ambition of public policy in this area being to separate the provider from the purchaser of services, in order that the rigours of the market are brought to bear on the delivery of welfare services, such exercises have become numerous and ever more tightly proscribed. In pursuing an 'efficiencies and effectiveness' agenda, government, and its associated funding bodies, have been at the forefront of establishing performance indicators and associated performance measures covering a whole range of welfare services.

The move to performance audit probably first appeared in relation to the community care sector. The pre registration and post inspection of residential homes was linked to the establishment of basic minimum standards, set down by the Registered Homes Acts of 1984 and 1991 (Bland, 1996). The Centre for Policy on Ageing, which had published optimal standards in its *Home Life* publication in 1984 (Centre for Policy on Ageing, 1984) then went on to issue further supplements in 1988, 1992 and 1993. Increasingly, local authorities and care homes themselves adopted quality assurance procedures linked to a more in-depth audit utilising performance indicators. The acquisition of BS 5750 ISO 9000 and other so-called 'kite marks' such as 'Investors in People' and the 'Citizen's Charter' are also very much part of this performance audit culture which in turn stems from Quality Assurance and Quality Management (Gupta and Docherty, 1998). Data collection and its analysis is one crucial means of showing that your organisation is meeting its prescribed targets.

Audit tools are now commonly built into legislation. In July 1998, for example, the government, in announcing its *New Deal for Regeneration*, stated that this programme would be subject to monitoring against Audit Commission defined efficiency standards. Similar performance indicators were developed for the *Healthy Communities* initiative and others were embedded in the Crime and Disorder Act, 1998. Public policy now operates within an audit culture that demands that those charged with the service delivery meet certain defined targets. Housing organisations are now required to operate to performance standards which, in England and Wales, are defined by the Audit Commission, and in Scotland by Communities Scotland (Audit Commission, 2002; Communities Scotland, 2001).

Research has played a major role in defining appropriate performance standards and then measuring subsequent organisational performance against these. In this context, the role of research is often to act as an arbiter of 'success' or 'failure' and has been a key component in setting the agenda for organisational change. Research can be utilised to justify or challenge current service patterns, or modes of operation. The results or findings of such work appear in committee reports, management plans and annual performance reports and then become the 'objective' basis for re-allocating resources to justify service reforms. Much of this output is not produced by the staff who are responsible for delivering these services themselves, rather it is originated by outside consultants. Given the potential repercussions that often arise from such studies, serious strains can emerge between those subjected to an evaluation exercise and those charged with carrying out the task. The rapid growth of performance audit has also meant that collecting, analysing and reporting on operational data has now become a routine task within all social welfare services. This, in turn, means that those working in the social welfare field have a clear interest in ensuring a rigorous and objective research process.

Time and time again, individual projects or programmes have been criticised for not having in place detailed records or descriptive accounts of what exactly has been undertaken during a specific period of time. Without such evaluative material it is impossible to assess whether the aims and objectives originally set for the project have been achieved. Such criticism is usually voiced when an outside evaluation is being undertaken, typically to support the case for continued funding. Having appropriate data collection systems in place, in order to generate evaluative information, is now seen as critical to the decision-making process in social welfare.

There is, however, much debate within social welfare circles as to whether such information and associated measures, as currently constituted, provide an appropriate measure of actual performance. Is the emphasis not heavily weighted on quantitative data that details the efficiency of managerial monitoring systems and, crucially, financial considerations, rather than qualitative data detailing the actual quality of care provision itself? (Allen, 1995; Kemeny, 1992). Do they indeed reflect day-to-day operational efficiency, or merely an ability to meet easily measured targets? This represents a challenge to all those engaged in social welfare work, and the policy and research community in particular.

Research and users

While research has a long association with the management of social welfare services, using research to better understand the needs and desires of service users has only recently become a feature in the planning and evaluation of service delivery. Techniques employed to elicit such perspectives include participatory appraisal, focus groups and co-counselling interviews. Broadening the focus of research to ensure that the experiences and opinions of users are accorded a distinct and separate voice from those providing the service represents a major shift in emphasis. The policy drive to ensure that a distinct customer focus becomes core to the delivery of all public services in large part explains this shift of emphasis (Rodger, 1999; Kirky, 1999).

While collecting and analysing performance data can provide some insight into user experiences of the services, new research agendas have recently emerged which seek to engage directly with the vulnerable, disadvantaged and, sometimes, quite badly damaged people who constitute so much of current service provision. Rather than accept the workers or managers interpretations of the users' experiences, research is now being asked to engage directly with users themselves. This development has major implications for the researchers, and critically those subject to the research. Dearling (1997; 1998) provides a simple example of gaining this perspective through interviewing a drug recidivist. He showed that 'Bert' had a perfectly clear view that prison wouldn't change his drug-taking behaviour nor his views on the subject, a perspective that might not be shared by the prison staff.

There is also another factor that needs to be carefully considered within a social welfare setting and that is, the threat the researcher may pose to those being researched. As many users of services are marginalised, they don't trust officialdom. Welfare staff, in turn, are often fearful themselves of management's intentions. Therefore, when constructing any user focused research, the researcher must *'convince the people that he or she does not represent a threat to their well-being and must be as honest as possible about the aims of the research'* (Howard, 1989: 54).

All researchers need to gain the trust of those they are working with. While this can be relatively straightforward, within a professional staff context, building trust and understanding with users can take much longer to achieve, if it happens at all. Yet, without such trust and understanding between the parties then it is difficult, if not impossible, to enter into any meaningful research dialogue. This imperative creates a series of issues which researchers not only need to be aware of, but have strategies in place to accommodate such demands within the research design. Critically, in this regard, an appreciation of the ethical basis on which any research with, about and for people should be fully appreciated.

To illustrate this point, just consider what impact research on domestic abuse has on the victims asked to recount their experiences in detailed interview sessions? While such information would be crucial to better understanding user needs in, for example, a women's refuge, the personal cost in recounting such experiences could represent a high price for an individual to pay in order to access such data. The twin issues of disclosure and confidentiality are also germane within this ethical context. Overall, it is important to consider what exactly is the value of the study to the commissioner, the researcher and those being researched? This is discussed in greater detail when the following chapter considers the issue of ethics. That said, if users are a core element in the study, then it seems only reasonable for those conducting the work to adopt methods which include, as a major element, a proper appreciation of the lives and experiences of those who are being 'researched'. Assessing how best to achieve this ambition is always an extremely challenging exercise. For some years certain researchers have argued for researchers to be pro-active in this process and to 'take sides' with user/user groups (Becker, 1967; Robson, Begum and Locke, 2003). Major external funders of social welfare research such as the Joseph Rowntree Foundation now specify that they expect user involvement to be a core feature of the research they fund. In their guide to prospective researchers it states, '*The Foundation has a commitment to exploring ways of ensuring that people central to the research are involved in, and empowered by, the experience*' (Joseph Rowntree Foundation, 1997: 1).

This stated ambition represents a considerable challenge, which should not be underestimated. User involvement in social welfare research can be a very empowering process to users when it helps challenge and perhaps change certain preconceptions held by the commissioners or researchers, leading to an enhanced understanding of the issue or their particular perspective. Yet, does enhancing user involvement in the specification of research not equally run the risk of compromising the study's robustness and objectivity? If the users advising the research study are uncomfortable with a particular line of questioning, or a particular research approach, should this automatically invalidate its use? When the requirement is to empower users and minimise the harm that can be done to communities subjected to research then the challenges are even greater, and the question arises are researchers best placed to offer such empowerment? Finally, researchers such as Gelsthorpe have suggested that the researchers' own perceptions are 'part' of the research. She argued that her interaction with the research subject was essential, '*I was concerned to record my experiences and interactions with prison, rather than so called "objective observations"* '(Gelsthorpe, 1990: 95).

All research is the product of negotiation and compromise between the various affected parties. Enhancing the power position of one party has great value if that particular perspective has generally been ignored. User involvement on these grounds has a lot to commend it. However, achieving a balance of views and perspectives from the various parties is certainly not easy to achieve.

Research, bias and distortion

At various points in this book ideas about how you should best 'construct' a research project are offered. This term is, however, used advisedly, given that the majority of social welfare research involves a process of negotiation between individuals and organisations. Each of these 'players' has both power and influence on the research process, and some have far greater power to influence than others. The players in this context include those funding the study and those carrying out the actual work. Those who are the subject of the research itself do play a role, but unless an active user approach is adopted this can often be passive.

Funders of large-scale studies tend to be the government, in one of its multi-various guises, as well as charities and research bodies. As large scale funders they tend to draw up distinct programmes of research which are designed to address topics that they consider to be of some importance. Clearly, in the case of the government, their research funding, in the main is used to support stated policy objectives. The charities and research bodies are also strongly influenced by government's policy agenda, with much of their funding seeking to support and influence government thinking and spending. However, they also have a role in trying to encourage government to take on fresh ideas.

Voluntary and statutory agencies tend to fund smaller scale studies, many of which have a direct operational and/or user focus. It is also the case that these bodies use their limited research resources to try and highlight issues which they feel government should be pursuing. Research, in this context, is often used to support overt campaigning purposes. Such organisations also employ the results of specific research studies to support funding proposals. Providing objective evidence of demand is becoming commonplace within what has become a highly competitive funding environment.

At the other end of the financial and influence stakes are individual researchers, who are generally undertaking their own studies; typically they are an academic pursuing their own research interests, or a student undertaking a dissertation, thesis or project. The worth of this research should never be undervalued. Given the lack of obligations to funders these studies can be more objective and often focused on topics often ignored by mainstream funders. It is this work which often helps change the direction of research and policy, feeding ideas up to the mainstream funders.

Those who carry out the work, the other partners or players, include: consultancy and academic institutions, specialist individual consultants and academics; contracted field-work or polling organisations; interested individuals, students and social welfare staff of every description. The working relationship between the players, funders, researchers and subjects is typically set down in a research brief. Such a document should:

- Specify the topic/subject to be researched.
- Establish the aims, method and research design, with anticipated outcomes and a timeframe for completion.

- Include any bids for funds, either through internal or external channels.
- Detail tendering, commissioning and contracting procedures, where required.
- Outline the case for the study, utilising the key bibliographic sources.
- Provide details of any specific moral or ethical issues which they think the researcher should address.
- Outline access arrangements to key data sources for any secondary analysis.
- Specify an agreement required between the funder and researcher as to what data collection instruments and associated fieldwork procedures should be employed.
- Specify similar procedures in relation to project management and monitoring procedures.
- Detail any preferences for the focus of data analysis.
- Outline the procedures for commenting on the draft findings.
- Specify the final report format and the requirements for any associated presentations and publications.
- Within a policy and practice context it may also detail a potential policy response timeframe, such as when the study is needed for a particular committee, conference, or whatever.
- The procedures that will apply when conducting a final project evaluation.

Setting down the research questions, the prime focus of interest, is undoubtedly the critical construction task. This, in large part, determines subsequent decisions about who gets invited to bid for, or do the research, what budgetary constraints apply and what 'strings' should be attached to the funding. The brief also details the client/contractor management arrangements. This baggage, or what social researchers refer to as their 'bricolage', is to a greater or lesser extent part and parcel of conducting any research study, and it clearly has a bearing on the final product.

It is also the case that the research equation is often significantly influenced by 'other' external factors. The brief often highlights a bias on the part of the commissioner. For instance, researchers are frequently faced with examining a problem that has been defined by the commissioner, reflecting their particular viewpoint or prejudice. Such questions are often hard to research, are certainly not value-free, and are problematic given the various dimensions of the problem or issue under scrutiny. At the same time it is also worth considering whether there can truly be an unbiased question. The word bias assumes there can be something that is unbiased and neutral, and that within a social welfare context is difficult to conceptualise. That is not to say there is not distortion and deception. This, in part, reflects the fact that the raison d'être for so much applied research is pragmatic, a reaction to situations as and when they arise, rather than being part of a considered and prolonged programme of investigation. This often means that the wrong question gets posed; one that is more a reaction to pressure, than a considered examination of the issue to hand. Alternatively, the right question can be in place but, due to constraints of time or money, the study can only ever hope to skirt around the topic. Local and national politicians, with their powerful associated bureaucracies, also have an expectation that research will provide agreed 'answers', 'solutions' or 'quick fixes' to the problems they have identified. Often these very same administrators also have a clear vision of what would constitute the required solution, and an expectation that the research will endorse this. Research, in such circumstances, is rightly viewed as a legitimisation tool for decisions that have already been taken, and as such hardly merits the label of 'research'.

The outcome of any study is determined by the weight attributed to different aspects of the evidence, as selected and interpreted by the researcher. Yet, from what we've already outlined, it is also the case that certain elements in this equation are often pre-determined by the initial construction process, the results of which are detailed in the brief. All funding organisations want 'value' from the research they pay for and this may lead them into an expectation that their organisational assumptions, strategic plans, ideologies or perspectives should take pre-eminence in the resulting study. The old adage *'who pays the piper calls the tune'* has some resonance in this context. Commissioning organisations can have a great deal riding on the results of a research study, hence their desire to control and if necessary manipulate the findings. That said, such pressure may not be explicit, but may be more implied with the various parties not always totally aware of the respective power and influence they hold. By introducing very significant distortion, prejudice and unwarranted assumptions right at the start the value of the whole exercise is undermined.

Recipients of research briefs, therefore, need to be alert to possible omissions in the conception of the research question. They also need to be alert to potential bias in how the work required of the study has been specified. The same goes for the consumers of research reports. If the initial conception is flawed, then this will impact on how the subsequent work is executed and how the results are presented. The construction of any research project can pose real dilemmas, and you need to be alert to them.

Given this backdrop there are occasions when a researcher might decide they are unwilling to undertake such a tightly prescribed commission. In other contexts the researcher may not have that luxury. If your line manager instructs you to undertake the work, as prescribed, then there may be little you can do about it. Academic institutions are often characterised as providing 'independent', 'objective' and 'impartial' research, whereas consultants may be viewed as being more amenable to meeting the clients' wishes. Yet, university researchers and their associated departments, in common with private consultants, now have research income targets to meet. Academic institutions are measured not only by the status of the different research projects undertaken, but also by the top line figure generated by their research activities. In such a competitive environment securing research monies can easily become the goal, rather than the nature of the commission itself. As should be obvious by now research is a commodity; a product that can be bought from a variety of suppliers. It is, therefore, far from being a uniform commodity given the marked potential for the wide variety of suppliers to deliver a very varied and different product. A survey reported in a 'lad's' magazine can provide one take on young male sexuality, quite another might emerge from a detailed study carried out by a respected academic institution.

In trying to minimise the influence of distortion, all parties, whether planning, executing or reacting to any research study need to be alert to its possible presence. Distortion acts to warp the actual research process and ultimately leads to false conclusions being drawn. However, it should also be acknowledged that completely eliminating such distortion is an impossible task. It is important to appreciate that all research is relative, in that one person's 'truth' is not necessarily shared by another. As one eminent social scientist put it, as researchers we all *'implicitly or explicitly, attribute a point of view, a perspective, and motives to the people whose actions we analyse'* (Becker, 1998: 14). We are all 'blinkered' one way or another for a variety of reasons and this affects our view and perspective on particular issues and society. In effect, as researchers, we are all part of the research. This issue is considered more fully in the subsequent section on reflexivity.

It is important not to dismiss the variety of perspectives that can be brought to bear on a particular research study, but instead try and appraise their respective value. Being alert to the presence and influence of distortion, then taking the appropriate steps to address such influences represents an important starting point in trying to improve the quality of any research. Undoubtedly, the most biased research is that which does not recognise its potential for distortion. Yet, on the other hand, the most committed research which explicitly states its belief structure, may produce some of the most illuminating research findings within a social welfare setting. This is particularly so where understanding behaviour and motivation is often of paramount importance. *'Dispelling stereotypes and myths'*, as Kimmel calls it (Kimmel, 1988: 23).

Research and politics

The hidden agendas, prevalent in so many research exercises are more often than not about control, and within the social welfare field this frequently has a distinct political dimension. It is also important to remember there are, embodied in most research studies, underlying and fundamental elements which can be traced back to ethos and ideology. Some of this was touched on in the earlier discussion of theory.

Political agendas are also often linked to media interest and can have a marked impact upon the framing of research questions in relation to crime, homelessness, drug use, sexual behaviour, gender, child abuse, ethnic minorities and more recently asylum seekers. The prevailing social, economic, political and moral climate of our society, as articulated by politicians and journalists, tends to determine what is considered an acceptable and unacceptable line of research enquiry, particularly when public funding is involved.

Additionally, there are well-articulated international, national and local perspectives which again help frame the parameters of any study conducted on what are portrayed as 'contentious' or 'controversial' topics.

Official attitudes towards drugs' policy provide a useful illustration of how such influences can impact on a specific research agenda. At different times in the last 20 years policy makers involved in drugs work have backed the funding of studies which have examined systems and methods to prevent, or reduce drug trafficking; approaches to reducing the effects of drugs as a nuisance at the community level; harm reduction approaches for working with drug users; and the effectiveness of drug education strategies. Such research operates in a highly politicised environment where adopting the high moral ground against drug use is the norm. The government sponsored 'Drugs War' and 'Scotland against Drugs' organisation and its populist 'Just say no' campaign which ran throughout the late 1990s all provide classic illustrations of this stance. Researchers working in this environment could not easily make a case to legalise some drugs, as one means of reducing street crime levels, given the direct link between drug users and petty crime. Such a stance, which has been argued by some senior police officers and certain drug workers, and is advocated by comparative research in countries such as the Netherlands (South, 1999; Marlow and Pearson, 1999), could herald an end to a researchers' credibility in carrying out officially backed studies in this field. Consequently, political expediency may be one of the most powerful determinants in such decision-making processes. That said, the drugs' research community in Scotland did play a key role in challenging the value of the 'Just say no' strategy given ever increasing drug use. 'Drug facts', the replacement campaign, effectively abandons the strict abstentionist position and instead advocates a harm reduction perspective, attempting to educate possible users about the health impacts drug use can have (Scottish Executive, 2002).

Research and reflexivity

As a researcher it is critical to understand your version of the truth will not be the only truth. In any research undertaken you will choose to lay emphasis on different elements and issues within the study. The decisions that underpin these choices will be very much influenced by your own personnel knowledge and experiences. It is also the case that no one individual has the capacity to look in all directions at once: we are not, metaphorically speaking, flies. It is, therefore, impossible to take account of all the possible perspectives in any one study. Rather what we do is to use our particular insights and perspectives to focus on what we consider to be the critical elements of the study, choices which are largely determined by our own particular 'bag and baggage'. It is this, which very much influences the way we address the specific research question. Also by observing phenomena, we engage in a process of making sense of it by inductive reasoning and reflection.

Kemeny (1992) makes a useful observation in relation to data, in that by itself it has no meaning. Meaning only occurs when the researcher captures and sets the data in context. Capta, the term employed to data with a meaning, cannot become such until you, as the researcher, capture and create its meaning. Fielding and Gilbert (2000), takes this point further by warning researchers about the dangers of employing secondary data, such as official statistics, in their own studies. When using secondary data it is important to know who has collected it, and for what purpose, because this has distinct influence on the presented data. Data, in itself, cannot be value free. Two researchers constructing their own studies of youth homelessness will collect their own data, and they are likely to also put their own particular interpretation on any official data collected on the subject. That, in turn, influences the results of their research. As Blumer (1969) notes, we all have a tendency to shape the world to fit our theories.

In constructing a piece of research it is important to acknowledge your own predilections, for as a researcher you are never 'value free'. This term implies that the researcher has a responsibility to ensure that they conduct any study in a totally neutral fashion, ensuring personal bias, or ideology does not contaminate the study. Traditionally, there has been a belief that the results of research should be objective: not unduly biased by the views of the researcher, or the organisation funding the study. More recently, a counter view has emerged which argues that 'value free' research is utopian and, quite unrealistic. Clearly the beliefs and attitudes of the researcher, and those of any commissioner, cannot be eliminated and will have an influence on their research. After all, such beliefs and attitudes have helped determine the choice of subject, and the subsequent adoption of a specific research method. So a more accurate position is that the selection of the topic is 'value relevant', both to the researcher's values and/or the values of any funders. 'Value relevance' should not be confused with trying to achieve 'value free' research. Those that argue against the 'value free' perspective suggest the adoption of a 'reflexive' position, whereby ideology and perspective are clearly indicated throughout the work, thereby sending clear signals to the reader that this research has been influenced in this particular way.

As a researcher you are not after 'the' truth because, given your own particular and unique background, your truth will differ from the truth as viewed by others. As a researcher you can never conduct research without reference to yourself, so multiple truths exist. Yet, that is not to imply that in research anything goes. There are distortions and lies that can be exposed by undertaking competent rigorous research. What reflexive practice seeks to do is make you aware of your own influence on the research you undertake and particularly on your interpretations.

The 'bag and baggage' you carry around influences how you will address an issue. It is now generally accepted that those undertaking research need to think carefully about the contents of this 'bag and baggage' and think how this might impact on the execution of the research work. Only once you have properly considered these issues can you then set in place measures to address, own up to and explain or counter balance such influences. For example, in examining the experiences of minority ethnic groups, would the research be enhanced by employing researchers who have a similar background to those being researched? Would a white middle class, middle aged male have much understanding and appreciation of the life experiences of minority ethnic groups? Would this lack of understanding not impact on the way the specific research questions were structured, and as a result distort the outcome of the eventual interviews? As Blumer (1969) so aptly put it, researchers often do not have an intimate acquaintance with the area of life under consideration. Further, would the presence of a particular researcher not potentially restrict the information being provided, or produce results which the interviewee thought the researcher would want to hear? If someone with the same ethnic background constructed the interview questions and carried out the interviews would a more comprehensive set of responses be produced? Then again, is there a danger here that such an approach could exaggerate and thus distort the responses? Reflexivity can become an almost philosophical process, but none the less important in so far as it encourages us to challenge our assumptions and praxis.

Researchers make a whole range of decisions when conducting a research study and, in doing so, this impacts on the study. Appreciating how researchers understand and experience the world is a part of the actual research work they undertake, and is central to the notion of reflexivity. You do need to recognise and reflect on your capacity to affect your research, and then make that transparent to the reader by alerting them to these potential influences and distortions. As an aside, it is also the case that only through conducting research can we learn and develop our understanding of the issue under examination. This, in turn, affects how we choose to examine and execute future research. It should also be pointed out that within sociology, reflexivity has another distinct meaning, namely the potential influence research has on the subject matter of the original research. Once published, social research can be read by the original research subjects. In turn, this might influence their future behaviour and undermine the validity of the original findings.

Understanding, knowledge and power

Through reading this introduction to social welfare research you will have quickly realised that, rather than being some cosy academic enclave, research is something that may be very important to your day-to-day work. We participate in and are affected by the consequences that arise from research. You will also have begun to see that for research to be of any value, it has to be undertaken in a competent and professional manner. Being aware of the research process, how exactly research gets formulated, is crucial to understanding whether such professionalism has been achieved.

In the following section the various stages in formulating the research question and selecting appropriate methods to address that question are more fully considered. In planning the project the various influences and pressures discussed so far have to be resolved, or at least considered. The assumptions and theories employed to provide structure and references need to be set down, as are the final research questions and the information required to properly answer that question. Our background and training will have an influence on these decisions, and that influence is something we need to be aware of. The expectations of research, either set by yourself or those funding the work, is also a consideration. Bias and distortion are easy to introduce into a study, but they will only produce a poor piece of work that will not be good research. However, the continual process of reflection is enhanced when researchers are honest about how they exert influence over the situation and the people being studied. So, once again, there are tensions between the pursuit of 'objectivity' and the need for researchers to understand the highly complex nature of social interactions, culture and the environment in which such interactions take place. Finally, in order to meet other defined objectives, it is important to be aware of the various agendas that any study seeks to serve. Understanding the process of research puts you in a strong position to challenge the validity and worth of certain studies and also to defend your own methodology. Understanding through knowledge is always power in the right hands.

Planning the Project

Part One of this book introduces you to research design, detailing each stage that needs to be properly considered prior to embarking on any research exercise. To a degree this planning exercise mirrors the work that goes into planning a holiday. When deciding on your next summer break you probably want to consider all the possibilities. Taking that analogy some destinations start out as favourites, given you may have visited them before or friends have recommended them. Others locations will be entirely new, demanding background research via holiday brochures and travel books. Having read up on these different places and opted for one location, you then need to decide how to get there and what to do once you arrive. It may be that you need to reconsider your initial choice of destination given the complexity of the travel arrangements, the quality of available accommodation or the lack of activity choices once you get there. Time and money constraints also play a major role in this later decision making process. Then there are the practicalities to consider, the passports to check, the money to find, currency to order and the clothes and sun cream to buy.

In involving yourself with the research process there are also a number of time-limited decisions required and a similar set of choices exist. In framing research questions you or colleagues need to carry out a fair amount of background reading in order to become acquainted with the subject and methods in hand. It may well be the case that the questions you want answered have already been considered by other researchers, with the results being published. Reading published work on the same topic may also set you off thinking about other more fruitful ways of addressing the questions. Through carrying out this background research, your choice of questions may change, or at least be further refined. As was noted in the introduction, it is often the case that you are asked to get involved in a research project that is ill defined, or not addressing the right questions. By undertaking this background reading, a more focused and useful set of research objectives should emerge and you are better equipped to challenge research inconsistencies.

Matching research methods to research questions is a vital element in the planning process. Some research methods, such as basic secondary data analysis, questionnaires and interviews may be familiar to you. It is also likely that other less familiar methods would be more helpful in addressing your particular questions. So once again, it is important to consider the full range of research methods open to you. Different skills are required to undertake different research methods, and these take time and effort to learn by you or your research team. In addition, there are also pre-planning and timing considerations that need to be thought through. Each method has its benefits as well as its possible drawbacks which again demand careful deliberation. It may well be the case that one approach, while producing good quality data, would be expensive in both time and money, so the 'next best' option may need to be substituted.

The second part of this book, **Putting a Project Together**, illustrates – with reference to actual relevant examples – each of the techniques commonly employed in social welfare research. Each individual chapter in Part Two considers one specific method. Each details which tasks they are best suited to addressing, listing perceived advantages and disadvantages. When deciding upon which method, or methods to adopt, it is crucial to have some idea of the work and staff time that will be involved in properly executing that approach, as well as any resulting consequences of adopting particular methodologies. While this part of the book provides a broad overview of the various methods, there is also an expectation that you or colleagues will read other more technical texts in order to gain a fuller understanding of exactly what is involved. The references found at the back of the book should provide a useful starting point for this additional reading.

In social welfare settings you will probably already know quite a lot about your subject, but in order to properly plan out and design your research you need to focus on the methods that are most appropriate. This will enhance the planning process and give you a clearer idea of the timescale necessary to carry out the work and, therefore, the costs. As with a holiday, it is only through careful planning that your original ambitions are tailored to meet the constraints imposed by the available time and money. Chapter One describes the key planning stages involved in designing a piece of social welfare research. It takes you through the entire research process, from refining the research questions through to publishing and presenting the final report. Only by fully appreciating what is required of your research can you possibly plan out how that is to be delivered. The more thought that goes into what is required, and what could go wrong, the better the end result. By anticipating possible problems, at an early stage, it is possible to address them and set in place appropriate contingency arrangements. Things can still go wrong but at least you will be better prepared.

Whether the work is being carried out by yourself, as part of a team, or is being contracted to outside consultants, the planning and design issues detailed in the following chapter are exactly the same. To properly undertake your own research work, or manage a research project being carried out by others, you always need to have a clear understanding of the research questions, the context for the research, and an appreciation of the research methods. Only through gaining this understanding and knowledge is it possible to ensure the research delivers on its defined objectives, within a realistic timescale and to budget. Chapter Two then considers the range of issues which need to be addressed when commissioning research from external consultants. A core consideration, in this context, is the need to draw up an enforceable contract, a document which largely emanates from designing a robust and considered research planning exercise.

CHAPTER 1

Planning the Research Process

> **CHAPTER OBJECTIVES**
>
> This chapter is designed to ensure that you:
> - Understand the various stages involved in planning out a research project.
> - Fully appreciate the significance of each individual element that makes up the research planning process.
> - Are able to utilise this planning approach to evaluate the worth of published research findings.

Introduction

The secret of achieving good research, as with many other activities, lies in its original conception, careful planning and good preparation. Conception is about design and vision, being able to define, and then further refine the specific research questions that you wish to address. Planning involves matching the demands set by the research questions to the available resources, whether these are financial, personnel or time. Put simply, planning represents a compromise between idealism – what you would really like to achieve – and pragmatism – what is possible within the constraints you have to work within. There is, for example, no point in planning a comprehensive study of youth homelessness in the UK if you don't have the time, personnel nor resources to properly carry this task through. Preparation is all about ensuring that all possible practical difficulties, which could impact on the execution of your research project, are fully considered and, if necessary, addressed as part of the project planning exercise. Again sticking with the example of youth homelessness:

- How would you gain access to the homeless records held by a variety of local authorities?
- Would all authorities be willing to allow you access to such data?
- What steps could you take to best ensure access to these records is achieved?
- What are the potential benefits, or disadvantages for young homeless people involved in the research?
- Are there ways in which the young homeless people could be involved in the planning or executing of the search?
- Do any data Protection Act restrictions apply?

Working out the answers to these questions, and then testing them, will largely determine whether the study is a starter or not. It is also important to recognise that the context of research within social welfare and the 'people services' must always be a central consideration when planning the process. Essentially, social welfare research will place much more emphasis on ensuring that research is planned *with* users and service providers. It also emphasises the fact that research about people, communities and service provision needs to avoid processes that are *done to* 'researched communities'. As far as possible, social welfare research should address ethical considerations. These are explored in greater detail within this chapter. Adopting methods of empowerment are critical in this regard.

Research design is a process that encompasses planning from its initial conception, through to its envisaged execution involving data collection, analysis and subsequent interpretation before, finally, reporting the anticipated results in some type of document. In conducting any research, each of these distinct phases needs to be carefully thought through, and then reconsidered holistically. If there are specific demands for disseminating the research, these are likely to have an impact on earlier planning phases. For example, if the research is needed to inform a committee decision, then the timing of that committee meeting will impact on the initial timescale for undertaking the research. If a particular audience has to be addressed, then the questions posed may need to reflect their specific interests in the study. For instance, in addressing the incidence of anti-social behaviour in a specific community the focus for the local community, the council, business interests and police may well differ. If a specific sample size is demanded, then the practicalities of ensuring that it can be achieved needs to be carefully considered. In conducting a study designed to examine and comment on existing procedures and associated work practices for dealing with supported accommodation placing, adequate time and resources would need to be planned to ensure a truly representative number of cases could be fully followed through. A small and potentially unrepresentative sample would produce only spurious results. Likewise the input of users as well as carers and managers requires forethought. Working the requirements out well in advance and having the necessary resources and timeframes built into the research, helps ensure such unsatisfactory results do not occur and that the remit is realistic and informs both policy and practice.

Too often the research task is viewed as being a set of incremental stages, with one leading on from another. In reality, the process of research is an inter-linked entity, holistic, where a lack of thought at an earlier stage can considerably diminish what is possible later on. The task set for this chapter is to ensure that you understand and appreciate the importance of undertaking a rigorous research planning exercise. The assumption here is that you will be involved in conducting a small-scale research project. However, if you are charged with the taking forward a major study, which could be commissioned from external consultants, you will require to go through exactly the same planning exercise. A fully thought through proposal, encompassing all the distinct elements of the project would still be required, even although you would not be personally carrying out the work. Understanding and appreciating the importance of each element of any research project is critical not only in designing an appropriate brief for the work, but it also ensures a framework for the subsequent project management once the work has started. Chapter 2 provides more detailed discussion of research commissioning and contract management. By fully understanding each part of the research process, as outlined in Figure 1.1 below, you can assess the significance of any published research findings to your own job, your workplace or the wider policy and practice environment.

The research process

Conducting research is a dynamic process and always needs flexibility in its application. However, without being mechanistic, it can be represented schematically as a continuum of twelve distinct stages. Each stage in this planning process is outlined within this chapter. Classifying each of these stages in this manner does not, however, imply that research planning, or the actual process of carrying out research, is either sequential or straightforward. The progression from one stage to the next is not always linear. In practice, the process usually involves many revisions of decisions already made, in light of later decisions. So if initial assumptions about how to conduct the study prove invalid, in light of preliminary investigations, then a revised or an entirely new approach might need to be developed. Alternatively, you may be forced to revise the specific focus of the research question if the initially proposed research method is considered unworkable. Depending on the nature of the specific research questions, research planning can become a very complicated and time-consuming exercise. It can, on occasions, resemble the old adage of 'one step forward and two steps back'. Hence, the importance of properly acknowledging the significance of the feedback loops, as detailed in Figure 1.1. Undertaking a series of revisions in light of reflection at all stages may seem tedious, but it will save considerable amounts of time, money and personal energy when the fieldwork part of the project is being undertaken. Just as important is the fact that, by working through the various issues thrown up at the planning and design stage, the quality of the final research findings and output should be greatly enhanced.

So the reality of research tends to be a far-more messy activity than the logical and rational sequence often detailed in the final report. When the research is being undertaken, the planning process continues in tandem to accommodate other changes and circumstances that were not fully considered during the initial planning exercise. As researchers involved in studying children noted *'doing research is a messy affair as dependent on negotiation, adjustment, personal changes and serendipity as on careful and meticulous preparation'* (James et al., 1998, 196). That should not, however, be taken as an excuse to skimp on the initial planning exercise, given things never quite work out as planned. Rather it is the exact opposite, namely that it is very important to try and plan

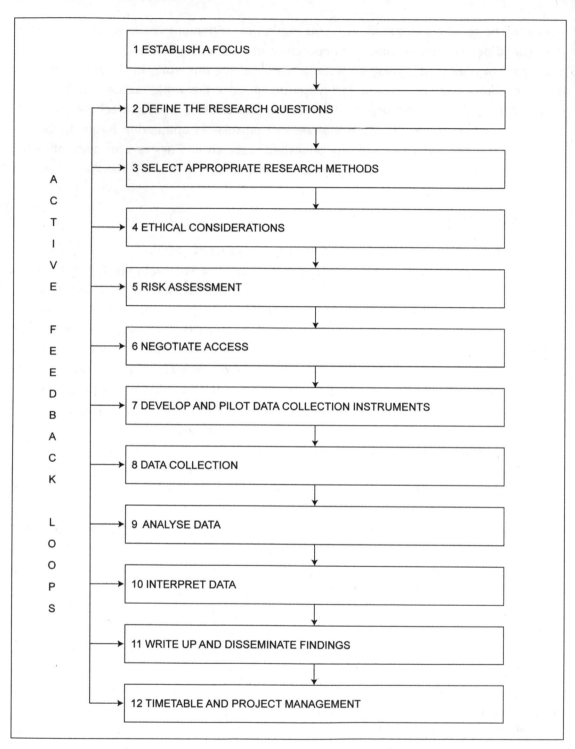

Figure 1.1: The research process

out, in a logical, sequential and comprehensive manner, all aspects of the envisaged research.

Establish a focus

Research design typically starts with a desire to try and find a way to answer a specific query, or help solve a particular problem. This can either emerge out of your own interests, or as an active response to service delivery problems. On other occasions, policy makers or managers need to update information on user patterns, cost, or performance. Beginning with a problem or query is frequently the starting point. Turning this into researchable questions is a different proposition. Only by adopting a clear focus for the envisaged study can a workable set of research questions emerge.

Initially, the questions or issues under consideration are likely to be very broadly defined and, as such, are not a suitable basis for focused research. In trying to focus the study, your aim should be to reach a position where specific research questions can be posed. To establish such a focus you will need to critically evaluate the sources of your current information and knowledge, then read around the topic, and decide whether this is indeed an area that would benefit from research. You might find that previous research has already answered the question you seek to answer. Alternatively, this reading may reveal that the problem was the consequence of a set of different factors entirely. This focusing should also help to identify the locations of relevant data and the people who would need to be considered for research, as well as potential research participants and partners. As an aid to illustrating how you establish a research focus the example of formulating a local youth homelessness research project is outlined.

Over the last decade, addressing homelessness, and youth homelessness, in particular, has been an important strand of public policy. In supporting this policy agenda a significant amount of research has been undertaken, both nationally and locally. It is also worth noting that a significant amount of this research work has been small scale and short term, so may be of limited value unless you are interested in the specific local context. In many cases, councillors on the social services committee will have instructed officials to report on the incidence of the youth homelessness and come forward with policy options to reduce this problem.

As the official charged with this task you would first need to read the published literature on the topic, to better understand why this type of homelessness occurs in the first place. Homelessness texts suggest that problems within the family, institutional child care failings and individual personal problems, often exacerbated by substance abuse, are major contributory factors in explaining the rise of youth homelessness (Kennett and Marsh, 1999; Fitzpatrick, 1999; Anderson and Tulloch, 2000; Anderson and Christian, 2003). Then there are the contributory influences of broader welfare policy changes that have, over the last twenty years, discriminated against young single people. Policy would appear to encourage young people to remain part of a conventional family setting until they are older, more mature and financially better equipped to set up their own home (Anderson and Morgan, 1997). Housing benefit and income support operate age restrictions, as does the national minimum wage. This all adds considerably to the difficulties of those who want to, or need to set up a home independently at a young age (Kemp et al., 1993). In addition, the demise of casual unskilled labouring employment in recent years, and a marked lack of employment opportunities for those with low academic attainment is another contributory factor (Maginn et al., 2000). Then there are the social and homemaking skills that need to be acquired, in order to sustain a viable tenancy, given that the lack of income makes owning a home an impossibility (Third et al., 2001). Finally, there is a significant problem inherent in identifying the full scale of youth homelessness since many young people will be effectively 'invisible', sleeping on friends' couches or moving to major centres such as London. Tracking any vulnerable group is a significant research issue (Green et al., 2001). Youth homelessness can be a result of the 'pull' factors, the bright lights and city life, as well as the 'push' factors already outlined.

Having gathered this background, much of which is well known, some of which is not, you and your colleagues then need to assess which of these factors is an influence on the youth homelessness problem locally. Are all these factors equally relevant, or do some have greater resonance in your particular area? In seeking answers to this question it would be helpful to sound out colleagues, as well as the views of other statutory and voluntary agencies, who work in this field.

The next stage is to try and outline the types of possible solutions. It is clear that simply finding suitable accommodation for young people to live in will not solve youth homelessness. Rather what emerges from the preliminary reading is a set of different contributory factors, some of which may be linked in the case of certain individuals, each of which demands distinct support needs. There are also a number of broader policy changes that could help alleviate the problem. While the local authority and various voluntary sector agencies can address some of the above issues, the broader social, economic and political factors are largely without their immediate control. This is not to say that any subsequent committee report would not highlight the impact of these broad policy issues in order that the council could formally raise them with government and other interested bodies in appropriate forums.

Accepting these constraints, but still seeking potential solutions, what other aspects of youth homelessness would you then wish to explore? One focus might be to examine the importance young 'runaways' have in adding to the homelessness problem (Wade, 2002). In this particular study, a representative sample of some 3,000 children, under 16 years of age, from six different parts of Scotland, were interviewed to ascertain their prevalence to running away from home. In addition, in-depth interviews were held with 37 'runaways' to discover their particular characteristics, experiences and needs. Interviews were also held with agencies involved in this type of work to get their perspective. The Scottish study, which was linked to a wider UK study, found little differentiation in teenage behaviour right across the UK. So the merits of working with schoolchildren, generally, or children more likely to be 'at risk', would be worth further consideration by any follow on study. Producing education packs on how to set up home and homelessness may, for example, have some merit. Also, putting 'leaving home' onto the school curriculum as part of the personal education process – as a natural course of events for most young people – is both desirable and destigmatising (Clark and Dearling, 1986).

Related to this would be a need to explore likely family backgrounds and the nature of family conflicts that help create young homeless people (Smith et al., 1998). In this qualitative study homeless young people were interviewed, across a range of household circumstances, whether living singly, with lone parents, or in larger family settings. Interviewing their parents complemented this, in order to gain some comparative perspectives. Family counselling and parenting skills are other potential avenues that need to be explored when looking for potential local policy responses. Developing responses to 'looked after' young people leaving care has been another focus for research. Most of those leaving care lacked core life skills, and 17 per cent of young women leaving care were either pregnant or were already mothers (Foyer Foundation, 1998).

Then there are the employment issues, and how specific projects designed to better prepare vulnerable young people for employment have faired (Maginn et al., 2000). This large scale national evaluation utilised a postal questionnaire survey, and then followed this up by conducting a number of local case studies on specific supported accommodation projects. The study had a particular focus on comparing how well foyer projects scored against other initiatives in assisting young homeless people back into work and independence. Interestingly, it found there was very little difference in the effectiveness of one type of approach or another. Again this may be something that could be pursued locally, with local employment initiatives being asked to focus on youth clients.

Finally, in the search for potential solutions there might also be some value in examining how other countries in Europe have gone about addressing this issue (Anderson, 2003; Arnstein, 2002; Edgar et al., 2002). In the UK local authorities often visit what they perceive to be successful foreign initiatives. The foyer model, for example, was originally developed in France, where there are some 450 foyers working with over 100,000 young people in any one year (Murray, 1995). Whether the cultural, social and political environments that operate in other countries make such policy transfer feasible is something the later chapter on comparative study will consider in greater detail.

So having spent time reading, talking and thinking about the broad range of issues and problems associated with youth homelessness you then need to narrow down the focus of your research. Clearly, you cannot be expected to research every aspect of the topic; that is neither the object of the exercise, nor is it realistic. Rather, you should try to narrow down the scope of the study to the point where you understand the broad parameters of the issue, and have identified how your specific interest can best be addressed, or not.

At this time, it would be useful to clarify just exactly what senior managers and policy makers expect from the research.

From what has been revealed by the literature review it may be that a report covering the generalities of the issue would suffice at this stage. Then you could suggest, in that initial report, that a basic monitoring exercise be instigated, over a fixed period of time, in order to determine the scale of the local youth homeless population and help reveal whether the problem is more representative of one particular aspect than any other. This could then constitute the first phase of the work, with the second stage focusing on the potential solutions to the actual homeless problem and needs of young people as uncovered by stage one. Having 'best practice' examples, gleaned from detailed case studies drawn from throughout the country, would be useful background. These might help both to focus and prioritise the nature of the research: highlight the likely problems to be encountered; and suggest potential solutions.

Having identified a strategy to address the problem in hand, you then need to give some thought as to the actual practicalities of conducting any proposed study. It is at this stage that you need to think about what scale of resources, in terms of time, finance and personnel, can be called upon to support this work. Given what you now understand about the issues, and the nature of potential solutions, would this be sufficient to do justice to the research you think is required? If the budget is already fixed, and this means you need to reduce the proposal to include, say just four case studies of good practice, would the resulting study still be capable of answering the questions originally posed? If the answer is no, can you make a case to ensure the study is properly resourced? Would one option be to present the key decision-makers with a two-stage research exercise, with the costs of the follow-on case study unspecified until the actual number of case studies needed was decided?

In making a case for resources it is also worth thinking about who might be interested in the results of this work. Would it just be your managers and the councillors, or is there a wider audience encompassing policy makers, professionals and the general public? If this is the case, then how would you propose to reach these different groups? What publication or dissemination strategy is required? Rather than just producing a research report and related committee papers, should you not consider press releases, journal articles, conference presentations and even a book? Each of these has a cost, which has to be borne either by the direct costs associated with the research project or from some other budget.

These are just some of the many practical questions that need to be considered right from the start of the project. While attempting to clarify both the nature and objectives of the proposed research, it is critical to think through the practicalities of carrying out the research, at the same time as trying to establish a tight focus. Only after properly considering all this information, holistically, can you really determine whether there is value in taking the research forward. The focusing task helps to clarify the issues surrounding youth homelessness, and appreciate its complexities. Only by going through this process can you establish whether there is, in fact, a workable focus for the study.

Defining the research questions

Research questions need to be realistic. They should clearly articulate the purpose of the research. They also need to provide the foundation on which you build the entire study: it will determine the focus of the literature review, help you decide what data is required and the direction and focus of subsequent analysis. Having worked to narrow down your general focus, as described above, you should now be in a position to formulate a specific research question, or set of related questions. Sticking with the youth homelessness example, this might lead to a question, such as, '*what strategies are open to a local authority in seeking to deal with youth homelessness?*' Or it could be a simple statement of intent, '*in order to deal effectively with youth homelessness, a local authority requires to develop a four pronged approach involving a schools' housing information pack, a family counselling policy, the development of a young persons housing policy and a youth employment strategy*'. Either approach will suffice, for the important thing is that you have a clear statement of the problem which identifies both the focus of the research – policy and practice options open to a local authority in order to deal with youth homelessness, and the limits of the population – the youth homelessness population and those who might be affected.

Many research projects, however, begin not with a question, but with a hypothesis; a tentative statement in the form of an assumption which is subject to verification, or refutation through subsequent research. An hypothesis can be written as a simple declarative statement; for example, '*the provision of local authority furnished accommodation is the best means of ameliorating the growing youth homelessness problem*'. Alternatively, such a hypothesis can be expressed in a slightly different way, namely, '*the provision of local authority managed furnished accommodation can help significantly in alleviating the growing problem of youth homelessness*'.

Formulating a research question, however phrased, also involves defining concepts and variables. In the above examples, the concepts of 'youth homelessness', 'furnished accommodation', 'significantly' and 'alleviating', are all terms that will need to be defined. Each would require a working definition that is coherent, unambiguous; and, if possible, framed in a way that makes it feasible to measure the relevant variables. As part of working through such definitions you would also need to consider what data would be required to adequately explore these concepts. It is crucial that such definitional aspects of any study are carefully thought through, given that they have a major bearing on how you subsequently structure the research. So having established your research questions clearly, in one or two sentences, and carefully defined the terminology, you can now move onto the next stage of the planning process.

Selecting appropriate research methods

Now that you are clear about what it is you want to research, the next stage is to think about the actual research strategy. How will you go about carrying out the investigation needed to answer the research questions? In establishing the focus of the study you will already have started to work through some of these issues. Clearly, in an ideal world you would choose the research methods most appropriate to providing focused answers to that particular research question or questions. In practice, however, research planning is often heavily influenced by practical considerations. As was noted earlier, certain research methods might be ruled out because they are too costly, or there is insufficient time or expertise available to properly carry them out. The failings evident in many research studies can often be traced back to the best method not being employed because of time and money considerations.

In the youth homelessness example, one effective research method might be to survey all local authorities involved in this work and then, from that information, select those projects that were judged most successful based on a measurement criteria drawn up by the project. This survey approach would be likely to yield both quantitative and qualitative data, but might be ruled out because of the time and costs involved. To get round this resource difficulty, you might then opt to only look at local authorities, which reflect a similar profile to your own. In limiting the research in this way there are likely to be implications in respect of its capacity to expose useful policy options and, therefore, the overall quality of the resulting research.

Resource considerations, however, are not always paramount in selecting a particular strategy. You may choose a strategy because it is one you already know and, thus, feel confident about using. It may also be the only method you have any knowledge of, particularly if you are new to research. The danger here is that by restricting your choice of research method, you also influence the definition of the research problem. Again this will have a bearing on the quality and wider applicability of the subsequent research output. As discussed earlier, Part Two of this book is designed to introduce you to the range of possible research methods that can be employed. But before you get to that stage, both the purpose of research and the likely availability of data should have been properly considered, as these have a clear bearing on the eventual method, or methods selected. The purpose and eventual use of research should govern the research method. Bear in mind that it is all too easy to become immersed in the details of research methods and, in the process, lose sight of the real aim of the research itself. In social welfare the aim is usually to help identify service deficiencies; help with needs' assessment; solve practical problems and produce ideas for future prioritisation of services and facilities.

Ethical considerations

Ethics are about the moral position adopted by the researcher and those funding that piece of research. Each of these groups has a moral obligation to protect people from any mistreatment, which could result from taking part in the research itself. Within the social welfare context this is given added impetus given so much of the work involves examining sensitive issues and dealing with vulnerable, damaged, isolated and disempowered groups. It should also be borne in mind that these two issues are not mutually linked. Ethics is primarily about politics, power and control within the research process.

Research ethics involves issues of confidentiality and where it is practical, offering a degree of privacy; agreeing informed consent with research participants; and, ensuring the proper protection of all research participants. It is generally acknowledged that the freedom to undertake research is bounded by certain professional and personal moral rules, and the methodological demands for the verifiability of any research undertaken. The one can, and often does compromise the other.

Too often researchers view the issue of ethics merely as a matter of securing informed consent from participants and getting access to issues agreed with the powers that be. While informed consent is an important issue, in its own right, it is not always clear that once it has been secured, researchers review its operation. Also how do you achieve informed consent from children, or from people with dementia? While you can explain what the research is about, will those taking part, understand fully what is being said to them? And are we, as researchers, clear about the pressure we exert when trying to get participation or participants? Agreeing to take part in a study can have major repercussions for any participant. For instance, within the introduction we noted the trauma victims of domestic abuse might be put through recounting their experiences. Similarly, when appraising the performance of a particular project, are you not indirectly making an assessment of the personal performance of the staff? Research does have other costs, which need to be properly taken into account.

Also while most researchers will tell those participating in the study what the research is about, are they as clear with them when it comes to explaining how it will be used? It is also the case that we employ different approaches with different people. Middle class professionals, being more articulate and enquiring, might get a more comprehensive picture of the study, than that supplied to the clients being interviewed.

Confidentiality is another important ethics issue, as it also sets down the relationship between the researcher and the research subjects. When undertaking certain types of study, often in a business environment, or when dealing with particularly sensitive material, commercial confidentiality agreements often have to be signed, prior to the research taking place. It's also very common for researchers to offer anonymity to participants in any study. Yet, do they continuously monitor whether such guarantees are being adhered to, and if they do breach such agreements whom exactly calls them to account? Offering such guarantees at the start of the project can be easy, but once you have some tangible results, do the limitations agreed not compromise the potential value of the research findings? Further, to adhere to the confidentiality agreement do you find yourself editing quotes, but in the process effectively compromise both authenticity and accuracy? Then there is the issue of what you do about storing the data you have collected, and then determining who can have access to it. You also need to think about how and when you will dispose of the collected data. So in working up a statement on confidentiality, you need to carefully think through the consequences. It should never be the case that once it's signed off, you then just go and do as you please.

Although it appears this discussion poses more questions than answers, that is what you should expect in reviewing the ethics of your research. What you need to do is raise questions, and then set about trying to address each of them to your and your funders satisfaction. Overall, ethics is about thinking through and setting down how you expect to protect those being researched, as well as the researchers themselves, when participating in a study. So in addition to issues of consent, privacy and confidentiality, when undertaking research on and with under-privileged and/or marginalised groups care should be taken not to reinforce stereotypical labels and stigmatisation. Further, plagiarism and theft of material from other researchers, groups or reports is clearly ethically unacceptable. It should also be the case that the interests of the client group being examined should not outweigh the demand to produce a truthful and objective account.

To help you in all of this task there are a number of professional ethics codes, which contain both professional and personal outlook. Perhaps the two best-known ethics codes within the social welfare area are the British Sociological Association (BSA) and Social Policy Association (SPA). These professional associations of academic and professional researchers stress an ethical expectation for the researcher, and for the wider discipline itself. Research funders now commonly demand a clear statement on ethics, and ask that you specify the ethics code you will adhere to when undertaking this particular piece of research.

While much of the debate on ethics focuses on those being researched, consideration needs to be given to the researchers themselves. This issue, is in part, covered by the Health and Safety considerations, detailed immediately below. But the personal well being of researchers needs more careful consideration. Conducting interview sessions or observational work in the workplace, institutions or people's homes can be exceptionally draining personally on the researcher. By not having the opportunity to discuss their own feelings about what these interviews are revealing can cause a suppression of feeling. Those interviewing victims of some kind of emotional trauma, whether they are victims of violence, or relationship breakdown, need to be given space to discuss through what they feel about their work, either with other researchers or an independent listener? But would such an arrangement tie into any confidentiality arrangements already agreed for the study? As noted earlier, when considering ethical issues you need to pose these type of questions, and then have answers to hand which accommodate the issue in a manner acceptable to your particular ethical guidelines.

Risk assessment

When planning out any research work it is also important to undertake a full risk assessment. Until recently this was never really given the attention it deserved. Too often individuals were undertaking interviews on their own, typically within people's homes, without properly considering the potential danger they might be putting themselves in. If you are to be in charge of the envisaged research project then you will be required to ensure that effective arrangements are in place to guarantee the health and safety of all staff members involved in executing that project. Where others are undertaking the research, you may wish to highlight specific health and safety considerations that the contractor needs to put in place within the research brief.

All employers have specific health and safety responsibilities in relation to staff undertaking any work-related business. Where such work takes place outwith the normal office context, then consideration needs to be taken of any potential risks colleagues could be exposed to. When undertaking such a risk assessment particular attention needs to be focussed on any staff members whom might be asked to work alone. Similarly thought needs to be given when individuals are expected to undertake work outwith libraries, offices and other places that would be covered by health and safety regulations. Undertaking fieldwork in premises where such regulations may be non existent, or are likely to be compromised, needs special attention. At the same time, it is important to bear in mind that all staff members have a responsibility to conduct themselves in a safe manner. It is also the staff members' responsibility to attend training sessions and observe the guidance issued to protect their own, and their colleagues' safety.

The areas of risk that need to be considered within any research context, and especially when undertaking the fieldwork element of any study, include all of the following:

- personal risk of physical threat or abuse
- personal risk of psychological trauma
- personal risk of causing psychological, or physical harm to others
- personal risk of being put in a compromising situation in which there may be accusations of improper behaviour.

As is evident from the above listing the risk assessment is very much a 'two-way street', in that it relates as much to the harm those working on the study might be exposed to, but also the harm that could affect those taking part in the study. In this sense, the risk assessment process should tie up with the ethical assessment of the envisaged study.

So what risks can you identify for all those who are expected to take part in the study? To do this properly you will require to conduct a full risk assessment of the envisaged research study. In such a risk assessment you will need to detail any locations or areas where staff working on the project would be expected to work alone. You would also need to detail any anticipated risks associated with undertaking the planned work. Having thought these through you will then need to detail, within the assessment, what steps you would need to put in place to minimise these risks.

Such a risk assessment needs to consider:

- risks to the health and safety of members of the staff
- risks to any others who may be affected by the fieldwork activities, namely, members of the public or clients
- appropriate levels of supervision should be defined detailing who is in charge at each stage, and when any subgroups are formed, whether there must be a leader for each of these subgroups.

Where fieldwork is conducted on the premises of another organisation, you need to be satisfied that the local safety procedures are adequate for the work envisaged and that the individuals concerned understand and comply with them. Where people are conducting client interviews, thought must go into where these sessions should take place. If it is important that such interviews are held on an individual face-to face basis, in someone's home, for example, then a robust reporting in procedure needs to be put in place.

Finally, general safety rules need to be set down for all those taking part in research, preferably through written protocols, supplemented by verbal briefings or advice. While the organiser of the fieldwork is responsible for ensuring that all safety precautions are observed for the duration of the activities, as was highlighted earlier each individual also has a responsibility for conducting activities in a safe manner both for themselves and for others. This may appear onerous, but it is crucial to get it right.

Negotiating and maintaining access

In planning to undertake any research it is important to bear in mind that it can take time to get an agreement to allow access to specific locations where the research will take place. In the case of access to vulnerable people or sensitive agency facilities, such as drugs counselling; 'looked after' young people; prisons and care homes, this is likely to involve reaching an agreement about what your work will entail, what documentary information you would want to access and what people you might want to interview. If it also includes accessing the clients receiving that service, the nature of the questions to be posed would also need agreement raising questions about confidentiality and data access considerations. There are ethical as well as practical issues at stake. Given the complexities that can be involved it is best to begin the process as early as possible. However, until you are clear about the actual research question, the methods to be employed and what exactly you want from the organisation and individuals involved in the project, then there is no real point in starting to negotiate access. If anything going into an access negotiation without a clearly thought through proposal will only reduce your chances of gaining agreement.

The first task in gaining an access agreement is finding out who it is you need to negotiate with. Many organisations, especially departments of local and central government, have agreed procedures in place for dealing with any research requests. It may be that you may first need to get permission from senior managers or administrators, so-called 'gatekeepers', before you can then approach the actual individuals you want to participate in the research. Negotiating access through such 'gatekeepers' can present problems. It is often the case that these people do not have a detailed knowledge of the specific work undertaken within the wider organisation, and therefore it is difficult negotiating with them. Again this reinforces the need to be clear about what you seek to achieve. Bear in mind that their prime consideration may be to minimise any interruption to the work of the organisation. So first getting past them, to access those you want to speak to, can represent a real challenge.

Being introduced and accepted by a management 'gatekeeper' also has its dangers, in that this may imply the study has the support of management, and the respondents you wish to engage with feel obliged to co-operate, or the exact opposite! You always need to make it clear, when introducing the research to any respondent that you act independently, if that is, in fact, the case. Where the management instructs an internal study that would clearly not be the case. As mentioned in the introduction, research, especially evaluations, often trigger concerns among staff and users/consumers, given the implications that can fall from such work.

The second problem concerning 'gatekeepers' is their ability to control which aspects of the organisation, or which individuals you eventually meet. You might know exactly who you want to have comments from, but they may be denied that opportunity in favour of others better versed in the 'official' line.

The detailed negotiation of access will, of course, differ from one research project to another. Whether negotiating through 'gatekeepers', or directly with respondents, there are four main points on which you will have to satisfy any prospective respondent. These are:

- Usefulness and significance – you need to illustrate why this proposed research is important.
- Reason for involvement – you then need to explain why their co-operation is being sought and what they would gain by taking part: put simply, what's in it for them.
- Purpose – then you need to be very clear about what sort of information you are seeking, why exactly you want this information, and what use will be made of it.
- Confidentiality – finally you will need to set down what degree of confidentiality, or anonymity, you can guarantee with the respondents involved with the study.

You might also want to think carefully about what it is you are actually seeking from the respondents. The acid test is whether:

... at some time in the future colleagues or other research workers ask you for co-operation with a project, would you be willing to give the same amount of time and effort as you are asking for yourself? If not, perhaps you are asking too much!

(Bell, 1999: 47).

If access is eventually granted, and there is no guarantee that it will be, there may be conditions attached. 'Gatekeepers' might, for example, demand the right to vet any material prior to its publication. They may also want someone to represent their interests on any research steering group, if such a body exists. In such instances, you would have to decide whether these conditions are acceptable and consistent with the aims of the research. While you might be happy enough for the 'gatekeepers' to check a draft of the report for factual accuracy, granting them an effective veto over publication may be harder to accommodate. In the *Shaping of Our Lives* study the opinions of 26 users of welfare services who were either disabled, or had learning difficulties gave their views on service provision and user involvement (Turner et al., 2003). One interviewee commented that, '*It feels like workers in the social and health care fields simply have no respect for service users as equal citizens*' (Turner et al., 2003: 3). It is this sort of finding which some organisations might not wish to be made public. If this was indeed the case then looking for another case study organisation might be the most sensible strategy. Again, you can see how by planning as much of the research in advance you can identify problems, and have the time and opportunity to remedy them. Hitting a problematic case study late on in the research could be catastrophic.

Gaining access can be a hit or miss affair. How many times have you received a postal questionnaire, and immediately put it in the bin? Access was achieved, but it did not result in the successful completion of a survey form. All postal surveys need a covering letter which should detail the four points noted above, as well as any other factors relevant to the particular study. The generally low response to postal surveys would suggest, however, that only a limited number of people consider their participation necessary. So not only do you need to get to the right person, but you also have to capture their interest. Again, using the youth homelessness example, if you opted to survey a wide range of local authorities, about their youth homelessness problem and their strategies for addressing this issue, you would need to think very carefully about how best to get the interests of those with a direct responsibility for this area. A general letter to the chief executive, or director of social services or housing may not be that productive. Careful pre-planning is essential. Overall, access should be viewed as a privilege, not a right, and it is up to the researchers to encourage and best facilitate that access and treat everyone involved with dignity and respect.

Developing and piloting data collection instruments

The next task is to think through the implications that will arise from developing a research instrument, or range of instruments. The most commonly used quantitative and qualitative methods are discussed in Part Two of this book. In the youth homeless example you would need to think about the best means to assess the local scale of youth homelessness. Gleaning statistics from the housing authority would be one method, but depending on the nature of their data collection they may present an underestimate. Undertaking an overnight survey of particular localities within a set of fixed periods may provide additional data. Your background reading is likely to suggest research instruments that may be modified to suit your specific purpose. For example, in deciding to employ a user attitude survey, as a means of appraising each of the case study homeless projects, you might collect a number of similar examples employed in other contexts and then use them to construct one for yourself. This approach can have its drawbacks, given that questions drawn up to deal with one particular set of circumstances might not be appropriate in your context. Also bear in mind what was said earlier about the 'bag and baggage' any one researcher brings to a study. So having gained some idea of what is involved, you may then wish to start to design your own specific research instrument.

Whatever the approach you will also need to build in time to properly 'pilot' any data collection instruments to ensure it fulfils your aims. The feedback derived from a properly executed pilot will usually help prevent costly errors. A misunderstood question, discovered late on in day, could negate all the answers given to that item, and could invalidate the entire exercise. A robust pilot will quickly highlight any such ambiguities in question wording, and should reveal potential gaps in the information being sought. This often happens when you get so involved in drawing up a range of appropriate questions and, consequently, lose sight of exactly what the questions seek to examine. Pilots also give you an accurate measure of just how long it will take a respondent to complete the questionnaire and, therefore, provide a useful estimate of survey time and associated costs. If you have planned and budgeted for a 30 minute questionnaire, and the pilot runs beyond that, you either cut back on the questions, reduce the number of individual surveys, or increase your budget.

Data collection

The next step is planning the actual fieldwork timetable: how you propose to collect the required data, having now worked out what data collection instruments are to be employed. This is the public face of research. Most people equate research with the ubiquitous market researcher who operates in town centres, clipboard in hand, asking unsuspecting passers-by a range of questions. What your actual fieldwork consists of will, of course, depend upon the specific research topic and the research instruments used. In most cases there will be a range of existing data sets, held either locally or nationally, that should shed some light on certain aspects of your chosen topic. Data on the incidence of homelessness are officially collected, but they will not break this down by age. Again this stresses the importance of conducting a rigorous planning phase as there is nothing more disheartening than finding out that the data you thought would answer some of your questions is not readily available from an easily accessible public record. Then there are the logistics involved in undertaking data collection to think about. How many people would be needed to carry out the youth homelessness survey? And what time, cost, travel and expenses would be needed to undertake the case study visits? Again can the budget and time limit you are working to accommodate these logistical concerns?

Analysing data

Having decided upon the research instruments, and negotiated access you now need to consider what sort of analysis you intend to be employed on the data to be collected. This might, at first sight, appear to be putting the 'cart before the horse'. But if you don't give some thought to subsequent data analysis, at the planning stage, then you may find that you have omitted to ask an important question, or that the question is there, but has been framed in an inappropriate way. This is of critical importance where you intend to conduct cross tabulations, that is comparing one set of answers to another, to see if a particular pattern arises. If the two sets of answers to be compared are incompatible, because of the original framing of the questions, then this exercise cannot be conducted. Attempting to address the issue prior to the study going 'into the field' again ensures the key objectives of the study are met.

Thinking about just how the data might be organised, classified and collated, in preparation for its subsequent analysis is another consideration in this part of the planning exercise. It is important to remember even a very basic research exercise can generate a significant amount of data. Given the steady advances in information communication technology (ICT) it is likely you would employ a specific software package to facilitate the data organisation and analysis tasks. While the software, Statistical Packages for the Social Sciences (SPSSx), is still very much the market leader in terms of large and complex quantitative data sets, greater use is also being made of standard spreadsheet packages for more basic number crunching exercises. In the analysis of qualitative data, there are now a number of packages that assist the researcher in organising and analysing the data generated from in-depth qualitative interviews. Chapter 12 examines the broadening application of ICT within social welfare research. Each software package has certain demands in relation to how it expects data to be presented, and this does have an influence on the data collection instrument. Again this illustrates the importance of ensuring feedback loops are utilised in all research exercises.

Interpreting data

As was mentioned earlier, the proposed framework for undertaking the data analysis should have already been well thought through, if not actually decided at this planning stage. The important point here is to plan enough time not merely for the mechanical operation of data analysis *per se*, but also to allow for the time consuming and mentally taxing task of interpreting the analysed data in light of the original questions posed. It is, after all, the interpretation of this collected data that is the core skill demanded of the researcher. Clearly, without good quality data, generated to answer a specific question, interpretation becomes a very difficult task, hence the need to plan carefully for its collection and subsequent analysis. Producing robust findings also requires the posing of clear research questions and the critical interpretation of the patterns that emerge from the collected data. To ensure carefully considered conclusions emerge it is vital to ensure there is time to examine and reflect upon all the elements of the research exercise. The basic error, which mars so much research, is that the conclusions appear to be independently formulated from the presented evidence. Too often this is a consequence of rushing to complete the task, and leaving insufficient time to properly consider what has emerged.

Writing up and disseminating findings

Having 'writing up' and 'dissemination' as part of the research planning exercise often appears, at first glance, somewhat illogical. Firstly, can all the writing, as detailed in Figure 1.1, really be left until the end of the research process? And secondly, how can you plan for the actual writing up when you have yet to undertake the research work?

In answer to the first point, writing up cannot be left until the end of the research exercise. Rather you should always plan to be writing, and then seeking feedback on drafts as each stage in the research process proceeds. Providing and getting comments on early drafts also helps to improve the quality of later stages in the research process. If your research has a steering group, its meeting time frame will be determined by when each element of the study is concluded and draft write-ups are available. This staging of tasks needs to be an essential part of the planning exercise and should act as a time tabling tool.

Considering the write up is also key to the research planning exercise. The essential element in writing an effective research report is being clear, right from the start, about who exactly your audience is and how best to communicate with them. To do this you need to know a great deal about the likely users of your research, right from the outset. How exactly do you envisage your research being used, and by whom? By addressing these questions you are better able to ensure the correct presentation format and appropriate dissemination strategy.

You should never plan research on the assumption that no one will read the finished account. Even if all you intend to produce is a basic research report you need to give some thought to promoting its wider dissemination. Dissemination comes in a number of forms. The report may be written-up in a variety of styles and formats. These range from the in-house photocopied summary report, through to the bound thesis for an academic institution. Beyond this, you might consider publishing a research article in a professional journal such as *Community Care, Community Justice Matters, Probation Journal, Benefits, Housing Today* or *Roof*. Alternatively, your work could end up becoming a chapter in an edited book designed to enhance best practice in a particular area. Clearly a review of youth homelessness intervention projects would have a wider audience than just the councillors and officials who initially requested it. But to achieve this end, the editor of such a book would have first have had to have heard about your work. One well-tried means of getting access to this wider audience is to use your research findings as the basis of a conference presentation. Again it pays to plan ahead concerning such matters, as some forms of dissemination demand long lead in times and these can only be accommodated with careful planning.

Another consideration which has moved up the agenda along with ensuring a much greater focus on user involvement in social welfare research, is how best to inform the respondents about the outcome of your study. It may be that you have already agreed some sort of early feedback as part of the access negotiation process. As noted above, it is quite common for 'gatekeepers' to insist upon the right to comment on drafts of any material throughout the research. Even when they do not, it is good practice to provide a forum whereby those involved in the research can comment on matters of accuracy, and express their own views about the conclusions you, or the commissioned researchers have drawn. If this is done prior to the publication of the final report it can help to improve the final product by ironing out inaccuracies as well as help strengthen particular arguments. It is also important to remember that the 'gatekeepers' are rarely those who are directly involved in the day-to-day work, which is the focus of the research. By presenting them with the results of the study you cannot always assume those 'at the coal face' will see a copy of that report. It might be useful, therefore, to negotiate for the inclusion of a short article in an in-house newsletter, in order to disseminate the basic findings, or to organise an in-house seminar on your work. The point here is that you should try, wherever possible, to make the findings of the study accessible to all those who gave both time and information, and made the study possible in the first place. As with all aspects of research process, the time involved in dissemination needs to be built into the research plan. Effectively managing this consultation feedback may also throw-up some sensitive issues with regard to confidentiality and anonymity.

Timetable and project management

Keeping to time is perhaps one of the most demanding tasks in conducting a research project. Throughout this planning work you should draw up a clear timetable with considered deadlines that have to be met. In this part of the planning exercise you need to bring all these elements together. As there never seems to be enough time to do everything that needs to be accomplished, careful planning can help greatly, especially if you follow these three simple rules:

- Construct a realistic timetable and when it comes to conducting the research stick to it. Make sure you know when the various deadlines fall, what has to be done to meet them, and what time you really do have available. Never work on the basis of an idealised notion of the time you would like to have. Think very carefully about just how long each task will take.

- Plan out a sensible sequence of activities. Think carefully about when each task has to be completed. There will be occasions, for example, when it is more efficient to be doing two or more tasks at the same time. Also pay particular attention to potential external factors that could put a constraint on your schedule. If you want to interview all the voluntary committee members involved in managing a youth homelessness initiative together, then there may be a limited number of dates available within the timeframe of the study.

- Build in progress monitoring dates to ensure you don't let the schedule drift too much. That said, your envisaged timetable cannot be set in stone. Sometimes it will be impossible to stick to the agreed schedule and you will have to make alterations to cope with delays, or unforeseen events. So ensure you build in some extra time to allow this to happen. The idea here is to try and deal with any problems, as and when they arise, then restructure your timetable, rather than let the whole thing drift.

Displaying your proposed timetable graphically, with the tasks on one axis and calendar dates on the other does make it easier to monitor actual progress. This also lets you see the impact holidays will have. By using this chart, as shown in Figure 1.2, you can tell at a glance what stage the research should be at, what progress you have made to date and what tasks remain to be completed. This is the key to ensuring good project management.

Appraising existing research

Most of the distinct stages in project planning outlined so far will also provide an aid to appraising the value and worth of published research material. Bear in mind that research appraisal, as a task, is also integral to conducting the first part of the research planning process, when narrowing down the focus of the study in order to refine the research question. Developing your research appraisal skills also allows you to quickly assess the value of a piece of research to your day-to-day work, or that of your organisation.

Research appraisal breaks down into four distinct stages, each of which is assisted by trying to answer a set of pertinent questions. As will be evident, these questions relate back to the research design process. It also illustrates the range of influences on the actual research process, as were discussed in the introductory chapter. In attempting to answer these questions, you will quickly build up an insight into the value to you of the research you are examining.

Community Care Evaluation Work Plan

Week Commencing	30-Sep 1	07-Oct 2	14-Oct 3	21-Oct 4	28-Oct 5	04-Nov 6	11-Nov 7	18-Nov 8	25-Nov 9	02-Dec 10	09-Dec 11	16-Dec 12
Data Validation												
Researcher 1	3	*	3	3	3							
Researcher 2		3 0.5		3 0.5								
Analysis												
Researcher 1						* 3	3	3	3	2		
Researcher 2		0.5		0.5			0.5		0.5			
Reporting												
Researcher 1										*		
Researcher 2							0.5		0.5	3	2 3	2 3

*Signifies meeting commissioning department.

Figure 1.2: An example of a research timetable

Clarifying the context of the research

- Who did the research and when?
- What were the stated objectives of the research and why were these issues raised at this particular point in time?
- Who wanted to know the answer?
- How were the results presented?

Assessing whether new research should have been carried out

- Were there any existing studies that could have provided the required information, or could have served as a model?
- Was there existing data that could have been employed?
- Was this special study needed, and if it was should this have been a one-off research study or a monitoring exercise?

Assessing whether appropriate methods were employed

- What methods were employed, and why?
- How well were the actual research methods applied?
- How were the results analysed?

Appraising the argument

- Does the evidence and the argument presented justify the conclusions reached?
- Do the conclusions answer the research questions?

By using the same set of questions, you also have a ready made quality control mechanism to use during your own research work, and if employed as your work progresses it should ensure that the resulting work has a sharper focus.

Clearly, the more research outputs you acquaint yourself with, the better prepared you are to undertake both research planning and research appraisal. You also do not need to be a full time researcher to become well versed in any particular subject area, or specialism. By getting into the habit of keeping up with developments in your work area you will soon be able to answer all the questions set out above, and should have little difficulty in planning out a new research study, as outlined by this chapter. The old adage that 'practice makes perfect' does not quite fit in the case of research planning. Rather it is more a case of practice markedly reducing imperfections and flaws.

Commissioning Research

Commissioning research or doing it yourself?

Up until now the assumption has been that you would be doing your own small-scale research, either alone or as part of a small team, which was connected either to your work or as part of a personal study. You may find, however, that some issues you are asked to investigate, or evaluate, demand a much larger workload impute than you or a small team can provide. It may also be the case that the proposed research needs a specialist researcher who has built up expertise in this area. It is also the case that there are a variety of research methods that are quite social welfare specific. Sutton (1997) provides a long list of these methods and it includes techniques for working in residential care and drug user settings, as well as group work. Further, not all research contractors will be familiar with particular social care professions and their client groups, and this knowledge base, or lack of it can also help you make the best choice. In such cases you need to know how to go about engaging a research contractor, such as a market research company, a specialist consultant or a university department, to undertake the work. A survey of local government research functions (Boddy and Snape, 1995) found that external researchers tended to be used when:

- The necessary substantive or methodological expertise were not available in-house.
- In-house staff could not complete the work within the allotted timescale.
- The research project involved large-scale survey work and, therefore, required more staff than were available in-house.
- The experience and reputation of a particular organisation or individual was sought to inform the research.

- Internal researchers might be viewed as being too close to the research questions, be biased, or unacceptable to some of the proposed respondents.
- Research was designed to deal with an organisational or management conflict.
- 'Independent' analysis was required to lend greater weight and validity to the research findings (particularly in relation to jointly commissioned work, when having one of the organisations involved undertaking the research might be viewed as problematic).
- Specialist data management skills and ICT software were required.
- Contracting out of some, or all, of the in-house research function was an organisational policy stance, or was considered to be a more cost-effective use of staff resources and facilities.

In practice the decision to engage external researchers will be determined by the nature of the research, internal organisational policy and, as always, by the availability of resources. Given you are, at some point, likely to find yourself in the position of commissioning rather than just conducting research, this chapter outlines the issues involved. These include drawing up the research brief, selecting potential research contractors, and tendering the work. Comments are also made in relation to managing the resulting research project.

The core document needed in order to commission a piece of research work is the research brief. This specifies the nature of the research questions, why you perceive the issues to be important and what is expected from the successful research contractor. It is the brief which provides the basis for the contractor's research planning and costing exercise. It is crucial, therefore, that the brief is comprehensive, clear and unambiguous. The stated research objectives should be feasible, within the time and financial constraints you have imposed on the proposed work. While it is usually open to the contractor to make their own recommendations in respect of research methods, it is always open to you, as the purchaser of these services, to indicate a preferred method in the brief. It may well be the case that, as a specialist contractor, they come back and offer a better means for achieving what you intended. Given these expectations the brief should emanate from a properly considered research planning exercise, as outlined in the previous chapter, and should never be something cobbled together some Friday afternoon!

Writing the research brief

Writing the research brief is the most important part of the commissioning process: it needs to be well thought out, detailed, clear and practical. As will be clear from Chapter 1 it is the brief that anticipates all aspects of the envisaged research and connects the various elements together. If this is not achieved then the objectives for the research are unlikely to be realised and valuable time, money and effort will have been wasted. The brief should mirror the research plan that emerges from the research planning exercise, as discussed in the previous chapter. The only two differences are likely to be that the brief will be more detailed in respect of certain management considerations, given the need to set down on paper all that is expected of the contractor. Secondly, there may be a degree of leeway in respect of the methods the contractor can/may employ in order to meet the stated research objectives. While the precise details contained in any research brief will vary from project to project they should always contain detailed information on the following seven elements. Organisations who regularly commission research tend to have clearly set down rules and procedures in place, and an expectation that these are strictly adhered to. It is always useful, therefore, to check whether such procedures are in place.

The context

The research objectives should be stated right at the start, followed by an outline of the thinking that went into shaping these specific research questions. Understanding the thinking and aims that informed the construction of the research questions allows the potential researcher to understand where you are coming from and properly consider the relevance of the questions. To ensure the potential research contractor understands properly the background to the proposed research, it is also useful to supply a résumé of this material, along with the details of the specific policy context. Then the envisaged aims and objectives you have set for the research should be clearly stated. While the stated aims describe the broad goals to be achieved by the contractor, it is the objectives that provide the detail of the specific tasks that require to be undertaken. It is also crucial that the stated expectations are achievable and realistic, given the defined financial and time constraints.

The most common failing in any research brief is to provide an ill-conceived, ambiguous set of research questions. The second fault is that the expectations set cannot be met by the resources made available. You also need to bear in mind that many professional researchers will not have a sufficient understanding of the very specific setting and professional cultures that operate within what can be very narrow social welfare networks.

It is often worthwhile, at an early stage in the initial research planning work, to consult with others who may have an interest in the subject you seek to have investigated, or who may become potential end users of any resulting research findings. For example, if as a community worker you were proposing to commission a neighbourhood audit, you might well find other council departments such as cleansing, parks, housing and roads might be willing to contribute to the costs in order to elicit specific information. By drawing in these contributions, more efficient and effective use of limited resources could be achieved and may well ensure your expectations are fully met. Further, such an approach should minimise any future criticism that other departments or agencies had not been given the chance to participate. It always helps to identify sources of expertise.

The anticipated method

The expected research method should be outlined, but as noted in the introduction above, this does not always need to imply that other approaches will not be considered, if that is what is wanted. The question here is about just how much flexibility prospective research contractors are to be allowed. Certain professional researchers, of course, take the view that they alone are best placed to decide upon detailed method design issues; that '*the researcher and only the researcher, should decide*' (Denzin, 1978: 331). Those commissioning the research may take a different stance given they are paying for the work, and want to be clear about what they will get for their money.

A more constructive approach would be to see research as a collaborative venture; where there is a bit of give and take in regard to the best methods approach. As the research commissioner you have to be clear about what you want, and have some idea about how this might best be achieved. But it is still possible, and desirable, to be flexible and allow the contractor to modify the envisaged methods or to suggest an entirely different approach if it will provide an answer, but in a different way than first envisaged. The difficulty here is that your budget may be based on using one specific method and, as a result, there may be limited room for manoeuvre if a better methods approach costs fractionally more. It is also harder to assess competing tenders if they adopt markedly different approaches.

Within the methods section of the brief you might also want to specify the need to pilot the approach and report back on this before progressing to the full-blown exercise. This is also the place to include any specific data quality control and reporting requirements.

Accountability

In social welfare settings, research accountability is not just to the paymaster. Users and customers, local politicians, policy makers, managers of various grades and practice staff may each regard the research outcomes as their property. How exactly you want these parties to be involved in the research needs to be clearly set down. This complex set of individuals and organisations will need to be properly consulted and kept informed about the research and its progress and these needs require to be identified as part of the initial research briefing process. That process, in itself, is likely to increase the list of potential contributors.

Expected research outputs

The research outputs expected of the contractor, namely final reports and any presentations should be clearly specified within the brief, given they will have cost and time implications for potential researchers. It is also common to detail expectations in relation to depositing the raw data, and any data analysis work carried out. It may be that the commissioner, at a later stage, may undertake further secondary analysis of the data set. Similarly any restrictions that might be placed on subsequent reporting or publishing of the work by the researcher should be clearly spelt out within the brief. Such restrictions are common in government funded studies, given the politicised policy environment in which much of this work is conducted.

Intellectual property rights

Intellectual property rights refer to who is deemed to own the information – the intellectual property – once it has been assembled. Is it the originator of an idea, the researcher, or the body that paid them to undertake the work? Put simply, in a contract research context, who can lay claim to an idea? For most pieces of social welfare research this is simply not an issue. But if there is some sensitivity about the findings, it may be that the commissioner places a restriction on where this material can be subsequently published. As noted earlier, this is commonplace in government research contracts covering active policy areas. Or if a particular appraisal method is developed to assess particular projects, or advise on future investment strategies, then there may be worth in establishing ownership given such tools may have some commercial value.

Management arrangements

The contractual requirements and any specific conditions, including the arrangements for monitoring and supporting the project, need to be clearly specified at the outset. It is now common for researchers to be asked to specify the ethics code they operate to, and provide data quality standard guarantees. Having in place, right at the outset, a specified means to monitor progress on these areas, and check on the quality of the work, as it progresses, is also important. The standard means of achieving this is to have an advisory group or steering committee. The use of the terms 'advisory' or 'steering' may indicate the style of involvement you and your organisation want to employ.

The function of these bodies is to offer advice and help to the researchers, and they can often help with access issues given they tend to be composed of people who have a direct interest in the research itself. Their key role is to help sort out any practical difficulties that can arise and act as a sounding board in relation to the written output. While the role of monitoring overall progress generally lies with the project manager, such groups do play a part, given their sequence of meeting dates is typically tied to key output dates. Your expectations or those of your organisation, for such a group need to be set down within the brief, given the researchers will have some role in servicing this group. Such expectations also need to be conveyed to advisory group members so they properly understand their role. Servicing this body and being dependent on their feedback also has a bearing on the research timeframe, given that sufficient time must be built in to allow people to read and comment on the different outputs. The costs associated with servicing such bodies also need to be defined and budgeted for either out of mainstream funds or from the specified project costs.

The actual membership of advisory groups or steering committees also needs to be carefully thought through, and agreed prior to the research being tendered. It may be that this group has some part to play in any selection process. Although some advisory groups have up to 20 members, limited membership to a small number of people is advisable, typically between six and ten, who have some expertise or direct interest in the research. Having an advisory group full of people nominated to represent departmental, or organisational interests, can quickly prove to be a disadvantage. If there is little real interest in the topic then dialogue at meetings can quickly become one way, and this can be dispiriting for both the researchers and the project manager. If different departmental perspectives emerge, which have not been fully considered in advance, then the advisory group could quickly degenerate into a battleground and in so doing become a serious problem for the on-going management of the research.

If you have any concerns about the feasibility of undertaking a particular research project, you may decide to phase the work, with the second stage being dependent upon the first being successfully achieved. By separating out two distinct stages, you have the option to terminate the contract if the preliminary results reveal only limited scope for follow up work. Phasing may also be useful when using new contractors for the first time, as it leaves you the option of employing a different contract researcher in the latter stages, if major problems arise.

Timetable

Setting down a clear and realistic timeframe is a critical component of any research brief. But the emphasis here should be on the word, realistic. Any organisation that commissions a piece of research, will be anxious about getting the findings when they want them, especially if this work is designed to inform an on-going management or policy exercise. The danger here is that deadlines set to meet management, policy or financial demands, compromise the time needed to properly conduct the research work. Financial imperatives are often the worst offenders, with multiple commissions being issued in January, with an expectation that these studies will be completed by the end of the financial year, merely to ensure a budget is spent.

Having a realistic timeframe is critical to contractors, given their need to meet the demands of other on-going work. So taking time in the planning exercise to properly consider a timeframe appropriate to the task in hand will pay dividends. Also remember, in a competitive market, contractors will often seek to win the contract first, then try and re-negotiate the timetable once the work is secured. Having a properly considered timeframe puts you in a much stronger position should such a situation arise. Only by having a clearly defined timeframe and a set of specific deadlines can you avoid the project being extended. The challenge is to ensure these are well considered and thought through.

While on the subject of timescales you also need to ensure sufficient time is set aside to allow selected contractors to respond to the brief and for you or a committee to appraise the submitted bids. Four to six weeks from issuing the brief to receiving bids is the accepted timeframe for most projects. Appraisal and interview, if that was considered necessary, can add another two weeks. Only in the case of small straightforward projects should a shorter timescale be considered. It is common to set down these dates within the brief so that everyone is clear as to what is expected of the tendering process.

Scale of funding

You need to be fully aware of the likely cost to undertake the proposed research and, as this will determine the budget, again, by conducting a proper planning exercise, you can work out the hours involved, multiply that by the range of associated day rate costs and then add on identified expenditure items to arrive at the budget figure. The cost of any project will depend on such items as research staff costs, bought in services such as surveying, travel, out of pocket expenses, draft report preparation, final report production and time to attend advisory group meetings and any specified presentations. It is difficult to make precise calculations, but it helps if you have some idea as to the likely range of costs. Again this reinforces the need to properly understand the work involved in undertaking the research. Whether or not you include an indication of the available funding for the project, in the research brief, depends on the practice within your organisation, and on the actual nature of the project. Giving some indication of price may increase the prospect of getting comparable bids, leaving the quality of proposal as the main criterion for deciding a particular contractor. On the other hand, if there is an error in estimating likely costs, it may artificially inflate costs. If you underestimate you might not get any bids back, or the proposals might omit much of what you want. Some organisations take the view that it is more appropriate not to include indicative funding information where the project elements can be clearly defined. This typically applies to work that involves the use of standard methods. Where the possible methods are more open-ended, providing funding information may be an essential part of the research brief.

Once you have completed compiling the draft research brief it is useful to have someone with an interest in the topic look it over and comment on it before it goes out to potential contractors. Often, when you are too close to a project, over a period of time, basic points of detail can be missed. An example of a research brief is contained in Appendix 1.

Identifying potential contractors

Once the research brief is completed you then need to find a suitable contractor to carry out the research work. Contractors who carry out social welfare research fall into one of four distinct categories, although it is not uncommon for one or more of these groupings to collaborate on a specific project. Market research companies, many of whom are well known polling organisations, are perhaps the best-known research contractors. They tend to specialise in large-scale opinion poll surveys, and are often used by other more specialist consultants to provide survey services. Some of the larger organisations employ a small number of specialists, in areas such as housing and planning, to offer specialist services and crucially generate work for their large survey business. Then there are the consultancy businesses, which offer specialist services covering the whole panoply of social welfare functions. Consultancy is also a very mixed bag in that it ranges from large generalist research businesses to an individual who has taken an early retirement package and can offer a very distinct set of skills. Then there are the university research departments, which as was noted in the introduction, can offer a similar profile to that of consultants. Given the preponderance of management and policy based research work, the main operators within this market are the specialist consultants and university research departments, especially those who have developed a particular expertise. University based researchers also often buy in field work services from the larger market research companies.

In choosing between an academic institution and a private consultancy business it is useful to consider the advantages and disadvantages displayed by both. As Hakim (1987) points out:

> The main advantages of university based research are that a greater depth of theoretical work will be brought into a project ... But because academics have competing teaching responsibilities, being in effect part-time researchers, the work may be subject to long delays, and the individualistic ethos of the academic community impedes team research ... The main advantage of the research institute and of specialist agencies are that their full time research staff can complete studies more quickly, and they are able to retain a variety of specialist and general support staff who are needed only on an ad hoc basis for particular aspects of a study – such as sampling experts, statisticians, data processors, or clerical support staff.
>
> (Hakim, 1987: 168).

It is also worth bearing in mind that the values and perspectives held by different researchers and agencies can also differ, and this will have a bearing on the resulting research output. Certain research organisations such as the Adam Smith Institute or the Institute for Public Policy Research are, in fact, party political think tanks. Political affiliations and tendencies are often remarked on in the media, in using phrases such as 'left of centre' or 'right wing'. In addressing this issue, May comments:

Social research takes place within a context in which many of its rules and procedures are taken for granted. These 'background assumptions', upon which research decisions and analysis are based, should be open to scrutiny. Without this in place, social research can so easily reflect the prejudices of society in general, or the research community in particular.

(May, 1997: 61).

Placing the contract

Most commissioned research, of any size, is awarded using some form of competitive tender. The advantages of a competitive process are that it:

- Helps ensure that the research is as cost effective as possible.
- Affords the widest choice from a range of expertise, including potential new contractors.
- Helps prevent contractors and customers drifting into a cosy long-term relationship, in which familiarity can breed, if not contempt, then staleness or complacency.

The most straightforward way of ensuring a fair competition is simply to advertise the project as widely as possible in an attempt to get all interested parties to apply. In this way, everyone gets an equal chance to submit a bid and you can then select the best option. In practice, however, this sort of wide-open competition can prove to be an expensive and unwieldy process for all concerned. You might attract a great deal of interest with your advertisement, which is good. Sorting through and making a selection from a large and varied number of rival bids will, however, take time and may not be as manageable. Operating some kind of quality control threshold will be impossible given the number of unknown applicants. A number of suitable researchers are likely to be put off because they are not convinced that the cost and time involved in preparing a bid is justified by their chance of success. Given these problems it is more common to invite expressions of interest from suitable contractors, and ask only those who positively respond to tender. This form of restricted, or closed competition, may seem less democratic, but it is likely to be more efficient and cost effective.

Organisations and agencies who commission research on a fairly regular basis often have built up a data base of 'approved contractors'. Such a database might contain information about contractors' knowledge of particular topic areas and their specialist skills in operating particular methods; their technical or specialist qualifications; their ability to mount an effective field work team, if needed; and their credibility and reputation based on their performance on previous projects. This information is then used to draw up a short-list of contractors who would then be invited to bid for a given project.

Those who do not have such a resource to draw on, which is the more likely scenario in social welfare research, could use their network to draw up a list of possible contractors. This group could then be contacted, asked if they were interested in the proposed project, and if so they could then provide a practice note detailing their ability to undertake the proposed project and listing any previous commissions in this area. This information, plus a letter of recommendation from previous clients, if so desired, could then be used in a final short-listing exercise. Those short-listed would then be asked to submit a bid on receipt of the detailed research brief. Such a two-stage competition also has the advantage of ensuring that the new contractors are not excluded from the bidding process. Putting effort into finding a range of potential contractors will pay dividends later on.

Whatever method is used to identify a short-list, it is best to keep the numbers invited to bid to a minimum. This usually means keeping the list down to six, or preferably less. Don't forget large numbers waste time for all concerned, as most contractors will be unsuccessful despite having spent time and resources in preparing a bid. If you are new to commissioning research and you don't know the market, increasing the numbers invited to bid might seem like a safer option, but bear in mind that you will also be wasting your time in managing and evaluating the unsuccessful bids. Also remember that if you get a reputation for wasting consultant's time they may be less likely to bid for future work. If you don't know the market the best option is to get advice from those with more experience about who is in the market, but then employ your own short-listing criteria.

Within a tendering context rival contractors are required to make sealed bids in response to the brief. The process is characterised by a high degree of confidentiality and a formal relationship between the customer and the contractor. The research is awarded to the contractor who best meets the research objects, and submits the lowest acceptable bid. This strict legalistic approach to tendering can, however, be counterproductive in that it hinders effective discussion and gets in the way of researchers developing a real understanding of the research problem. In practice, the approach is often modified in some way, perhaps to encourage researchers to suggest alternative methods and/or to allow them to discuss the research brief before submitting a bid. By getting in touch with a number of potential research organisations prior to a specific brief being tendered some of this creative dialogue can take place. This also allows these researchers to undertake some preliminary work prior to the brief being received, and should improve the quality of the submission. However, it can also be a process which is subject to abuse, when commissioners use the contracting bids to amend and re-tune the final research outline – a point amplified in the next section.

Not all research projects go out to tender. There will be certain circumstances where it is not necessary or desirable. Where it is clear, for example, that only one contractor has the particular expertise necessary to undertake the project; direct negotiation may be the preferred option. Direct negotiations may also be pursued where a research company or academic institution has exclusive access or ownership of data or specialised research facilities. With small-scale projects, contracts worth less than about £10,000, the administrative costs associated with tendering may be disproportionate. In negotiating the price for a particular project, however, you need to have a good grasp of the actual costs involved. Checking out the cost of similar work undertaken elsewhere can provide a useful 'benchmark' against which to assess the selected contractor's price.

Selecting the successful bidder

How do you choose the most appropriate researcher from amongst the bids you receive? In formal tendering the choice is apparently simple; you take the lowest bid. It may be unwise, however, to make the decision on cost considerations alone. The lowest bid may not be the most appropriate. There is always the possibility that a bid, which is significantly lower than the others, has misunderstood the requirements of the brief. If you are concerned that a bid is abnormally low, the resources detailed in the bid should be carefully examined and then re-examined before comparing them with the other submissions. If the bid is acceptable on quality grounds, the potential contractor could be asked about any serious discrepancies in the proposed resources and if satisfactory explanations are not forthcoming it is probably best to reject that bid.

All bids should be evaluated against a range of criteria, which include competence, quality, and creativity, as well as cost. In considering a bid you should ask yourself the following questions:

- Does it demonstrate a clear understanding of the requirements from the project?
- Does it demonstrate the level of ability needed to undertake the analytical, technical and data handling aspects of the project?
- Does it comment constructively on any conceptual, methodological and/or data related problems that might be anticipated and on how these might be addressed?
- Are there suitably qualified and experienced staff available for all aspects of the project?
- Do the researchers seem prepared to work closely with you (and you with them)?
- Does their proposed timetable appear to be realistic and achievable?
- Are the costs, staffing and other resources clearly specified and adequate?
- Do the researchers appear likely to produce high quality results and be able to present and communicate findings clearly and succinctly?
- Does the proposal conform to a professional ethics code?
- What quality control guarantees can the contractor provide?

Social welfare research also requires contractors to understand the culture and professional boundaries of the work, or services, or social problems being researched. In practice, interviewees may need to exhibit high levels of empathy with the topic to be researched; understand complex questions regarding confidentiality and be particularly well attuned to issues such as racism, gender, ethnicity as well as health and safety. In some cases you may decide to interview all or some of the prospective contractors, perhaps to clarify some aspect of the design and get a view on how you could work with them. Such interviews should only be conducted when the contractor has a reasonable prospect of being awarded the contract. If you intend to ask all potential contractors to an interview, or to make a presentation in support of their bid, this should always be stated within the brief. If possible the date and format of the interview or presentation should also be stated at the outset. You may even have to consider paying expenses for short-listed contractors, as you would for job applicants.

You should also never use such a competition as a means of trawling for ideas, or alternative solutions to your specific research problem. There will be times of course when one or more of the rival competitors make a suggestion which improves the initial research design; indeed suggestions and modifications to enhance the brief are to be encouraged. However, using such suggestions in a narrowed down second stage tendering process may raise the question about the abuse of intellectual property. If a scoping exercise is required, then pay consultants a fee to do this. Never run it on the back of a tendering exercise.

Finally, successful and unsuccessful contractors should be advised of the outcome of the selection process as soon as possible. Contractors may find it helpful to have some feedback on the perceived strengths and weaknesses of their bid, but the details of their competitors' bids should of course remain confidential.

Research contract

Having selected a contractor, you should formalise this through issuing a legally binding contract. The format for such a document and the procedures for issuing it will vary depending on the organisation you work for. For those who do not have such arrangements in place an example of standard contract letter is provided in Appendix 2. This document typically sets out the purpose of the research study, the respective role of contractor and customer, its timescale and any other contractual conditions which are relevant such as fee management arrangements, expected outputs and the ownership rights of the research data and any resulting products. This concludes the commissioning exercise, and now all you have to do is manage the work.

As you can see it takes time to properly plan out all aspects of any research study and a bit longer to produce a robust and comprehensive research brief. It also takes time for contractors to prepare good quality proposals in response to the research brief and for you to properly scrutinise these bids and award the contract. Understanding the research process, in a broad sense is critical to all this planning. As an aid to improving your understanding the next section of the book considers the broad range of methods that can be employed in that research process. Section Three then looks at the aspects of the research process which involve analysis, theorising and presentation.

PART TWO

Putting a Project Together

The previous section outlined what was required when preparing and planning out a research project. This second part examines the various methods you can employ in order to collect data and information as part of research. Having first considered some basics about what exactly it is you are attempting to measure or record, the following chapters then get you thinking, in some detail, about different data collection instruments. The topics covered include: how you go about undertaking a literature review; what issues you need to consider in relation to measurement; and what considerations should be taken when drawing up a sampling frame. A range of the more common data collection methods are then considered, each within a separate chapter. This part of the book concludes with a chapter on the value of comparative research, a growing issue for social welfare research, and another on the increasingly important role that computers and information communication technology plays in the research process.

The research strategy you adopt depends very much on the nature of the data you want to collect. The research questions determine the type of evidence you need to collect, and to some extent also dictate the methods you can employ. Consequently, the theory, concepts and values that underlie your research have a key influence. Careful thought needs to be given, at the outset, to ensure that the research design will ensure the required data is collected. An equally crucial consideration, which is the focus of the final part of the book, is whether the collected data can be analysed and interpreted in a way that addresses the original research questions. Again, all of this reinforces the need to carefully plan out the study to ensure all the components, the research questions, the proposed data collection instruments and the envisaged analysis mesh together.

It is important that you choose a method, or methods, which are most appropriate for your field of investigation. While a number of different methods could assist you in your task, some will be more appropriate than others. In this part of the book we offer a toolkit approach to research methods. If you want to put a nail into a wall, you would choose a hammer in preference to a screwdriver. While it is possible to put a nail into a wall using a screwdriver, the effort involved is far greater and the end result might not be as good as that achieved by using a hammer. Similarly, if you wanted to know about how people behave in a given set of circumstances you might feel that observational methods would be a more fruitful approach than getting all the individuals concerned to complete a self-assessment questionnaire.

The decision about which method to use will also involve consideration of other more practical constraints. Inevitably, this often boils down to questions about time and available resources. If resources are limited, then using a longitudinal study to follow through the impact of a major change in service delivery, such as the introduction of personal social care packages over a five-year implementation timeframe, might have to be cut back. Undertaking two short, but linked questionnaires for staff charged with this task, which build on from an analysis of basic operational monitoring data, might have to suffice. Time constraints can work against the research in other ways. If, for example, you want to observe the meetings of the local authority's social services committee charged with this task, or those of voluntary groups providing some of the support services, there may only be a limited number of opportunities available during the life of the research project.

While the resources to be expended on research represent one consideration, there are others. Getting agreement to distribute a brief questionnaire to staff employed on a particular project, or initiative, might be straight forward, but getting approval for you to be an observer of the project with unrestricted access to the projects records might prove that bit harder. Again these factors will, inevitably, influence the final choice of methods. Adopting a method that might prove difficult to follow through will present a major risk to the study. In such circumstances, either a different approach is adopted, or alternatively, a workable fallback position is set in place.

It should also be acknowledged that personal preferences also play a part. For whatever reason, some researchers appear to favour one method over another. In such instances there may be a temptation, either consciously or unconsciously, to frame the research questions in a way that suits this preference. As a means to overcome such familiarity, this section exposes you to a wide range of different methods and approaches. To enhance your understanding of these methods and approaches reference is made to specific studies which have employed particular methods, so that you can check out, in detail, just exactly how they utilised that particular research instrument.

While the following chapter arrangement, in considering one separate method at a time, might suggest only discrete choices are available, it is more useful to consider combining methods. Different tools can be employed to complement each other and make the overall research task more robust. In assessing how well an after school club operates, two distinct approaches could be employed. To get an understanding of how the club functions, on a day-to-day basis, and how it engages with the kids, participant observation might be considered the most appropriate method. Spending time in the project watching what is carried out and how the children and staff interrelate will provide one insight. To set the parameters for using this method it would first be necessary to examine the original objectives set for the club, as detailed in its funding proposal, and then assess the records to see how well these aims have been met overall. This documentary work and associated basic quantitative work will throw up issues that you might want to focus on in the participant observations sessions. Interviewing those involved in delivering the service, the paid staff, the voluntary workers and the committee members would also add another qualitative dimension. In terms of public accountability appropriate education and social services officials, as well as councillors might also need to be interviewed. Then there would be a need to get the opinions of those in receipt of this service: just what exactly do the kids make of it? By combining a range of different research methods in this way it is possible for the study to examine the same set of issues, but from several perspectives. It also allows one method to feed into and help enhance another approach. As a result, the overall quality of the assessment will be greatly improved. The successes and achievements of the project would stand out, and be tested. Any conflicts or contradictions should also emerge. This process of combining methods is called triangulation and is a useful means of establishing the validity of different, but related data sets. Where the same point arises out of different research approaches, then this finding is clearly more robust than one that has only arisen out of a single research method approach.

The following chapters, therefore, provide an overview of the key methods available from the social welfare research toolbox. It is up to you to decide which tools, and in what combination, are best suited to the task in hand.

Grounding the Research

Introduction

Reading and familiarising yourself with all available literature on your chosen subject area is a critical part of any research process. Such focused reading not only helps you refine your research question, but it also encourages you to examine how certain theories might help in working through the research design. While accessing relevant published work is the core task discussed in this chapter, don't forget that what's missing from the literature can often be as important as what is already there. It is, therefore, crucial to conduct literature searches systematically, ensuring that at all times you take concise and accurate notes and reference details which can easily be referred back to at some later stage in the study. Having sought out and retrieved all the relevant published information it is then necessary to make sense of this material by undertaking what is termed a literature review, a synthesis of the issues and arguments you have unearthed. This work will then feed directly into the planning and refining of the eventual study. This chapter outlines the key steps necessary to carrying out these tasks.

Library searches

How then do you locate relevant published material? For most researchers the two main options will be either the Internet (which we deal with later in this chapter and in Chapter 12) or libraries. According to Bell (1993), libraries can seem like an Aladdin's cave to researchers, filled to capacity with resource material. Yet, among such riches it is easy to get lost. To avoid this pitfall it is important to understand how your library is organised. First, find out about the reader services the library provides. This allows access to the published materials held in this library, as well as information on how to access relevant material held elsewhere. It is unlikely that the library will meet all your immediate needs, but most have borrowing arrangements with other libraries, which collectively should offer a better selection of relevant material. University and other specialist reference libraries are the best sources for research literature, but access is likely to be more restricted. It is therefore worth checking first with the library about their access requirements. If you are not a registered student, for example, you may be granted only limited reading and/or borrowing rights in a university library. Further, there is likely to be a charge for using these services. Access issues are an important consideration here, given that many of the new electronic resources are paid for on a subscription basis and this either restricts availability or incurs a payment for their use.

Secondly, bear in mind library staff are an invaluable aid to finding the published gems that you seek. Their guidance and skills can help greatly in locating relevant material, but to get to that point you first need to know what you are looking for. In working out your research questions you will have already identified certain key words which encompass the various parameters of your particular subject area. Such words are critical in allowing both you, and the library staff, to access information. The advice, that you should make friends with the relevant library staff and always be polite, patient and remember to thank them, is well worth taking to heart (Vaughan, 1982). They are the gatekeepers of information and are a significant resource in themselves.

Libraries contain a wealth of sources that are useful in conducting research. These include:

The catalogue, which lists all the stock, held by that particular library. For each publication held, the catalogue details the author, title, date of publication, place of publication, and a set of keywords or brief text about the subject area covered by the publication. Catalogues are now held electronically, rather than on paper or microfiche, making searches far easier. Almost all electronic catalogues access material through a keyword system, so as long as you have the key words which fall from your research question, you should be able to locate likely publications. Although library catalogues have become far more standardised, there can still be small variations in how they operate. Such standardisation has the advantage that it is now possible to search through the catalogues of a number of libraries on-line to locate material.

Journals and periodicals are the main source for up to date research. Many are now available as e journals. Refereed journals – those in which the published articles have been subjected to peer review by a panel of experts in the field – are usually considered more authoritative than non-refereed journals. The latter tend to be the professional journals, while the former are academic. The main refereed journals in the social welfare field are: *British Journal of Guidance and Counselling, British Journal of Criminology, British Journal of Learning Disabilities, British Journal of Social Work, Childhood, Children, Child Abuse and Neglect, Critical Social Policy, Disability and Society, Employment and Society, Environment and Planning, European Journal of Social Work, Family Policy, Gerontology,*

Health and Social Care in the Community, Housing Studies, Howard Journal of Criminal Justice, International Social Work, Journal of Social Policy, Journal of Social Welfare and Family Law, Journal of Social Work Practice, Policy and Planning, Policy and Politics, Social Work in Europe, Social Policy and Administration, Sociological Review, Sociology, UK Youth, Urban Studies, Welfare Digest and Work and Youth and Policy. Other professional journals and magazines include *Criminal Justice matters, Community Care, Drug and Alcohol Professional, Health Services Journal, Housing, Roof, Housing Today, Social Work Education* and *Young People Now*.

Abstracts provide bibliographical information and summaries of published journal articles. Such abstracts allow you to get some idea of the relevance of the article to your research. If it appears useful then you can seek out the full article. If it does not, then you have not wasted a lot of time in searching out and reading the entire piece.

An index, classified by subject area, can also help you locate relevant published work. While the catalogue is the primary means of finding books in a particular subject area, indexes are essential for locating journal articles and other periodical sources. One good source for accessing material is the on-line *Web of Science* facility. This holds the Social Science Citation Index (SSCI), which covers all social science disciplines including psychology, sociology and health. It also covers the Science Citation Index (SCI) which encompass all science disciplines and the Arts and Humanities Index. To access this facility you have to first register as a user. All university libraries are linked and students can get access. Outwith the university sector access to this facility varies.

BIDS (Bath Information and Data Service) is another bibliographic service for the academic community within the UK, providing access to bibliographic data, scholarly publications and research data. BIDS also provide access to the Ingenta Journals; some 5,000 full-text electronic journals accessed via a full text on-line or fax service transmission. The International Bibliography of Social Sciences (IBSS) is also accessed via BIDS. As with the *Web of Science* you require to register as a user to utilise this facility.

SCIE (Social Care Institute for Excellence) is the successor body to the National Institute for Social Work and is based in London. In 2003 SCIE joined forces with the University of the West of England (UWE) to establish the UK's primary library of social work material, accessed through the CareData data base. Located in Bristol, this site holds 30,000 books and 3,000 journals. Although still in its infancy SCIE should quickly become a national resource. SCIE is on-line at *http://www.scie.org.uk*, with the electronic library for social care at *http://www.elsc.org.uk*.

There are other 'bibliographical instruments' such as Silverplatter and Cambridge Scientific Abstracts. These are commercial index facilities that are provided on a subscription basis to libraries. Access to these resources will very much depend on the type of library. University and research libraries will have access, so external readers may be denied access, or will be required to pay. Provision within public libraries will vary. Then there is the British National Bibliography (BNB), which provides information and an index of all books printed in a particular year. The British Library in London compiles these annual listings from all the publications deposited with them given their Copyright status. This information is available on-line at *http://www.blpc.bl.uk*. The British Library also has a dedicated service covering social policy, via the Social Policy Information Service (SPIS). Then there is the Applied Social Science Index and Abstract (ASSIA). ASSIA is continuously updated and is made available either as a public access catalogue (PAC), accessed either on-line via a subscribing library or a CD-ROM. Social welfare topics are also covered in the British Humanities Index. This is a more general listing, but has the benefit of being readily accessible in most public libraries. Two other useful on-line bibliographic search facilities covering social welfare topics are Sociological and Social Services Abstracts, and Social Work Abstracts.

Each of these indexes draws from a specified set of publications (including academic journals, professional journals, magazines and newspapers) which are detailed by the index. When conducting a search you can either include all the publications listed, or just those you choose to select. The index will then generate a list of all publications that match the key words you specify. For each publication the search provides a full bibliographic title, an abstract and a key word describer. From this information you can quickly decide whether there are particular articles that would be worth searching out from the library shelves or ordering either electronically or via inter library loan. If the information generated is incomplete you can then use the descriptor information to further refine your key word search. To illustrate what such a search produces, ASSIA was employed to generate articles published between 2000 and 2003 on the topic of 'young people's housing'. The following items were listed:

Title: Clark, S. (2000) 'Talkin' 'bout regeneration', in *UK Youth*, 102, 34–5.

Abstract: Describes how a young people's video project challenges people's assumptions about a housing estate at Rushenden in the Isle of Sheppey.

Descriptor: Housing estates; renewal; young people; attitudes; videotape recording; Rushenden; England.

Title: Brent, J. (2001) 'Trouble and tribes: young people and community', in *Youth and Policy*, 73, 1–19.

Abstract: Southmead is a large housing estate on the northern edge of Bristol, England. Young people are persistently seen as a major problem that prevents the formation of community. However, young people continually engage in collective activities that bear certain strong resemblances to what is generally labelled 'community', except that their activities are not approved of. Looks at young people in relation to ideas of community, including issues of sociality, collectivity, locality and power. Gives examples of adult views of young people, followed by accounts of young people's own communal actions, and relates these to theories of community, including that of 'neo-tribes' described as unstable 'effervescent communities', that challenge the nostalgic idea of community as 'warm togetherness'. Suggests that the behaviour is related to Southmead being a place of class and poverty. It involves the power position of young people, in terms of their rights, the resources available to them, and the way power is exercised upon them.

Descriptor: Housing estates; young people; social behaviour; local communities; Bristol; England.

Title: Kemp, P. and Rugg, J. (2001) 'Young people, housing benefit and the risk society', *Social Policy and Administration*, 35, 6, 688–700.

Abstract: Draws on debates about the risk society to examine the impact of the 'single room rent', a restriction in the housing benefit scheme that applies to single people under 25 living in privately rented housing. Drawing on qualitative interviews in six localities in England, it examines young people's ability to gain access to and afford privately rented accommodation while receiving housing benefit. Argues that the single room rent restriction has not only cut their housing benefit entitlement, but also created more uncertainty for young people.

Descriptor: Young people; housing benefits; rental housing; risks; England.

Title: Holdsworth, C. and Solda, M. (2002) 'First housing moves in Spain: an analysis of leaving home and first housing acquisition', in *European Journal of Population*, 18, 1, 1–19.

Abstract: Examines young people's first housing acquisition in Spain. The majority of young Spanish people leave home to buy a property and to live with a partner and/or child. Examines the extent to which this transition dominates first housing moves during the 1980s and considers the ways in which wider family networks facilitate leaving home to buy a property; examines characteristics associated with deviation from this normative route. Finds alternative transitions, particularly moving into rented accommodation, are more common among young people from more advantaged backgrounds, and those living in northern Spain.

Descriptor: Young people; housing; first; purchasing; leaving home; Spain.

Title: Bolland, J. (2003) 'Hopelessness and risk behaviour among adolescents living in high-poverty inner-city neighbourhoods', *Journal of Adolescence*, 26, 2, 145–58.

Abstract: Ethnographic literature on inner-city life argues that adolescents react to their uncertain futures by abandoning hope, leading them to engage in high levels of risk behaviour. Tests this relationship using a survey of 2,468 inner-city adolescents, asking questions about hopelessness, violent and aggressive behaviour, substance use, sexual behaviour and accidental injury. Nearly 50% of males and 25% of females had moderate or severe feelings of hopelessness. Moreover, hopelessness levels were predicted for each group, as were risk behaviour patterns. Results suggest that effective prevention and intervention programmes aimed at inner city adolescents should target hopelessness by promoting skills that allow them to overcome the limitations of hopelessness.

Descriptor: Young people; hopelessness; risk behaviour; poverty; inner cities; USA.

Title: Dekel, R., Peled, E. and Spiro, S. (2003) 'Shelters for houseless youth: a follow-up evaluation', in *Journal of Adolescence*, 26, 2, 201–12.

Abstract: Followed up 345 Israeli youngsters who had been residents of two shelters for runaway and homeless youths, 6–12 weeks after their departure. Telephone interviews were conducted with the youngsters, their parents, and social workers in the community. A majority of the youngsters had either returned to their family homes, or had been placed out of home. Their residential stability was found to be low. Post-shelter place of residence was related to length of stay at the shelter, amount of contact with their family while at the shelter, and manner of departure. Findings lead to a typology of shelter uses, and also raise questions about the extent to which shelters achieve their declared goals.

Descriptor: Homeless young people; sheltered accommodation; follow-up studies; Israel

Title: Rokach, A. and Orzeck, T. (2003) 'Coping with loneliness and drug use in young adults', in *Social Indicators Research*, 61, 3, 259–83.

Abstract: Loneliness is a subjective experience which is influenced by one's personality, life experiences, and situational variables. The study examined the influence of Ecstasy (MDMA) use on the coping strategies of loneliness. The Ecstasy users were compared to Non-Ecstasy users and to a group of young adults in the general population who are non-users of drugs. 818 participants volunteered to answer a 34-item yes/no questionnaire, reflecting on their loneliness experience and the ways in which they coped with it. The strategies examined included Acceptance and reflection, Self-development and understanding, Social support network, Distancing and denial, Religion and faith, and increased activity.

Results revealed significant differences between the scores of the Ecstasy users and the other groups.

Descriptor: Ecstasy drug; drug abuse; young adults; loneliness; coping strategies; Canada.

Title: Turner, H. and Butler, M. (2003) 'Direct and indirect effects of childhood adversity on depressive symptoms in young adults', in *Journal of Youth and Adolescence*, 32, 2, 89–103.

Abstract: Using a sample of 649 college students from New England, examines whether cumulative trauma in childhood and adolescence is related to depressive symptoms in young adults, and explores the mediating factors that operate in this association. Results indicate clear differences in cumulative trauma by socio-demographic characteristics. Higher trauma is associated with both early onset of depressive disorder and later depressive symptoms.

Descriptor: Colleges; students; depression; predictors; adversity; social environment; childhood experiences; stressful events; indirect effects; New England; USA.

Title: Vazsonyi, A. and Pickering, L. (2003) 'The importance of family and school domains in adolescent deviance: African American and Caucasian youth', in *Journal of Youth and Adolescence*, 32, 2, 115–28.

Abstract: Examined the importance of the family (closeness, monitoring, and conflict) and school (grades, homework time, educational aspirations, and commitment) domains on a sample of adolescent African American and Caucasian youth. Found that: developmental processes including family and school domain variables and deviance were very similar for African American and Caucasian youth. Both developmental domains revealed independent predictive relationships with a number of different measures of adolescent deviance in both groups and the two domains uniquely accounted for 25 percent and 37 percent of the variance explained respectively in African American and Caucasian adolescent total deviance.

Descriptor: Young people; deviant behaviour; predictors; families; schools; ethnic differences; USA.

Academic theses, relevant to your subject area, will generally be held in the relevant university library and can be read on the premises. Some libraries also offer inter-library loan facilities. There are comprehensive indexes of theses such as the ASLIB Index to Theses, which again is available on-line. Accessing a relevant thesis can provide you with a solid review of the literature as well as an insight into the method issues that arose. Theses may be particularly useful if you are researching for a higher degree, as they will give you a feel for the format, style, and expected standard of work. Using such sources can encourage plagiarism, so take care in how you use this material.

Inter-Library Loan, as noted above, allows books and journal articles not readily available in the local library to be forwarded, at a cost, to your library. To get a copy of a book or photocopy of a journal article through the British Library Inter-Library Loan system can, however, take a few weeks. It is envisaged that this paper based transmission system will be replaced by one involving the electronic downloading of articles, which then can be printed off in the library, or on your computer. Books, given their size, are still likely to be posted out, but with the advances in information technology, especially the use of Adobe Acrobat Portable Document File (PDF) files, that could change before too long.

Finally, mention should also be made of the specialist library facilities offered by IDOX (previously the Planning Exchange). Their library is dedicated to the broad range of local government services such as education, social services, planning, housing, environmental issues and economic development. For subscribing members, in the main local authority policy and research sections, a weekly abstract of all material received by their library is provided, broken down by topic. Then the different topic listings are consolidated on a monthly basis. Members request items and these are posted out. As a subscription organisation this service is beyond the reach of individuals, but it may be possible to access it through your employer.

Internet sources

As will be evident from the last section, the Internet has, in less than ten years, completely revolutionised information searches. If you have access to the World Wide Web you can search for your particular topic of interest, again using keywords. Surfing the web, using a search engine such as *Google* or *Yahoo* or *Ask Jeeves,* will provide no end of potential material. If you are familiar with the techniques involved in electronic data searches then the web should present few difficulties. But whether this will produce the information you require is quite another matter. Be warned it is easy to get drowned in material, so you need to think carefully about how you can best access what you need. Some training in search techniques, which is covered in Chapter 12 on ICT, would be useful. Remember accessing web sites can be addictive and as such is highly distracting to the task in hand.

Given the mass of information out there it is worth starting your search through the use of gateways. Libraries, especially those who cater for a specialist client base often have on-line contacts that will assist the information demands of their specialist readers. Within the social welfare field these often include the SCIE resources already detailed, SW Bubl Link/5.15, Catalogue of Internet Resources for Social Work, the Social Sciences

Information Gateway (SOSIG) and the Social Work Gateway. Within these sites you can then access specialist sites that keep people up-to-date with developments in their particular field of interest. Some better known sites are CareData web, child data, legislation direct, social science abstracts and sociological abstracts.

The Joint Information Services Committee (JISC) *http://www.jisc.ac.uk*, a government funded body that provides advice and opportunities to use ICT in further and higher education provide another useful gateway. This site provides information on bibliographic sites, on-line publications, subject gateways and relevant data services, a topic discussed in more detail below. It also has an interesting digitised collection of early pamphlets on social policy covering topics such as poverty, the origins of the welfare state, health, housing, pensions and unemployment insurance.

In addition to accessing information sources, the use of e-mail provides a major advance in basic information technology, rapidly linking people with information to share. E-mail topic listings are a facility that allows you to receive any information posted by e-mail to a particular listing site. Within the British context this facility is provided by JISC, via JISCMAIL (formally mailbase), located at the University of Newcastle. To access this facility type *http://www.jiscmail.ac.uk* and from the home page navigate to the inventory of listings. Under the Social Studies heading you will find 96 Sociology, 26 Social Work and 24 on Gender Issues listings. Having selected the particular listing, or listings, which best covers your particular interest you can register with them. Then all material passing into this listing will automatically be copied to your e-mail address. Similar facilities are available through out the web, and in certain instances on-line discussion groups on various topics have been created. Posting a message to appropriate listings could be a useful means of exploring the parameters of a particular research topic. Such a message would have to include a very clear outline of the proposed project and a request for any comments or suggestions. Be advised that the advice you receive is only as good as those who choose to offer it. These facilities are constantly developing and it is clear that their research applications will expand greatly over the next few years. (See Chapter 12 for more details).

Finally, it is also worth keeping up to date with the Joseph Rowntree Foundation *http://www.jrf.org.uk*, which specialises in funding social welfare research. Their comprehensive web site provides details of on-going research programmes and relevant funded projects and all *Findings* publications which briefly detail each of the Foundation's completed research projects. It also provides a good set of links to other relevant sites.

Sources of other information

Remember that in surveying the literature, consideration should also be given to statistical material, as well as to written texts. The best site to consult is ukonline *http://www.ukonline.gov.uk*, the official UK government hub, which links all official government departments. If your area of interest falls within Scotland, Wales or Northern Ireland you will probably be best advised to go directly to the devolved administrations web sites *http://www.scotland.gov.uk*, *http://www.wales.gov.uk*, *http://www.northernireland.gov.uk*. Such sites provide a vast array of information, such as reports, consultation papers, press releases, and in some cases basic statistics. Perhaps the best known data set is the Census, but each and every government department possesses statistical information, which are considered core to their day-to-day operations. Accessing such data can involve a great deal of knowledge and navigation, so it is often useful to first consult government publications on what published statistics are available. All official statistics held by government are detailed in the Guide to Official Statistics (Office for National Statistics, 2000). This current guide is also available in PDF format at *http://www.statistics.gov.uk*. Ask for assistance when first exploring this very specialised area, given the mass of data available and the variety of locations in which it is deposited. There is also a gateway facility available that should ease access to government departments' public data sets, at *http://www.inforoute.hmso.gov.uk*. Remember each government department produces its own annual abstract of statistics so the data available is massive. Whether it is held in a format that suits your particular research interest is an entirely different matter. One benefit of the move to e-government is that it is sometimes possible to access more detailed breakdowns of available statistical information. Census and local unemployment data, for example, can be provided at neighbourhood scale, useful if you are asked to undertake a neighbourhood audit. Digests of official statistics such as Social Trends, which is produced annually and Economic Trends, which is published monthly, are good starting points. Regional Trends, also produced annually, is a very helpful source for regional comparisons.

Planning the search

With such a wide array of sources to choose from it is essential that you plan your search carefully. It's all too easy to waste valuable time browsing library shelves, or the web for material that turns out to be of little, or no real relevance to your research topic. Although conducting a literature search is not an exact science, the following steps should help you avoid the above pitfalls:

- Be focused – start by making sure you have a clear sense of what it is you are looking for. Well thought out research questions will always provide the necessary focus.
- Define your terms – what are the key words that best describe your research area? For example, if you are researching 'housing options for the disabled', your key words might include disability, impairment, mainstream and supported accommodation, access issues, adaptations, and welfare advice'. Most systems only allow three key words, so you have to employ different combinations to see what information was available. In most search facilities there are 'or' and 'and' facilities. The 'or' command broadens the

search so that you can find as much as possible on your topic. Once that has been achieved, you want to narrow the field, so the 'and' facility is employed. It may also be important to define the limits of your search in terms of geographical areas (e.g. UK only, Europe, USA), time scale (1995 to present), language, and so on. The trick is to cast your net in different, but related ways, and then see what re-occurs. At the same time you may discover individual items of interest.

- Ask for help – if you are not familiar with the library, or have not used certain of its up-to-date facilities, ask for help in identifying and using the most appropriate search facilities whether a general or specific catalogue, CD-ROM or an online search facility.
- Use what you find to access more – find and read the relevant books and journal articles (using the Inter-Library Loan service if necessary). Citations found in these publications will provide links to other related and useful material.

Taking notes

Finding literature is always a time consuming business, even using the information technology now available. The importance of taking good notes, as you progress cannot be stressed enough. Having to redo a library or web search because you have forgotten to note the proper source is not only a waste of time, but is also extremely frustrating. So to avoid this problem always take good notes about the source of any reference as you go.

Once you have found the book or article it pays dividends to develop the habit of taking good notes and proper reference details right from the outset. How you choose to keep your notes and in how much detail is to some extent a matter of personal choice. The following information is the minimum necessary for research purposes:

1. The author's surname and initial or first name. Note too whether the named author is an editor, rather than the sole author of the book. When referencing an edited collection, the author of the individual chapter has to be acknowledged as well as the editor.
2. The date of publication. This information is found on the reverse side of the title page. Try and ensure you are using the most up to date edition.
3. The title of the book or article.
4. The place of publication and publisher's name.
5. For a journal article, note the name of the journal, volume and issue number, and the page numbers of the article. Take care if you abbreviate the name of a journal. Use only accepted abbreviations and not your own idiosyncratic shorthand because you could get mixed up between similarly titled journals.
6. The International Standard Book Number (ISBN) or the International Standard Serial Number (ISSN) in the case of journals are unique reference numbers. Again this is found on the reverse side of the book's title page, along with all the publishing details, or in the contents page of a journal or magazine. Such reference numbers are useful if you plan to order a book or article through Inter-Library Loan.

7. If the item was found in your local library you might want to record the specific catalogue reference so it can be easily located in the future. If you are using a number of libraries, it is also worth noting the actual library where the item was found.

8. A brief comment or abstract of the contents of a book, chapter, or article might be useful as a reminder of why the item was considered noteworthy in the first place.

Presented below are typical examples of notes made on a book, an edited collection, a research report and a journal article.

Traditionally, researchers would have recorded all this information on a card index system, and then used that to organise the collected information in a variety of ways. Now simple database packages have replaced the need for card indexes. Most on-line bibliographical sources allow the user to download items from a search into your personal

---

Connors, C. and Stalker, K. (2003) **The Views and Experiences of Disabled Children and their Siblings: A positive outlook**. London: Jessica Kingsley. (ISBN 1-84310-127-0)

Based on data gleaned from one-to-one guided conversations with disabled children, their parents and siblings, this book examined the effects of disability on disabled children. In the past, while parents and professional perspectives were well recorded, this is not the case for the children themselves. The two-year study, which was carried out between 1998 and 2000, involved 26 disabled children aged between 7 and 19. It sought to consider the children's understanding of disability; the way they negotiate the experience of disability in their every day lives, their perspective on relationships with professionals and the services they are offered and, finally, their siblings' perception of the effects on them of having a disabled brother or sister. The book's main objective is to use this work to develop further a childhood model of social disability. It also illustrates effective ways of communicating directly with disabled children and how this could assist mainstream, specialist and statutory providers.

Figure 3.1: An example of notes on a book

Anderson, I. and Sim, D. (eds), (2000), **Social Exclusion and Housing: Context and challenges**. Coventry: Chartered Institute of Housing. (ISBN 1-9000396-39-4)

A collection of individual essays that take as their starting point the view that housing is very much a key cornerstone of the Labour government's social exclusion agenda. The editors' introduction details the establishment of the Social Exclusion Unit and the National Strategy for Neighbourhood Renewal. Argues that in order to develop effective responses to social exclusion there needs to be a sound understanding of the issues and pressures, which affect the housing system. Chapter Two provides a useful historic discussion of the policy notion of social exclusion, and how it has replaced notions of poverty and deprivation within government policy circles. Part 1 provides a standard geographic discussion of the distribution of inequality, while Part 2 reworks that in relation to specific groups such as the homeless, minority ethnic groups, lone parents and young people. Useful chapter provided by David Webster providing a critique of the current debate on lone parenthood. Argues that economic downturns and the resulting rise in unemployment are a major cause of this social issue. Getting lone parents back into work under New Deal works for women with appropriate skills, but not for those who are unskilled and are having to look for work in stagnant or declining labour markets. Part 3 looks at the role of housing as an intervention mechanism in social exclusion policies. Concludes that exclusion, as a contested term, has a limited value but if we talked more about the social consequences of exclusion from social welfare services it might be more useful highlighting the inter-linkage between services. Also argues that there is value in using the Scottish term of inclusion, rather than exclusion.

Figure 3.2: An example of notes on an edited collection

Anderson, S., Brownlie, J. and Murray, L. (2002) 'Disciplining children: Research with parents in Scotland', **Central Research Unit Research Paper**. Edinburgh: Scottish Executive. (ISBN 0-7559-3428-8)

This official report presents recent research on parental attitudes to disciplining their children. The research was carried out between March 2002 and August 2003, to tie into a Scottish Parliament debate about banning the physical chastisement of children. It used qualitative interviews of couples, individuals and focus groups to explore the issue initially, before using that information to draw up a quantitative survey of 692 Scottish parents. Most parents saw smacking as a 'normal' part of parenting, a deeply imbedded part of Scottish parenting culture. There was a noticeable class dimension to its use, however, with the middle classes being more reluctant to smack. The smacking of children under three was, however, not considered justifiable. Shaking, hitting around the face or head, or using an implement was also considered unacceptable, constituting abuse rather than disciplining. Smacking was emotionally charged leaving parents feeling both guilty and upset. Heightened expectations about parenting and reduced parental control were seen as core in this debate. Parents raised concerns about the work-life balance, loss of routine in family life, and pressures on both themselves and their children in relation to material expectations. Children were felt to be more assertive and less accepting of adult authority. Parents were also concerned that they were now being held to account for behaviour of their children.

Figure 3.3: An example of notes on a report

Bowes, A. and Domokos, T. (1998) 'Negotiating breast-feeding: Pakistani women, white women and their experiences in hospital and home.' In *Sociological Research Online*, 3:3, September *http://www.socresonline.org.uk*.

Article argues that breast-feeding is a socially constructed and socially controlled practice. The paper draws on data from a research study of women from diverse ethnic and class backgrounds. Argues that breast-feeding women in hospital are generally subordinate to professionals, but remain active in the negotiation of breast-feeding. At home, health visitor support is especially significant. Breast-feeding appears to be a lonely struggle, and the end of breast-feeding is caused more by outside influences. Successful breast-feeding projects are most likely for white, middle class women who have effective stocks of knowledge, and can negotiate concerted action with health professionals. Women belonging to socially excluded groups have greater difficulty in the negotiation process, and their breast-feeding projects are less likely to succeed. Whilst influenced by patterns of constraint, breast-feeding projects also show marked individuality.

Figure 3.4: An example of notes on an article in a journal

database. Again take care not to amass a substantial database of information, much of which you will never get round to reading. Use the abstracts to decide whether this or that article, or book is of direct relevance to your specific study. Try to seek out the key texts and articles, rather than constructing a large, comprehensive and unwieldy bibliography. Getting to the right texts is the crucial task, rather than building up an elongated list of publications. Be clear about what you need and try not to become seduced by the technology.

References

It might be useful to select the referencing system you intend to adopt in your final report before you begin taking notes. Figures 3.1 to 3.4 above have employed the Harvard system. Originally developed in America it now has almost universal application. Another, the British referencing system was developed by the British Standards Institution (BS 5605)

(BSI, 1978). Information on the various referencing systems should be available from your local library. Your own organisation may have a preferred 'house style' of referencing, in which case that is the one you should adopt. The important point to remember, no matter the referencing convention you adopt is that it should be both thorough and consistent. To get a clear idea of how the Harvard referencing system functions in relation to the range of published output consult the bibliography at the end of this book.

Reading critically

In reviewing the published work for your own study it is important that you critically read material, because it is your opinions on that work, collectively, that is the basis of the all-important literature review. Being a critical reader is often easier said than done. It is all too common to find:

> *The uncritical review, the furniture sale catalogue, in which everything merits a one paragraph entry no matter how skilfully it has been conducted. Bloggs (1975) found this, Smith (1976) found that, Jones (1977) found the other; Bloggs, Smith and Jones (1978) found happiness in heaven.*
>
> (Haywood and Wragg, 1978: 38).

One way to develop this critical habit in both your reading and subsequent writing is to scrutinise published research work and ask the same sort of questions of it as you would be expected to have answered in designing your own research project. Such an 'evaluation' should Include topics such as:

1. Research question – what is the research question hypothesis and is it a valid and relevant question?
2. Literature review – is the review relevant and up-to-date; are the links between theory, earlier findings, and the study being reported clearly and explicitly?
3. Sample – who are the research subjects, how were they selected and are there aspects of selection that might limit the wider applicability of the results?
4. Data collection – how was the data collected and what steps (if any) were taken to ensure reliability and validity?
5. Presentation of findings – was the data analysed appropriately and were the resulting findings clear and concise?
6. Conclusions – do the conclusions follow logically from the analyses, and critically does the data actually warrant these conclusions?
7. Ethics – does the research meet accepted standards of ethical practice?

All research is dependent on reading to a greater or lesser extent and it is, therefore, important that you read critically, widely and with a clear purpose. The above review of critical reading very much mirrors the previous discussion, in Chapter 1 on appraising existing research.

Literature reviews

In setting the context for any research study you will be expected to produce a critical review of the available literature. A literature review serves two purposes. Firstly, it provides the context, the background to the current research: it should give the reader an insight into the state of knowledge on the chosen research area. If possible it should also identify any gaps in current knowledge that the research proposes to fill. Secondly, it should illustrate that the researcher can locate the relevant literature, summarise it and consider its relevance to their particular study. A literature review should not, therefore, be a mere reiteration of all the items found as a result of the literature search. Nor should it be simply a catalogue of books and articles read. Rather it should demonstrate a critical awareness of the literature within the subject area, through careful consideration of relevant work.

The precise details of the literature review, illustrating the depth and breadth of coverage, will depend on the nature of the project. You would not expect as much from a brief internal research report, for example, as you would from an academic thesis or project. Nevertheless, all literature reviews require three things of you, the writer:

1. That you be selective in your presentation of the literature. You will have to leave out some things, perhaps many things, which you have found from your searches. This may be frustrating, but it is a discipline that must be learned.
2. That you only identify themes or features in the literature that are relevant and of particular interest to your study.
3. That you discuss the range of relevant literature, not simply that which supports your position. A good literature review should compare and contrast different aspects of the literature.

The success of any literature review, however, is in the reading that underpins it. Reading for research is not like reading for fun. That is not to say it cannot be enjoyable, but simply that it demands that you read widely, that you read carefully and that you read with a purpose. Delamont (1992) identifies three types of reading with a purpose: reading on and around your topic; reading for contrast; and reading to develop analytical or theoretical concepts. The important point here is that you need to read, and when writing this material up for the literature review, it has to be critical, while maintaining a sense of scepticism and curiosity.

The literature review is critical in grounding your study. It will indicate to the reader whether this is a study that has been rigorously conducted, drawing out key issues from previous work in the field, or merely a very basic appraisal, or monitoring exercise. The literature review is also fundamental to helping you properly understand the nature of the issues. It is crucial that you spend time on the literature review because it will have a major influence on the planning of your subsequent study. If you rush into fieldwork, before concluding a solid literature review, the quality of the eventual research outcomes will suffer.

CHAPTER 4

Documentary Techniques

CHAPTER OBJECTIVES

This chapter is designed to ensure that you:
- Recognise both the value and practical difficulties associated with using documentary techniques.
- Appreciate the various types of contemporary document that can utilised in any study.
- Understand the importance of historic method when assessing the value and worth of any document considered relevant to social welfare research.

Introduction

Almost every social welfare research project will involve you in examining and analysing a range of associated documentary material. The term 'document' in this context refers to a broad range of written sources, encompassing official reports, internal management reports, as well as the full range of day-to-day filed records, often referred to on mass as 'archival material'. Also included within this broad term are all non-written sources such as film, video and photographs, as well as slides and audio recordings. The procedures and skills necessary to undertake documentary studies closely replicate those outlined in the previous chapter, in relation to literature reviews. It is also the case that documentary work can often constitute one distinct part of any literature review exercise. It is important to try and ensure a clear appreciation of the range, content and quality of all available documentary material associated with your own particular research interest. Documentary material also provides other insights into the proposed study area, and this is extremely valuable when planning the research project. As was emphasised in the previous chapter in relation to the literature review, it is crucial that, as a researcher, you never rush into the fieldwork. Time spent seeking out and reviewing the available documentary records, in the same way as books, journals and related relevant studies, pays dividends. The better the information you start out with, the more robust the planning and refining exercise. This, in turn, will result in a more tightly focused study. On occasions documentary work also throws up some innovative and novel research questions, which might not have been considered if the preliminary focus of background reading was solely based on published secondary sources.

While documentary work can be used to explore the parameters of a proposed study, as a method in itself it can generate material which can either supplement a study, setting a piece of research within its historic context, or alternatively be the prime means of conducting a research study. A useful example of the former is Garland's work entitled *Punishment and Modern Society* (1990) and more recently his follow up book *The Culture of Control: Crime and Social Order in Contemporary Society* (2001). Both works partly draw on archive material to illustrate how notions of punishment and rehabilitation have changed over time, and how these changes are reflected in the changing structure of the criminal justice system. In the recent past, Garland argues, we have seen concerns with welfare and deprivation give way to a new criminology focused on individual choice and social control. Social solutions to crime have now given way to economic ones. All this leaves Garland asking whether crime policy has started to become part of the problem, rather than the solution.

The critical skills required to undertake this type of work are very much those of the historian and, on occasions, the investigative journalist. Historic method involves the researcher in first locating the relevant material. So the first question you need to answer is where exactly I will find this type of information. Then having located the material, the next task is to select that which is relevant to your study. This involves you in a rigorous questioning of the document's specific purpose and then asking exactly why you are consulting it. It is the selection, evaluation and utilisation of available evidence that is the cornerstone of all good research. The purpose of this chapter is to detail the various issues involved in adopting such an approach when seeking to utilise documentary material.

Documentary research

Documents are divided into what are termed either 'primary' or 'secondary' sources. Primary sources are those that came into existence in the period under research; contemporary written reports or material collected by those who witnessed, or were engaged in the execution of a particular project, event or initiative. An example of such material would be the minutes and supporting papers of a social services committee, or those of a voluntary body's management committee, recording the decisions and action points relating to both practice and policy. The documentary record would also include any records generated by these organisations regarding their services, facilities and initiatives, as they carried out their day-to-day work.

Secondary sources are, by contrast, someone's interpretations of these events, based on their consideration of these very same primary sources. Secondary sources, largely published material, were the core consideration of the previous chapter. The pamphlet produced to celebrate the twenty-five year history of Glasgow's community-based housing associations would be a typical example of secondary documentation (Robertson, 1997). This document drew on primary sources such as official reports, minutes and various other contemporary publications as well as the recollections of both committee members and staff. Use was also made of photographic material that recorded the work these bodies undertook over that extended timeframe.

This material revealed that the community-based housing associations viewed themselves, at the time of their creation, as being a tangible example of resident participation within the local planning process, a form of community-based action designed to stop the wholesale demolition of their tenemental neighbourhoods. The documentary record also provided substantial amounts of information on the technical and administrative skills needed in order to improve some 30,000 tenement flats, while retaining the resident population. If only secondary sources had been relied upon, then the emphasis might have focused more on current notions of community empowerment, achieved through the process of housing renewal. Politicians and administrators from both central and local government would also have received greater consideration, given their ability to influence the 'official record' of events. Thus the grass roots roles played by many community activists and community workers would have been passed over, or merely recorded as a footnote. Only by bringing together both sets of sources, the primary and the secondary record, can you decide where the emphasis in recording this part of history should lie. At the same time it is also important to appreciate the subtle differences that exist within primary sources. All primary sources can be further sub-divided into what are termed 'inadvertent' and 'deliberate' sources.

Inadvertent sources

This refers to primary material that is used, by the researcher, in a way not originally intended. These are typically the myriad of material generated by the day-to-day work of public administration. Examples would be the formal minutes that record the decisions taken at the various meetings held. Then there would be the whole range of administrative records, everything from the job descriptions, organisational structure, wage records, client records, funding and financial records and all correspondence, whether letters, newsletters, or press releases and clippings. The guidance material produced by government departments or their specialist agencies also has some value, given the emphasis it places on certain issues, at a particular point in time. Clearly much of this material has a distinct and limited operational focus. For instance, using this to try and determine whether the core policy objectives were being met might prove a bit fraught. Examining policy statements, the management plan, the business plan, and the performance audit might prove more productive. But clearly, public pronouncements and what happens on the ground can be markedly different. By carefully considering certain bits of operational data and analysing it in the right way, it is possible to reveal where the operational priorities lay, and this would tell you far more about a project, than merely noting its stated objectives in the business plan. That, after all is the basis of so much of the monitoring and appraisal culture, which currently operates in the public sector. So, despite the bulk of this material appearing mundane, given it is generated from very practical day-to-day work, if properly analysed it can prove to be far more interesting than first assumed.

This is not to say, however, that such material does not present the researcher with problems. Given the ephemeral nature of so much of management material it rarely survives as a complete entity. The lack of a complete record can limit your capacity to draw out clear conclusions. It is also common practice to construct reports in a way that emphasises one set of issues, while downplaying the significance of other equally valid points. So a literal interpretation of one particular report, without reference to a body of other related documents, could easily result in misconceptions arising. A good example is the way that organisational performance information is generally constructed to fit with the stated strategic ambitions of the organisation. Within youth work the activities undertaken can be defined as being either 'community based', with some services being available to all or most age groups in the locality, or tightly focussed on 'processed offenders'. While the performance information will reflect a particular focus this may act as a gloss on what the agency is actually doing. This is especially the case when agencies need to fund work they want to do within budgets that may have proscribed policy and practice 'strings' attached.

It is also the case that records are written with a narrow operational objective in mind. There is never any real thought given to how these could be subsequently classified and analysed. As a result, they can prove very unhelpful to subsequent study. For example, the terms employed in many basic forms tend to be vague, and as such are difficult to classify and compare. In a study of housing allocations based on medical criteria the records held by general practitioners proved especially hard to classify, given the vagueness and variety of terms applied (Smith et al., 1991).

More often than not, records reflect more about the recorder, than the particular topic in question. In Booth's (1889) pioneering work on the living conditions of London's poor, use was made of School Attendance Officers' official case reports to isolate out the conditions in poorer neighbourhoods. Aware of how the personal biases of the attendance officers could influence how they recorded each truant's case, Booth first held interviews with the officers about each individual case. He then used the results of this interview to address what he considered biases before coming to his own views about the living conditions of truants (Englander and O'Day, 1995). All of this implies that a great deal of care needs to be taken when using basic documentary records.

Deliberate sources

This refers to those documents that have been produced with the intention of influencing future researchers. These include autobiographies, memoirs, diaries and letters, all of which are intended for later publication. Then there are the various documents of self-justification. So while inadvertent sources, at least initially, appear straightforward, deliberate sources also need to be treated with caution.

Richard Crossman, Labour's Minister for Housing and Local Government under Harold Wilson's first administration of 1964–66, produced perhaps the best known diary of that period (Crossman, 1976). Crossman's intention was to illuminate British politics from the inside, more than anyone had done before. And he certainly succeeded in doing just that. His diaries caused a sensation, in that they detailed the Wilson government's decision-making process from the perspective of a very recent cabinet minister. Such a document has the explicit aim of preserving a particular perspective for the future. There is, as a result, a tendency for the evidence provided in such a publication to be either incomplete or inaccurate. Information that might show the author in a bad light may be amended, or ignored. Such sources are, therefore, tricky, and demand careful consideration. That said, such deliberate sources can also provide a unique insight into how decisions were made, often illustrating various considerations and tensions that are never made part of an official record. Official reports or minutes always imply a consensus in decision-making. Again, only by reading a variety of sources can you hope to come to a view on what actually happened, and what were the key issues in that decision being reached.

Witting and unwitting evidence

Both types of document also provide what is referred to as witting and unwitting evidence. Witting evidence is the information which the author of the document wanted to impart, whereas unwitting, or 'hidden' evidence, is everything else that can be gleaned from the document (Marwick, 1977). Studying the speeches made by government ministers, about the role and function of councils in relation to social services would certainly reveal the stated objectives set for social policy at the time. In the 1980s, 'extending personal choice' and 'giving people greater responsibility for decisions' would be very much to the fore. The unwitting material would reveal much about the government's faith in market solutions and their desire to stimulate greater consumerism in relation to the delivery of the full range of council services. Privatisation and the desire to create markets within all social welfare services were the means to facilitate popular consumerism. There was also a marked shift towards accepting the residualisation of certain communities and the acceptance of basic welfare solution role for those unable, or unwilling to compete within the market. Perhaps more confusing was the considerable political and financial support given to voluntary initiatives and volunteering. Politically this was seen to be good, because it helped foster self-help and independence. It was also not in the public sector, but rather was viewed as being quasi-private, which made up for the lack of any real private sector interest in this work. Within many welfare settings it also encouraged innovative practice, which some commentators have suggested has been less actively supported by New Labour (Holman, 2000).

All documents contain unwitting evidence. The challenge for the researcher is to be able to identify its existence and then assess its actual significance. Again analysis and interpretation are the critical skills required of the researcher.

Practical issues

Historic studies

History is not what happened in the past, rather it is what we can know and, therefore, interpret about what happened in the past. History is constrained by the information that can be obtained and by how an individual chooses to interpret that information. In order to be able to interpret documents you have to be aware of the context in which the document was produced and that requires obtaining a broad, as well as a specific knowledge, of both the topic and period under consideration. This can only be achieved through reading a broad range of secondary and primary sources. Without such background knowledge and understanding the significance of specific documents could easily be overlooked. At the same time, there is always the danger that with such knowledge and understanding you may opt to over-emphasise the significance of material held in a document to justify your particular interpretation of events. Historical study is, as a consequence of these two parameters, in a constant state of flux. Our understanding of past events is constantly being reassessed through either the reinterpretation of existing documents, or through the discovery and interpretation of new ones. The fact that our understanding of the past is influenced by understanding of the present also ensures that historical events are always being revisited and therefore reinterpreted.

Historical studies of social welfare *per se* are not that common, but they do exist. South (1999) edited a collection of contributions entitled *Drugs, Cultures, Controls and Everyday Life*. As most people are aware, perceptions of drug taking are very much constructed at a particular point in time. South (1999) notes that historic studies of drug use have concerned themselves with both the construction and deconstruction of realities, rules and the meaning of actions. Even the use of the word drugs is problematic when it comes to assigning meaning. In both historical and geographic terms, drugs have been subject to prohibition and legalisation. Alcohol and cannabis are just two of the most obvious examples. Adopting a historic perspective on the subject helps us to see how far some drug use has been legalised and legitimised, such as the case of prescribed tranquillisers. Using drugs to escape one's everyday existence has, at various times in history, been both castigated and praised. The examples of opium dens, the widespread use of laudanum as well as the use of mescal by many Indian tribes, each designed to reach a state of ecstasy have been lauded in the past (Rudgley, 1993). Then there is the example of tobacco, once considered a socially acceptable habit, but is now falling out of favour, being banned from restaurants, pubs and public places in locations as diverse as New York, Amsterdam and Brighton. Given the dominant policy focus of so much contemporary social welfare research, there is a tendency to avoid trying to set any new study within its wider historical context. The resulting lack of historic social welfare studies could provide a rich seam for future researchers to mine.

Document searches and selection

Document searches need to be as comprehensive as possible. As noted earlier, it is extremely helpful when drawing up the initial research design to have a reasonable knowledge of what documentary material is available. Optimistic assumptions about access and/or the contents of documents can often undermine the initial aspirations of a research project. Much of the documentary material used in social welfare studies emanates from national governmental archives in London, Edinburgh, Cardiff and Belfast and the many policy and professional agencies, such as the Social Care Institute for Excellence, the Policy Studies Institute, the Institute for the Study of Drug Dependency, the Centre for Policy on Ageing and the National Society for Prevention of Cruelty to Children.

The recent advent of devolution, resulting in the creation of a Scottish Parliament, and Welsh and Northern Ireland Assemblies, merely builds on from the previous territorial government departments that had responsibility for the administration of these localities. As such each of these 'national' archives hold a comprehensive collection of all associated policy-based material. Given the legal distinctiveness of Scotland, and the requirement on many occasions to enact separate legislation covering similar policy initiatives – even prior to the establishment of the Edinburgh legislature – the Scottish Executive (previously the Scottish Office) tended to have a more comprehensive policy archive than its Welsh or Northern Irish counterparts. There are also national archives such as the British Library in London, where collections of papers by eminent individuals, and other documentary material are often left to the nation.

The problem with national governmental archives is that they tend to record the views of the government of the day, reflecting their own distinct perspective on events. Work on the local implementation policy is beginning to illustrate that while national government may have promoted a particular policy for specific reasons, it does not necessarily follow that it was implemented in different local areas for the same reasons (Robertson and Bailey, 1996). To gain an understanding of the interplay between national and local policy objectives, as well as ambitions, it would be necessary to consult both national and local archives. By doing so, a better appreciation of the policy formulation and implementation processes would be gained.

Such document searches have been made easier by the recent development of local archives. While archives previously covered either national records, or those relating to the creation of large urban settlements, smaller rural localities were rarely well served. Local archives resulted from the creation of larger local government administrative units (1974 in England and Wales and 1975 in Scotland). The more recent phase of local government organisation, in the mid 1990s, which broke up a number of the larger authorities, has had a negative impact on these local resources.

There is, however, no really comprehensive archive. National and local archives contain many gaps. Only by using both can some of these gaps be filled. With the advances in information technology, locating material within this extended archival network has greatly improved. It has also improved the quality of the catalogue records held, given the standardisation requirements of many database and cataloguing systems. Occasionally specialist books have been published which provide a guide to using specific archives. Regional archives are not so well funded and you will invariably find some material which has never been properly catalogued. This is also true for many local collections such as those held in local museums.

What is actually held in any archive tends to be haphazard. It all depends on what has been deposited by local government officials; what the original collector of the material was interested in; what may have turned up in lawyers' offices; or even what has been retrieved from skips on the way to the municipal tip. Chance plays a major role in determining what ends up being deposited in an archive. A good example of this is the archive held by the Heatherbank Museum of Social Work, located in Glasgow Caledonian University campus. This museum focuses on social care and social welfare developments in Scotland over the past 200 years. The archive element reflects the particular interests of its collectors, Colin and Rosemary Harvey. The first grouping of material is concerned largely with the poorhouses of Scotland, and the associated administration of the poor law. The second grouping is a collection of relatively recent medical and nursing equipment, most of which is no longer in active use. In addition, the archive has recently acquired the Archive of the Association of Directors of Social Work. So, if your interests coincide with this collection you have an invaluable data source, but clearly this only applies to a very specialist group of researchers. Other university archives tend to be just as eclectic, holding the papers of eminent academics and renowned local public figures of the past.

While archive searches provide one avenue, the most widely used starting point for many documentary studies is the local history section of the public library. The Glasgow Room of Glasgow's Mitchell Library is rightly famous, as is the Edinburgh Room in Edinburgh's Central Library and Liverpool's Picton Library. Mention should also be made of the four Copyright Deposit Libraries – The British Library in London, The National Library of Scotland in Edinburgh, the National Library of Wales, in Aberystwyth and the National Library in Dublin – which by law require a copy of everything published to be deposited with them. It has to be said, however, that the individual collections are not uniform. Finally, a trawl of second-hand bookshops, and especially those with specialist catalogues can often throw up gems and get you started on a documentary study. One key text or a useful report can then lead to other sources, as revealed by bibliographies, abstracts, footnotes and indexes, the so-called 'tertiary' sources.

Clearly, you could spend many hours, days or even months digging out such material. As time is money, you need to adopt a strategy that allows you to explore what's available and from that make a selection. Given what has been said above, this can only ever be a bit 'hit-and-miss'. If you have some familiarity with the different categories of evidence this will help you decide what is fundamental and what is less important, thus controlling your final selection. The danger is that digging out material becomes a substitute to getting on with evaluating the worth of the selected material. You will have to use your own judgement in deciding whether you have got what's required. Perhaps the most crucial decision in the selection process is ensuring you achieve some corroboration of the selected material. Always try and ensure that the key findings from one source can be corroborated from other contemporary sources. That is not to say the points being made should be identical, rather that the pattern of events appears consistent.

Official records as research sources

Official records refer to the full panoply of government papers. While Hansard, green papers, white papers and acts of parliament represent the official published outputs of government, there is substantially more information to be gleaned from the associated reports, files, notes, press releases, briefings and minutes of meetings. Using such an archive also has its potential pitfalls.

First, it is hard to find out from the catalogue exactly what is held within a particular topic file. Such official records can contain a wide diversity of material, much of which may prove to be of limited value. Secondly, as was noted above, what is archived is often an incomplete record. While this would typically imply certain documents may have been lost on the way, within the official archive civil servants or ministers can request concealments in respect of specific documents, or topics. As a consequence, it is almost impossible to know whether what is being presented is a comprehensive record of what is held. It is also the case that any researcher working on these types of papers will have to sign the Official Secrets Act, which can limit what they can report.

Thirdly, as with all archive documentary material, while reading through these files you need to be aware that civil servants are often asked to prepare proposition papers which may, or may not, fully acknowledge the other side of any argument. That said, taking the time to read the hand written comments, often found in the margins of these reports can provide an insight into official attitudes, and perhaps the counter arguments to certain ideas and initiatives.

But the real downside of using these archives is that official records are often constrained by issues of access and confidentiality. Not all public documents are readily accessible. Many are classified as being 'closed' or 'restricted'. Official papers, those that refer to Cabinet discussions and decisions, typically operate to a 30-year rule – namely that access is denied to the public for a period of 30 years. For example, January 1996 was the first opportunity that the public had to access the 1966 cabinet papers. Only then could Crossman's interpretation of events, as detailed by his diaries, be reassessed and perhaps re-appraised.

Restricting access and insisting on concealments is supposed to address concerns about security and confidentiality. Certain documents could contain information that is of a personal nature – certain criticism or observations could be considered hurtful to the people concerned, or to their relatives. Hence, the general operation of the 30-year rule. At the same time, it is worth stating that the UK government has a reputation for secrecy, and that all tiers of government feel uncomfortable with the concept of open access to all public information. This is a culture which will find it hard to adjust to the requirements of the Freedom of Information Acts, recently passed by Westminster and the Scottish Parliament. Although there has long been moves to promote more open government, and much discussion about the need for transparency in decision-making, it would be hard to argue that this has resulted in greater openness. Rather, minutes of meetings and associated background reports have tended to become more terse and, therefore, difficult to follow. Minutes, as noted earlier, also tend to be a record of decisions, rather than a report on the discussion that took place prior to that decision being taken.

It is also important to be aware of the presumption that lies behind the presentation of specific statistics. The old adage that there are, 'lies, damned lies and statistics', is extremely apt. Statistical information presented one way reveals a particular pattern. Yet, quite another interpretation could be arrived at if the data had been presented in another format. To gain some insight into this it is worth reading the commentaries that accompany Census statistics. Changing conceptions about work and employment, through time, clearly illustrate the changing status of different types of employment (Hakim, 1983). It is these interpretational norms that determine the way that statistical information is presented. Change the perspective and quite a different picture can be created. Understanding the broad policy context, in which the statistics have been prepared, will make you alert to this issue. As with all documentary work it is critical to question the motives of the source. What was the specific purpose of a particular document, or set of statistics? Can it be interpreted in a different way? So in order to fully appreciate the limitations of documentary research it is worth detailing the standard historical method that is employed in pursuing this type of work.

Adopting a critical approach

As will be clear by now the major difficulty in respect of documentary work relates to bias. People are selective in what they choose to record and, more importantly, what they decide to leave out. It is, therefore, important to be alert to the possibility of bias, due to selectiveness and manipulation. Documents should never be viewed as neutral artefacts. Consequently, they must be treated with great care and a fair measure of scepticism (Platt,

1981). Those who adopt a more critical approach to documentary sources would go further and argue that the principal objective of documentary analysis is to explore the hidden or unwitting meanings that may be present within the document. As with literature reviews, critical awareness of the source and the context in which these documents were produced is all-important.

> *What counts as reasonable fact in a casual conversation, in a courtroom, a scientific laboratory, a news interview, a police interrogation, a medical consultation or a social security office? What is the nature of social organisation within which these facts find support? To what vicissitudes, exigencies and considerations are the formation of these facts responsive?*

> (Heritage, 1984: 94).

In order to pursue this approach properly it is necessary to adopt both an external and internal criticism of any document in question.

External criticism

External criticism of a primary source is a means to try and avoid misrepresenting, or being misled, by the information provided in the document. Through this approach of questioning the status of the documentary source, you are trying to assess whether it is both genuine and authentic. External criticism of a written text would include such questions as:

- Was the supposed author of the document known to be contemporary with the document?
- Is there any collaboration supporting their authorship?
- Is the document consistent with other information known about the author?
- Is the document typical of the author's style?
- Is the style consistent with other documents produced in the same period?

Internal criticism

Having established that the document is genuine, internal criticism attempts to establish the credibility of the document's actual contents. Internal criticism considers questions such as:

- What is the nature of the document? Is it a letter, a policy statement, or the minutes of a meeting? How many copies would have been made?
- How did the document come into existence? When, where, and for what purpose was it produced?
- What does it actually say, and in what sort of language?
- How long after the event was this record made?

- Did the source of the information actually witness the event? If so, is the author a reliable observer?
- Was the primary witness, the source of the information, able to tell the truth?
- Was the primary witness willing to tell the truth?
- Is the document complete? Or has it been altered or edited in any way?
- Is there any external corroboration of the events described?

While many of these questions will have no relevance to the specific documents you are studying, they should not distract you from the main objective, namely to assess whether the contents of the document reflect facts or biases. As noted throughout this chapter, the author of a particular document will rarely set down the assumptions and beliefs that underpin their particular point of view. By drawing out such biases, and then understanding where they come from, the study will be greatly enhanced through making a considered and critical review of the available material. The previous discussion on reflexivity, in the introductory chapter, provides some useful insights into this issue.

Much of the discussion in relation to this research method would appear to be common sense. Yet, too often such basic common sense is ignored. Documentary work should not be regarded as a 'filler', a means of padding out a few pages with essentially boring background material. Through adopting a rigorous and critical approach to documentary work there is much to be gained from its proper utilisation. Indeed, it can be fascinating to trawl through a range of documentary sources, in what essentially becomes a form of detective work. Only through gaining experience of this type of work will you develop better critical awareness skills and a true appreciation of the value this approach has to all research work.

CHAPTER 5

Measurement

This chapter is designed to ensure that you:
- Understand the basic issues associated with measurement.
- Understand the various approaches to measurement commonly used in social welfare research.
- Appreciate the issues associated with validity and reliability in relation to measurement.

Introduction

Measurement is the process by which theoretical concepts are given a tangible, measurable form – 'operationalised' to use the technical jargon. While certain issues or topics prove easy to measure, many topics within the realm of the social sciences present more complex problems. The familiar concepts of weight or height present few measurement problems. The concept of weight is universal and deciding whether two items have the same weight is straightforward. There may be different scales in use in different parts of the globe, but converting from one to the other is straightforward.

But what if you cannot get agreement on the concept, or a definition of the term you are using? For example, what exactly is deprivation, or poverty, or household income, or social exclusion, or social class or level of addiction? Each of these issues can be viewed as a vague concept, difficult to define. Only once you have set down your definition of the concept, or term, being used can you then set in place a set of measures to give this definition tangible form.

In evaluating an outward-bound project, funded on the basis of introducing deprived young people to a broad range of outdoor pursuits, you would first need to agree with the project what its objectives were, and then decide upon measures to see whether these were being achieved. Defining the notion of deprived young person could be difficult, given the range of views on what constitutes deprivation. But you will need such a definition to be able to measure whether those taking part on the various trips and activities came from the target group. Measuring the activities that took place, and getting various perspectives on the value and worth of these activities is a slightly easier research task.

Similar problems have faced researchers looking at the operation of youth justice schemes. Some of these projects are aimed only at serious recidivists, some first time offenders and others are viewed as being preventative, seeking to offer young people 'at risk' or 'in trouble' alternatives to offending. Obviously, being able to compare the performance of these different programmes is useful to future sentencing practices. Martin (1997) tried to grapple with this problem in one of the most extensive research studies undertaken into the range and scope of community-based programmes for young and juvenile offenders. She explained, however, it was necessary to alter the categorisation process for programmes as she went along, given what was found on the ground did not fit the initial expectations of the research team. *'At the outset, this work was only going to focus on sentencing options, but it soon became clear that many practitioners were often using programmes in ways which did not fall into the category of sentencing'* (Martin, 1997: xiv). Direct comparisons between similar programmes are, therefore, fraught with difficulties.

Working out the appropriateness of the actual measure, or set of measures to be employed, can be challenging. Household income provides a useful illustration of the issues involved, and this particular topic is more fully examined by the Family Resources Survey (FRS). In trying to ascertain household income you first have to agree for each household member whether it is gross income, that is income before tax is deducted, or income net of tax. Those on lower incomes typically know what they earn as an hourly rate, while higher income groups would know the gross figure. Most people would not see interest from stocks and shares as income, but the Inland Revenue takes a different view, and so this income needs also to be recorded. Then there are various welfare payments, such as Child Benefit and Family Income Supplement, if that is paid. To ensure robust income data is derived from the British Household Panel Survey (BHPS) a total of five separate questions are asked. Only then can a reliable and comparable measure of household income be derived.

Different countries also tend to employ different measures to explain the same phenomena. A good example of this is proved by the diagnostic addiction measures employed by those involved in drug treatment work. There is a standardised measure, the Addiction Severity Index (ASI), which was developed in the United States. A variation on this measure was devised for Europe, the Euroasi. But in addition, within the UK, there is the Maudsley Addiction Profile and the Crista Inventory, which is favoured by the Scottish Prisons Service amongst others. As there is no agreed diagnostics instrument to measure drug addiction in the UK, or elsewhere, it is almost impossible to get a comparable measure of the level of addiction. This proves problematic when you wish to explore whether one particular treatment programme achieves better results with particular client groups.

The importance of measurement is that it provides a bridge between the abstract world of theory and the observed world of people, objects, or events which researchers want to explore and explain. Without measurement both the social and physical world would only be explicable in terms of theory. But whether the one particular measure is the best means to achieve such understanding is a vexed question. While we can agree that having a measure is useful, does that particular approach to measurement, of that particular phenomena, not have its own limitations and constraints?

This chapter provides a basic overview of measurement issues within social science research. The main themes to be explored are units of analysis, actual levels of measurement and the concepts of validity and reliability. Each of these broad themes has implications for any subsequent statistical analysis. They also throw up issues that require to be considered in relation to the links between measurement, theory and analysis. The chapter also touches upon the long-standing debate, within social research, over the merits and demerits of qualitative and quantitative measures.

Measurement and meaning

Measurement is the means of representing a theoretical concept. Theories represent a basic classification system that approximates to the real world, but they are not in themselves the real world. To articulate this concept, within social research, multi-dimensional measures are employed. While the concept of social class, for example, can eventually be reduced to a single measure, the concept involves a number of dimensions such as occupation, income, wealth, heredity, status and educational attainment. As no single measure can encompass this diversity, researchers, when measuring social class, will use two or more dimensions to generate their approximation of social class. This approximation provides a measure of the concept, but crucially not an encapsulation of the concept itself. It is also open to challenge by those who would say this, or that aspect of social class is over, or underplayed by that particular measure. All this might seem a little esoteric, but it is nevertheless an important point to remember. It is all too easy to get caught up with measurement and forget that it is only a means to an end – to understand and explain the social world – rather than an end in itself.

Crime provides another valuable illustration. If crime is the concept you are trying to measure, what is it that you mean by crime? While certain activities are regarded as illegal, could they all be classed as a crime? Speeding is illegal, but given what a sizeable proportion of the population break speed limits every day, should this be included in crime statistics? How do you find out how many crimes have been committed? One way is to ask the police, but police data only records reported crimes. It is generally agreed that as much as a third of all crimes committed do not get reported, and the rate on non-reporting varies markedly depending on the nature of the actual crime. So simply adding a third more crimes to the statistics would, therefore, produce a highly inaccurate measure.

Another approach would be to ask the public what is their experience of crime. This is exactly what the annual British Crime Survey (BCS) does, but again it illustrates the merits and limitations of any such measurement exercise (Coleman and Moynihan, 1996). Each year in England and Wales 40,000 people are interviewed and asked about their experience of crime. A less regular parallel survey is also carried out in Scotland (Duff and Hutton, 1999). This data is then used to construct tables of different crime victimisation rates, per 10,000 of the population. Yet does this produce a more accurate measure of crime? The simple answer is no. What it provides is another measure, but a measure with its own limitations. As this is a survey of individuals, drawn from the household post code files, then anyone not on it is automatically excluded. So crime inflicted on students, hostel dwellers, those in institutions and in prisons is not recorded. Some of these groups are likely to experience a higher incidence of crime. The survey also excludes people under the age of 16, again a group who experience a great deal of personal crime.

Then there is the fact that this survey only focuses on crimes inflicted on the person. Vandalism to bus shelters, train stations and derelict buildings are not reported. White-collar crime would also not get reported, as the victim here is the business or employer (see Anderson, 1999; McGuire, 1994; and Bottomley, 1981). So the BCS provides one measure of crime, and this can be compared to previous surveys to indicate changes in the pattern of crime. But as with police statistics it is certainly not 'the' measure of crime. Drawing policy responses from the data provided therefore needs to be treated with some care, given the limitations of the data set. It follows that a true measure of crime would be impossible to achieve. That is not to say the current BCS could not be improved upon. Used in conjunction with other measures it has value as one of many constructions of crime. Newburn (2003) in the *Handbook of Policing* describes 'crime analysis' as being '*the synthesis of police and other relevant data to identify and interpret patterns and trends in crime.*'

A further example of the challenges posed by measurement relates to evaluating the costs of user involvement in housing management. A team from Sheffield Hallam University set themselves the unenviable task of trying to devise instruments to assess the real costs to social landlords of giving choice and involvement to both tenants and leaseholders in the modernisation of their homes (Cole et al., 1999). On the ground this can involve anything from allowing colour choices for front doors, through to providing multiple choices in relation to refitting bathrooms and kitchens. The study also focused on what identifiable benefits tenants gained through the use of tenant satisfaction surveys. What the research team found was that while the process of evaluating the total costs of tenant involvement and choice was hard to track, given many costs are subsumed within total operating budgets, it was possible, however, to identify mechanisms that could assist both landlords and their tenants monitor such costs and benefits more effectively.

Quantitative versus qualitative measures

This brings us neatly to a debate that has exercised social researchers for decades; the debate on the relative merits of quantitative and qualitative measurement. Quantitative measurement refers to the use of numeric measures of social phenomena, while qualitative measures use data derived from interviews and observational techniques to arrive at an assessment. The details of the debate need not detain us, but it is worthwhile making one or two points at this stage. Put simply, the quantitative side of the debate argues for the pre-eminence of a 'scientific approach', one that produces quantifiable results and generalisable conclusions. From this perspective qualitative measures, such as participant observation, or detailed interviews tend to be viewed as unscientific, vague and inherently value-laden. Those who favour qualitative measures, on the other hand, counter that social reality is too complex to be reduced to mere empirical 'facts'. What exactly are these so called scientific measures measuring? For them the techniques of quantitative research can only reduce social reality to numeric categories which destroy their essential meaning.

Representing the debate as a dichotomy between qualitative and quantitative measures does, however, tend to polarise opinion. Quantitative researchers are encouraged to ignore the potential insights afforded by qualitative measures and vice versa. In reality, different styles of measurement are needed to help investigate and make sense of different social phenomenon. It is only the degree, or level of measurement that varies. Qualitative and quantitative researchers may have very different, often antagonistic views about the nature of the research process. Yet, these differences should not necessarily dictate the measures or methods of data collection they used. Dey (1993) uses a T'ai-chi Tu diagram to illustrate what he considers the dynamic balance between qualitative and quantitative data.

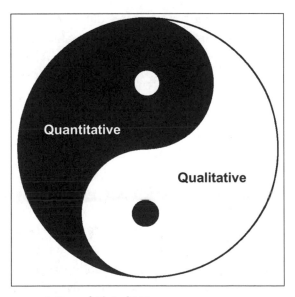

Diagram 5.1: Symbolic representation of T'ai-chi Tu.

The diagram reflects the mutual dependence of both types of data. It indicates that meanings cannot be ignored when we are dealing with numbers, and numbers cannot be ignored when we are dealing with meanings. Each complements the other, though at lower levels of measurement questions of meaning are uppermost, while at higher levels of measurement, questions of number loom largest.

(Dey, 1993: 28).

Units of analysis

Critical to any understanding of measurement is the unit of analysis concept. Put simply, the unit of analysis is the person, event, or social structure that is being measured in the research. If you were interviewing, for example, young single people about their experiences of homelessness, the unit of analysis would be the individual men and women interviewed. If, on the other hand, your interest was in the provision being made for these young single homeless people, the unit of analysis would widen to include the local authority housing department, local voluntary organisations engaged in tackling youth homelessness and the actual hostel accommodation provided. It is not unusual, to find more than one unit of analysis within a single study. A study of single homelessness, to continue with this example, might have at least two units of analysis; the individuals who are homeless and then the organisations that provide housing and welfare support services dedicated to their needs. The unit of analysis is critical when it comes to deciding upon the actual measurement tools to be employed in any particular study.

Levels of measurement

There are four levels of measurement: nominal, ordinal, interval and ratio. The level of measurement achieved then determines the types of statistical procedures that can be employed to analyse the collected data. Measurement, at its simplest, operates at the nominal level. With nominal measurement it is only possible to differentiate broad categories such as sex or marital status. Where the concepts being measured are defined more clearly, it may be possible to make finer distinctions whether at the ordinal, interval, or ratio levels of measurement.

Nominal

Nominal level measurement involves naming, or labelling, whatever is being observed. The object of study has to have the capacity to be categorised – whether these are objects, persons, attributes, or behaviours – in order to distinguish between them. For the measure to be effective the nominal categories must be mutually exclusive and exhaustive. What this means is that an observation should fit one, and only one, category. The appropriate nominal category should then be available for each and every observation. When you join an organisation, for example, whether it is as a member of a sports club or as an employee in a voluntary organisation, you will usually be given an identification number. This is a nominal category that distinguishes you from all other members of the organisation. This categorisation is exclusive because the number is unique to you. It is also exhaustive, because every member has a number. Beyond this the number itself has no meaning: it is simply a label and does not signify that someone having a higher or lower number is any more or less important.

The more categories you create the more accurately you can offer a representation of 'reality'. However, it should also be appreciated that our particular understanding of reality varies, and therefore the range is one of shades and gradations.

> *The world is not to be divided into sheep and goats. Not all things are black or all things white. It is a fundamental of taxonomy that nature rarely deals with discrete categories. Only the human mind invents categories and tries to force facts into separated pigeon-holes. The living world is a continuum in each and every one of its aspects. The sooner we learn this concerning human sexual behaviour the sooner we shall reach a sound understanding of the realities of sex.*
>
> (Kinsey et al., 1948: 16).

In a recent discussion paper by McManus (2003) the way the categorisation of sexual orientation has changed over time is discussed. This study notes that with the growing interest in sexually transmitted disease, and in particular AIDS and HIV, the health and social policy communities require to have more robust definitions of sexual orientation. The range of qualitative studies focusing on sexual health and lifestyles all need to define, describe or group their particular populations of interest. The paper notes that a variety of terms now appear in the literature, including sexual orientation, lesbian, gay, bisexual, transgender and gender identity. As the terms are applied in a variety of ways, there is an obligation on researchers to clearly describe the definitions which they apply. This publication offers help in this regard, and shows how far society's understanding and acceptance of sexual orientation has moved since the Kinsey Scale of Sexual Orientation, which drew up a six point categorisation between heterosexual and homosexual. As such it provides a good illustration of how everyday reality catches up with the researcher's reality. Even so, the reality is likely to be a construction only true in one, or some countries and cultures, while in others not at all. At the end of the day, all 'definitions' are social constructs and as such, they may vary through time and from place to place.

As there is no order, or degree element to categories constructed at the nominal level of measurement, limitations are imposed on the analysis and subsequent interpretation of the data. The main limitation concerns the use of measures of central tendency, or averages. These are employed to convey additional information about the collected data. There are three such 'averages':

1. The mean – the arithmetic average, which is derived from adding together a series of scores and dividing by the number of observations.

2. The median – the middle value in a set of scores.

3. The mode – the most frequently occurring value or score.

As you cannot add, subtract, multiply, or divide nominal scores, the mode is the only appropriate measure of central tendency for nominal data. To show this, suppose you had conducted a neighbourhood profile and had found the following distribution of employment status among the 400 residents surveyed:

Table 5.1: Employment status in Drumbog

Employment status	Category code	Number in category
Full-time employment	1	190
Part-time employment	2	100
Student/higher education	3	45
Unemployed	4	35
Retired	5	30

The code, (1) full-time employment, (2) part-time employment, and so on, is simply a label that represents each discrete category – no order or degree is implied. Consequently, calculating the mean or the median of the category code would produce an entirely meaningless number. The same is true for the category number. If you add together all the counts in each category and divide by the total number of observations this gives you zero. This makes no sense. Nor is employing the median any more helpful. There are 400 observations and, therefore, the median or middle value must lie between the 200th and the 201st score, in this case between '1' and '2' giving a median of 1.5. But this also makes no sense because if the above list was ordered in a different way, then a different median would result. The mode is useful, in so far as we can tell that more people (190) in the sample are full-time employed, making it the most common employment status.

Ordinal

There are of course many situations in which the researcher needs to go beyond such a simple classification in order to measure with more discrimination. One way to do this is to attempt to order, or rank responses in some way. Ordinal measurements do just this. They allow the researcher to make a judgement that one item is ranked above or below another. What it does not do, however, is to make statements about how much above or below. For instance, suppose that in your neighbourhood survey you collected banded income information based on each respondent's net income. Those residents who were in Category 4 income band in Table 5.2 are in the top 12.5 per cent of all residents, in terms of their income. Yet, without more precise knowledge of the actual net income paid, the ranking does not allow the researcher to say how much better off certain individuals are in relation to other residents.

Table 5.2: Organisation salary scales

Salary scale	Category code	Number in category
Below £15,000	1	275
£15,001–£20,000	2	95
£20,001–£25,000	3	80
Above £25,001	4	50

Ordinal level data is an improvement on nominal level data, but it still has clear limitations. Again these limitations are most obvious in terms of the statistics that can be derived from the information. Calculating the mean for ordinal data in Table 5.2 would be just as meaningless, as it was for nominal level data. You could, of course, use the mode, which in this case would be 1. It is more usual, however, to use the median as the basis for statistical comparisons when using ordinal data. This is also in category 1 indicating the neighbourhood is predominantly a low-income area.

Interval

Interval level measures have all the properties of ordinal measures, and, in addition, have equal intervals between the scores. This equal spacing means that you can make judgements about the degree of difference. Temperature is perhaps the best known example of an interval scale. If the temperature in a house is 40°C, then we can say that it is twice as warm as a house in which the temperature is only 20°C. The same applies to income. If you have a net income of £30,000 a year, then you earn twice as much as a colleague earning £15,000.

Yet there are problems in interpreting interval level data, because of the involvement of an arbitrary anchor point. The anchor points on the centigrade scale, for example, are the temperatures at which water freezes and boils, 0 and 100 degrees respectively. In practice, however, there are few limitations on the types of analysis that are appropriate to interval level data. If it is possible and/or practicable it is best to design measures that produce the highest level possible because you can always step down levels – from interval to ordinal to nominal – but not vice versa.

Ratio

There is one further level of measurement, namely ratio, which combines all the attributes of the interval level with an absolute zero point. The Kelvin scale of temperature uses an absolute value of zero, which represents the total absence of heat. Unfortunately, there are few, if any meaningful examples of ratio levels of measurement within the social sciences. Income might seem to be an obvious exception, with zero representing a total absence of money. Having no income is a rarity, as most people have some access to cash, albeit that it may not be paid to them directly. So the zero measure would rarely be used. If income was then used to indicate socio-economic status having no money would not imply someone had no socio-economic status. In this case using income as a ratio level measure would not be appropriate.

Validity and reliability

Whatever the level of measurement being used in a study, it is important that the measurement should yield both reliable and valid results. Validity refers to how well an item measures what it is supposed to measure. Reliability is concerned with the consistency of the measurement; will the test or method yield similar results in similar situations?

Table 5.3: Validity and reliability

Correct reading	Meter A Reliable and valid	Meter B Reliable but not valid	Meter C Not reliable or valid
58000	58000	58005	58160
58500	58500	58505	58800
59000	59000	59005	58905
59500	59500	59505	59123

Table 5.3 above, shows the readings from three separate electricity meters. It is designed to illustrate the significance of validity and reliability. Meter C runs erratically; sometimes it reads over and at other times it reads under. What measurement the meter records are clearly useless. It is not valid, because it does not measure what it is supposed to, namely the amount of electricity used. Moreover, the meter is not reliable since it fails to measure consistently. Meter A, by contrast is both reliable and valid; it measures what it is designed to measure and it does this accurately. But what about the worth of meter B? It always measures exactly five units over? The reading is clearly not valid, since the measure of actual power use is consistently wrong. Yet it is reliable, because it measures consistently. So although a test is reliable, this does not imply it is valid. For a test to be valid, however, it must also be reliable.

Unfortunately, in most social welfare research contexts the issues of validity and reliability are less clear-cut. Poverty indicators provide a useful example. There are a number of measures of poverty, such as the receipt of particular welfare benefits. Given that nationally agreed criteria apply, such measures also provide reliable measures for conducting comparisons between one location and another. However, it is questionable whether these measures of poverty are valid, given that the means tests involved treat certain personal savings in different ways, thus creating a potential variation in actual poverty. So while welfare benefits can provide a reliable measure, it may fail on the grounds of validity given the potential in variation in incomes of recipients. Also, the cost of living, particularly in respect of food and transport costs, varies considerably across the UK. This would affect the relative measure of poverty – what money can buy – in different locations. The value of any measurement criteria, in terms of its validity and reliability, clearly needs to be tested and its worth agreed. Only then can it be judged a worthwhile measurement tool within a particular research context. In order to do this there are a variety of validity and reliability tests that can be commonly applied. The following tests are applied to Census questions, to ensure that the information being generated through this massive nation-wide survey is of use to the variety of users that rely on this data.

Testing validity

There are three basic techniques for assessing the validity of a measure: face, criterion-related, and construct validity. The nature of the particular research task and the availability of resources will influence the choice of what validity technique to use. If you are planning a small-scale study, for example, it is unlikely that you will have the resources to go beyond a consideration of basic face validity.

Face validity

Face validity is a subjective method, whereby opinion and judgement are the sole means of determining validity. At its simplest, face validity may involve no more than the researcher reflecting on whether the test measures what it was intended to measure. A more sophisticated method might involve drawing on an assessment of the measure by a panel of judges' deemed expert in the field. This would provide a stronger form of face validity, but it is still a limited test given it is entirely dependent upon the value judgements of the judges, no matter how eminent. Selecting an expert in youth work to comment on the measurement approach adopted for an assessment of elderly day care facilities may not be the most appropriate use of expertise, but there may well be useful parallels. Such an expert might prove more helpful in commenting upon the appropriateness of performance measures developed to appraise the work undertaken in youth clubs, or outward bound projects. In turn, that might provide useful tools that are transferable to the day care setting. Face validity, while hard to defend on scientific grounds, can offer a useful starting point. After all, if you cannot demonstrate face validity, it is unlikely that other methods of assessing validity will be convincing.

Another good example of face validity is provided by Peter Townsend's measure of deprivation, which was very much an eclectic mixture of what he considered to be the basic necessities of life, relative to society as a whole (Townsend, 1979). Adopting this measure would be one means of assessing poverty within a community, given Townsend's credentials in poverty research. The original definition is however somewhat out of date, given that relative notions of poverty have changed in the intervening quarter of a century. As opposed to expert validation you could interview a representative group of people encompassing a variety of backgrounds to find out their assessment of what constitutes a 'necessity' these days, then use the results to construct a more up-to-date and relevant measure (Pantazis et al., 2000). The pioneering work carried out for the 'Breadline Britain' (Mack and Lansley, 1985) study did just that, and this work has subsequently been built on by the Poverty and Social Exclusion Survey of Britain (Gordon et al., 2003). Both these studies adopt a similar approach to face validity, in that they use a survey of the public to determine what standard of living is considered unacceptable by society. The robustness of the resulting measure is confirmed by the high degree of consensus that existed, despite the marked differences in the commentators personal circumstances.

Criterion-related validity

A more powerful tool, criterion-related validity, makes use of statistical measures such as correlation coefficients to assess validity. There are two common types of criterion-related validity; concurrent validity and predictive validity. Both types are similar, in that they use criterion measures and statistical correlation as a means of assessing validity. The correlation validity coefficient ranges from 0 to $+1$, with scores closer to $+1$ indicating the stronger the criterion-related validity.

Concurrent validity relies on authoritative measures, rather than authoritative individuals or experts to assess validity. Quite simply it involves comparing a new measure with an existing and valid measure. For example, if you wanted to test the self-esteem of young offenders, you could use a standard test such as the Rosenberg Self-Esteem Scale (Rosenberg, 1965). The Rosenberg measure uses 10 self-assessment questions that have a 1 to 4 scoring, and from this a self-esteem measure is calculated. You could then assess the same group of respondents using both tests, and then compare the results. If your test were equally as valid, you would expect your scores to be statistically correlated to the published criterion.

Predictive validity is about predicting future outcomes on the basis of an initial test. Sticking with the youth justice focus one example of such a validity test is used to predict re-offending rates, based on age, sex and previous convictions. Using this test you could predict the outcome with a cohort of young offenders, and then await the actual outcome after a fixed period of time. Then, with the predicted and actual results in place, the two sets of results could be compared. Predictive validity, in the form of a correlation coefficient between subjects' predicted award classification and their actual classification (the criterion), establishes a correlation coefficient. As with concurrent validity, the closer the coefficient values to $+1$, the more valid the test.

Overall, criterion-related validity is a valuable tool, but one that needs to be used with care. The difficulty with this form of assessing validity is that it relies heavily upon the quality of the criterion measure. How can you be sure that the criteria, the pre-existing test against which your new data is being assessed is in fact valid? Are the predictive measures of re-offending accurate? Similarly, a strong correlation on predictive validity may be flawed by faulty outcome measures. Are the actual re-offending statistics valid, after all it only measures those re-offending who were caught by the criminal justice system, within a defined timeframe? This might suggest that both the original predictive measure, and your data on re-offending, has its limitations.

Construct validity

Construct validity is the most complex approach to validity and involves comparing new measures with pre-existing valid measures. In this sense it is similar to concurrent validity. The difference, however, is that construct validity attempts to correlate validity with different methods of measurement and with measures of different concepts.

In a study of young offenders, a specially devised questionnaire could be used to ascertain their personal self-esteem. However, the type of instrument being used might unduly influence the correlation between this new instrument and an existing question-naire test, given both are questionnaires. If, however, the new questionnaire was correlated with an existing questionnaire and another method, such as an interview, you could be more confident of the validity of the new measure. Organisations such as Viewpoint are developing interesting hybrids of interviews and questionnaires using self-assessment tools to gain young people's views.

The extent to which a measure does not correlate with measures of a different concept is also considered in assessing construct validity. Suppose the new measure of self-esteem were contrasted with a questionnaire identifying individual social networks. A high correlation between the two measures would not be expected, given they are measuring different concepts.

Construct validity is a powerful means of assessing validity. It is also a complicated one that usually involves the use of multivariate factor analysis and, as such, is perhaps best left to those who have the necessary resources and expertise.

Assessing reliability

As noted earlier, validity is about the ability of an item or test to measure what it is supposed to measure. Reliability is concerned with the extent to which a measure is internally consistent. Validity is about external consistency of the measure. As noted above, the reliability of a measure says nothing about its validity. Both in the case of the electric meters, or the use of welfare benefits as a measure of poverty, a measure can be reliable, but invalid. There are many ways of assessing reliability, most of which involve statistical correlation. The most common techniques are: inter-rater, test-retest, split-half, alternate forms and item-total reliability.

Inter-rater reliability

As the name suggests, inter-rater reliability involves more than one person making judgements on a measure. For instance, if you have several people involved in undertaking an addiction assessment of the clients of a drug project, they each might be asked to measure the addiction scores for the same group of clients. If each person scores each client in the same way, correlating the scores from each would provide a measure of inter-rater reliability. A high correlation between those carrying out the test would suggest that the measurement was reliable.

Test-retest reliability

The test-retest approach simply involves repeating a measure after some time has elapsed. In theory at least, if the measure is reliable, subjects should achieve the same scores on both occasions. Another way of assessing the reliability of your addiction measure, for example, would be to have them repeat the test some time after the first one was conducted. All things being equal, they should produce exactly the same score on both occasions. There are problems, however, with the test-retest approach. Observed differences between the test and the retest might be the result of an actual change in the respondents, or the situation, rather than an indication that the measure employed is unreliable. In the case of the addiction measure, for example, the practice which the testers will have gained in using the measurement during the testing phase might have an impact on the subsequent retest measures. With practice they might well have become more proficient. Alternatively, the clients' dependency on drugs may have changed between the two surveys.

Split-half reliability

The split-half reliability approach is a variation on the test-retest method. Essentially what you do is develop twice as many items as needed to measure the concept, administer the instrument using all the items, then split them into two equivalent halves at random – say by odd and even numbered items – and correlate the two halves. The idea is that, if the test is reliable, the scores between the two versions should be strongly correlated. As before, the higher the correlation, the greater the reliability. The difficulty, of course, is in assuming versions of the measure are readily comparable in both content and difficulty.

Alternate forms reliability

This approach is the same as the split-half method, except that two completely separate, but equivalent, versions of the same measure are compared. One method is to give the same group of respondents' different versions of the measure at different times. In this way they are tested twice, once with each equivalent measure. Alternatively, the same measure might be administered to different groups of respondents. In either case, a correlation coefficient is calculated from the scores to assess the alternate forms of reliability for the measure.

The success of the alternate forms approach relies on the true equivalency of the two versions. Developing such items can be a difficult and time-consuming business. Add to this the need for two separate administrations of the measure and clearly to use the alternate forms approach demands access to considerable resources.

Item-total reliability

Item-total reliability assesses the internal consistency of a measure by correlating the score on one item, in a measure with the total score on all the other items. If each item on a measure is reliable, then you can be more confident of the reliability of the measurement in total. If a measure contains many items, calculating the correlation for item-total reliability can be a time-consuming exercise, even when using a computer.

Although these approaches to assessing reliability can be used either with achievement or attitudinal measures, they are more usually applied to the former. Attitudinal measures are harder to assess, since attitude is generally much less consistent than aptitude. That does not mean, of course, that it is not just as important to try to establish the reliability and indeed the validity of any attitudinal measures you employ.

Linkages

As noted in the introduction to this chapter, measurement is only valid in the light of theory. Without clearly defined concepts there is no point in attempting to define valid measures. The important point about measurement is that its function is to provide a link between theoretical concepts and social reality. Theory should guide your research, but it is measurement that enables you to test out your propositions and the associated theories. The measurement instrument needs to focus on the dependent variable that emerges from your hypothesis or theoretical proposition.

In choosing to conduct a study aimed at addressing the question: 'What are the factors associated with offending among young people?' you would first carry out a literature search on the various theories and explanations that might help answer this research question. This literature review would throw up both structural and individual explanations for youth offending. The structural explanations might focus on the socialisation of adolescents into adult society, changes in the labour market and the consequent growth in youth unemployment as well as changes in the welfare system, especially for those under 18. Individual explanations would focus on individual circumstances and the life experiences of these young people to date. From the literature you might consider that the concept of 'social networks' or 'social connectedness' seemed especially relevant in explaining youth crime patterns. Such 'relationships' or 'networks', which an individual has by virtue of family, friends, neighbours, colleagues or other acquaintances, have both an individual and structural component. While the theory of social networks is complex, the basic hypothesis in this context would be that the stronger the individual's social network, the less likelihood of participating in crime, unless of course, all friends and family members were criminals!

To take this concept further you would need to work out a means of measuring the number and strength of young person's social networks. That would involve assessing the importance of family, kinship, and friendship ties as well as whether they have membership of any formal organisations. Workplace relationships would also need to be assessed and measured. Such a measure of an individual's social network would require scoring all contacts within their social network, as well as a relative score for whether these contacts were 'weak', 'strong', 'positive' or 'negative' ties. Once that measure was devised, and refined in light of other tests it could then be used to see whether it did provide a means of explaining a propensity on the part of young people to commit crime.

Overall, measurement should never be viewed as a mere technical exercise. Rather, it is an integral part of the research process. By thinking about measurement issues early on in the study you are forced to focus more clearly on what are the important concepts. This in turn will help you to design a more rigorous research study.

Sampling

Introduction

In an ideal world a research project would focus on the entire population you wish to study. But clearly this would only be feasible if the population you wanted to study was reasonably small in number, or where the study had unlimited access to resources. Unfortunately, these conditions rarely exist; hence the need to select a sample from the population you are interested in. Suppose, for example, you want to explain why certain young people opted to use recreational drugs, while others do not. Clearly it would be impractical to interview all young people about their attitudes towards the use of recreational drugs. So to get round this logistical problem a sample of this population can be employed. At its simplest then, a sample is a compromise between obtaining complete information from the population, which is the focus of your study, and making best use of the time and resources available to carry out the research. Yet, sampling can offer the researcher far more than this. The aim is to achieve what is called 'synecdoche' – a part of a whole which can be interpreted as representing the whole (Becker, 1998). As Becker puts it, the '*logistics of sampling are arguments to persuade readers that synecdoche works, because it has been arrived at in a defensible way*' (Becker, 1998: 66).

Moser and Kalton (1983) go further by suggesting a number of advantages that sampling has over an enumeration of the whole population. The main advantage of sampling is that it is cheaper to conduct, because fewer people are required to collect and analyse the data. Sampling also saves time, since it is quicker to analyse and process the data gleaned from this smaller group. It also makes for greater accuracy, as sampling size allows checks to be made on the design and implementation of the data collection instrument. The small number of staff involved also makes it possible for the researcher to train the interviewers properly, and then to check on the accuracy of the completed interviews.

This issue was touched upon in the previous chapter, in relation to the reliability and validity of measurement. Sampling also makes it possible to collect and deal with more elaborate information about individual cases, albeit in a smaller number.

Two terms need to be clarified at this point. Firstly, when a sample is selected it is not necessarily people who are the unit of analysis, or the entity being sampled. Given the broad focus of social welfare research the unit of analysis can be schools, projects, initiatives, policy papers or basic management information. Secondly, the term 'population' refers to a discrete group of units of analysis, and not to the population in the conventional sense. For example, in a neighbourhood audit of deprivation, the unit of analysis might be all the local residents, the head of household or particular groups within the wider population. In research that examines how social services designate some children as being 'at risk', the unit of analysis might be cases that have been put on the 'at risk' register, or alternatively all cases currently being investigated. It is the researcher who defines the actual population in question. The important point is that the sample should be representative of the larger group, namely, the researcher's defined population. If you have properly selected your sample then your findings from the sample survey should be representative of the entire population. If the sample is not representative, the results are likely to be unrepresentative of this wider population. In the neighbourhood illustration used above, clearly a sample drawn from the entire population would seem to be the most appropriate to assess local deprivation. The other two categories, being unrepresentative of the entire population, are likely to produce distorted results.

The classic illustration of the dangers inherent in flawed sampling, comes from a public opinion poll conducted for the *Literary Digest* during the 1936 United States' Presidential Election campaign. Car registration records were used to identify a sample of voters for this survey. In 1936 car ownership in America was far more restricted to the wealthy than it is today. The *Digest* then telephoned the selected car owners, thus further reducing the representativeness of the sample; given telephones were also still very much the preserve of the wealthy. The survey results predicted a landslide victory for the Republican Alf Landon, yet it was the Democratic contender Franklin D. Roosevelt who comfortably won the day. No doubt the wealthy people contacted were solidly Republican, but there were others within the voting population who adopted a different political perspective.

Similar sampling problems still arise today. The recent growth in telephone polling at election times ably illustrating the point. Most people now have access to a telephone, and there is almost universal coverage. In the past this was not the case, and there was a danger that relying on a sample drawn from telephone subscribers would have excluded a distinct group within society, causing a skew or bias in the survey results. Yet, similar problems emerge today, despite almost universal telephone coverage. For example, a considerable number of people choose to go ex-directory, and it may well be that this is a more common practice with certain groups within society. Then there is the added complication that there is no longer one universal telephone directory, but rather a fragmented coverage, given the growth in new telephone providers as a result of deregulation. Then there has been the massive growth in mobile phones over the last 10 years, and the subsequent loss of a proportion of landlines. So just how do 'telephone surveys' draw their sample, given the population is now harder to isolate? An added complication in using this survey tool is that the researcher can never be sure who exactly they are speaking to, introducing another potential distortion. Finally, the time of day when respondents are phoned is also likely to affect who is contacted at home. As a result of all the above, telephone polling, which was at one time seen as a reliable universal survey tool, is now better suited to specialised surveys focusing on distinct and definable populations.

Other examples are provided by the ubiquitous market researcher seen sampling people's views on a range of issues outside the local shopping centre. Such passers-by are clearly not typical of the entire population; rather they simply happen to be available, at that time and in that place. Drawing your sample from these shoppers probably under-represents those people in full-time employment, those at school or in higher education, or those who choose to shop elsewhere. To get round this problem, market researchers typically operate a quota sampling system, in which they are required to interview only people who fit their pre-defined profile. So if you have ever wondered why such interviewers appear not to be interested in your views, but just those of others, this may be the reason. Television 'phone-in surveys' are perhaps the best illustration of an unrepresentative sample, given they typically attract only those who watch daytime television and then only those who can be bothered to respond. Such groups are unlikely to be representative of the watching TV audience, let alone the entire population. Everyday we read in the papers, or hear on radio and television that 'a recent survey showed'. Given what has been said so far, this evidence should be treated with a great deal of scepticism. Such surveys rarely, if ever, provide details of how the sample was designed.

Types of sampling

To avoid the more obvious problems of unrepresentativeness, a range of sampling techniques have been developed. There are two broad categories of sampling techniques; random (or probability) sampling and non-random (non-probability) sampling. Within these broad categories there are a range of approaches. Table 6.1 summarises the main advantages and disadvantages of some of the more common approaches to sampling.

Random sampling

The best way to achieve an unbiased sample is to use some form of random or probability sampling. A random sample is one in which every unit of the population has a known, independent and equal chance of being selected. The National Lottery numbers, for

Table 6.1: Sampling techniques

Type of sampling	Characteristics	Advantages	Disadvantages
Random sampling			
Simple random	Assign each unit in the population a unique number then then select the sample using random numbers.	Easy to analyse; requires minimal prior knowledge of population; free of possible classification errors.	Does not make use of any knowledge of population characteristics; larger errors from same sample size than stratified random sampling.
Systematic random	Choose a random starting point within the sampling interval (n) then select every nth unit for inclusion in the sample. The natural order of the population is employed.	Easy to draw and check; where population is ordered with respect to relevant characteristic, gives stratification effect which reduces variability.	Estimates of error likely to be high where there is a stratification effect; if sampling interval is related to a periodic ordering in the population, there may be a an increase in variability.
Stratified random	Identify strata in the population by certain characteristics (e.g. age, sex) and then select at random from each stratum.	Assures representativeness in respect of the properties which form the basis of the classifying units, thus reducing variability; decreases chance of failing to include members of population because of classification process; characteristics of each stratum can be estimated, and comparisons can be made.	Requires accurate information on proportion of the population in each stratum, otherwise increases the error; if stratified lists are unavailable, may be too costly to construct with possibility of faulty classification and, hence, increased variability.
Multi-stage cluster	Randomly select hierarchical groups (clusters) from the sampling frame. Select the sample at random from these clusters.	Can save time and costs if clusters are defined by geographic area; requires lists only for units in selected clusters; characteristics of the cluster as well as those of the population can be estimated; can be used for drawing subsequent samples because it is the cluster and not the individual unit that is selected and, therefore, the substitution of units may be permissible.	Larger errors for comparable sample than with other probability samples; requires the ability to assign each unit to a unique cluster, and an inability to do this may result in duplication or omission of units.

Non-random sampling		
Quota	Classify the population in terms of relevant characteristics, determine the desired proportion of sample in each strata, and then decide on quotas for fieldworkers.	Sampling and conducting fieldwork is efficient and relatively cheap, since units can be selected to be close to each other.	Introduces bias with the fieldworker's classification of respondents and non-random selection within classes.
Purposive	Target individual units on the basis of pre-existing information (e.g. 'exit polls')	(As above)	(As above)
Snowball	Purposely select the starting point and then ask respondents to nominate other suitable subjects.	(As above)	(As above)

example, are selected at random by placing numbered balls of equal size and shape into a machine that rotates them. Each time the machine spins, each ball has an independent and equal chance of being selected. As the balls are removed from the machine, after each selection, the odds will change, but the remaining balls still have an equal, albeit different chance, of being selected.

Simple random sampling

A simple random sample assigns a number to every item within a sampling frame and then selects a specified number of items, as a sample, at random. The sampling frame is simply a list of all the items in a chosen population. It could be the household post code address file, the electoral register for a particular locality, a complete client list of a project, over a given time period, a complete list of local authority social services departments, the entire payroll of an employer, or whatever. Suppose, therefore, you wanted to draw a sample of 100 staff members, to be interviewed about their attitude to the service quality within the social services department. One way to do it would be to give each staff member a unique number and then use a table of random numbers (or computer generated random numbers) to select the sample.

Such a procedure can, depending on the size of the required sample be rather tedious and time consuming. Further, its value is dependent upon the accuracy of the sampling frame. Using the example noted in the previous chapter, in relation to the National Crime Survey, drawing a representative sample of the population using the household post code address file was criticised because it excludes those who reside in hostel accommodation, and those in institutions. Such exclusions may be an important part of the population for your particular survey.

Systematic random sampling

One alternative to the laborious method of numbering all the units within a sampling frame is to use systematic random sampling. The technique is similar to simple random sampling, but instead of numbering all the items within the sampling frame you select every nth case from a randomly chosen starting point, to generate your sample. For example, taking your list of 5,000 residents within a particular neighbourhood, you would calculate the sampling interval (n), which is required to produce your sample of 100 residents. This is achieved by dividing the population size by the sample size – in this case 5,000 is divided by 100 to give a sampling interval of 50. You then select a random starting point between 1 and 50, using a table of random numbers, and then pick every 50th case thereafter until you have generated the required sample.

Problems can arise with this approach where there is some non-random order to the sampling frame. When conducting surveys in Scotland, for example, where four-storey tenement housing is prevalent, if you choose to select every eighth house to sample. In doing so you could end up with all the selected households residing at the same floor level, say two up, and this might distort general views about the quality of the local neighbourhood amenities. The sample might also be systematically biased where the sampling interval corresponds to a particular characteristic of the population. In a survey drawn from surnames, for example, you might end up with a higher than expected number of Scots or Irish given the concentration of Scot's and Irish surnames starting with the letter M, for Mc and Mac. The same is true for Pakistani surnames starting with K, such as Khan, or Sikhs with both S and K, given the common usage of the male Singh and female Kaur surnames. So before adopting this approach to sampling think carefully about the possibility of systematic patterns occurring within your target population which could distort the randomness of the resulting sample. Similar problems could arise if, in sampling client satisfaction with the service, you draw your sample on the same day at the same time each week. It may be the case that distinct types of client come into the centre on certain days, or at certain times of the day. This pattern of client behaviour might then skew, or bias the sample.

Where such a problem exists with the sampling frame, the solution might be to randomise the frame before then selecting the sample. This simply means that you try to ensure that any of these systematic patterns are broken up. With a very large sampling frame, such as a household post code address file, the telephone directory, or an electoral register this would clearly be impractical, and may not be necessary. As a general rule you should randomise the sampling frame wherever possible.

Stratified random sampling

The basic principle behind random sampling is that because the sample is drawn by chance, it is likely to be reasonably representative of the population. In using the simple approaches outlined above, there is always the possibility of over-representing one particular category. For example, the sample could select more women than men, or older people than younger ones, or fewer minority ethnic groups. The stratified sampling approach attempts to improve representativeness by drawing separate samples from different strata of a population, using a characteristic that is thought to be important. If you are conducting a household survey within a particular neighbourhood you might first stratify the sample to ensure both the age range and ethnic mix found in that locality are properly represented. If the Bangladeshi population, as noted on the most recent Census was 23 per cent of the local population, you would try to ensure the selected sample achieved the same representation. This, of course, assumes you have a good knowledge of the target population.

Stratified sampling can also be employed to boost the representation of a particular group, to ensure you have adequately covered their position or interests. A common problem in many surveys is that given the small size of one cohort, or group within your sample it is often difficult to say very much about them. This is a common problem in relation to most minority ethnic groups, because the sample throws up just a few cases, too few to draw any general patterns or inferences from their responses. To get round this problem, you could employ a stratified sample to boost the size of a particular group within the sample. The British Household Panel Survey (BHPS) does exactly this for the Scottish, Welsh and Northern Ireland cohorts because if the sample was drawn on the same basis as for England there would be too few cases in these other areas to produce any meaningful data. With enhanced numbers from these national groupings the BHPS can then be more confident about the results they generate for these localities, and can compare responses on key issues across all the UK nations.

The crucial point is that there needs to be some rationale for stratifying the population. In other words, you should have some reason, perhaps based on previous research knowledge or theory, for grouping the sample by say minority ethnic group, sexual orientation, or disability as opposed to adopting some other variable such as drug dependency, or self help group client.

Cluster or multi-stage sampling

Cluster sampling is useful when there is no readily available sampling frame, where one would be difficult to construct, or where the population is so geographically dispersed that a simple random sample would be beyond the resources of the project. This approach to sampling can be carried out in stages; first you select the clusters, then you sub-sample within clusters. A random sample of say 100 households, scattered across a small town, is unlikely to yield more than a handful of responses in each area or street. However, if you first selected four or five areas at random, and within each area four or five streets, then from these, four or five households to interview, you would have a cluster sample which would provide more detailed information about the range of neighbourhood types across the town.

In many cases, cluster sampling will be a more convenient option than a simple random sample approach. There is, however, a price to pay for such convenience. Cluster samples tend to produce more sampling error than simple random samples. This is because they involve more sampling steps and error is incurred at each step of any sample design. Thus, all things being equal, two steps produce more errors than a one step approach.

Non-random sampling

Random sampling may be difficult or inappropriate in some research situations. When surveying 'rough sleepers' for example, or people with dementia it is clearly impractical to conduct a random sample, as you would have no real idea of the prevalence of either group within the general population. Generating a random sample of such groups is hindered by the fact that no easily accessible, or accurate record exists for a wide range of so-called sub groups within the general population. In addition, in the case of 'rough sleepers' the adoption of a normal sampling frame, such as the household post code address file, would be useless given this group does not conform to the residence norms associated with the population at large. Difficult to access groups, a common enough phenomenon within social welfare, as well as small special interest groups, provide another example of where non-random sampling techniques are more appropriate to achieve an effective sample.

Random sampling may also be inappropriate when conducting qualitative research – where the generation of either figures or statistics is less important than exploring specific views and experiences. Non-random samples are often easier and cheaper to achieve, but with such sampling methods, neither variability nor bias can be measured or controlled. This can be a serious problem and certainly one that should be carefully considered before adopting a non-random sample strategy. Controlling access to sampling units will compound this problem. For instance, a social welfare agency or department may want to present research findings that are either supportive, or critical, of certain aspects of service delivery. This can lead the agency to encourage the selection of respondents who will convey one, or other perspective, thus invalidating the value of the associated findings. In such cases random selection techniques should be insisted upon.

Quota sampling

As with any sampling technique, quota sampling starts from the premise, firstly, that the sample should be drawn from across the population and, secondly, that the main characteristic(s) of the sample should match the incidence of that characteristic(s) within the population. The actual procedure starts by dividing the population into an exhaustive number of mutually exclusive groups, or 'strata', such as age, sex, occupation, through to a range of known preferences within the population. The distribution of these characteristics, within the population, may be found in Census data, or it may have to be estimated from other sources. Using a large-scale sexual health survey example, each interviewer involved in conducting the fieldwork would be given a particular group to find, and told the actual number and 'type' of people to be interviewed. For example, they may be told to obtain 50 men and 50 women, and then from this find equal numbers of straight, gay and bisexual people within certain age groupings. The numbers to be drawn from each sub-group would require being proportionate to their actual (or estimated) prevalence within the research population. How the individual respondents are chosen is often left to the ingenuity of the interviewers, just so long as the defined quotas are filled.

Such lack of control over the selection of respondents can act to undermine this approach, given its potential as a source of bias. Steps can be taken to improve quota sampling, but even with these improvements it still falls far short of random sampling in guaranteeing a representative sample of the population. Moreover the improvements tend to undermine the main advantages of quota sampling, which is its quickness. Quota sampling is comparatively cheap and easy to use. There is no need for a comprehensive sampling frame, and no need to call back if a particular respondent is unavailable; you simply replace them with someone else, or another case which 'fits the bill'. That is why, despite the problems of bias, it continues to be popular especially with those engaged in research and opinion surveys.

Purposive sampling

In some situations you might want to focus your research on a small geographic area, or on a relatively small number of people. In such cases you might purposively select your sample. The 'exit poll', is perhaps the most obvious example of purposive sampling. What exit polls do is to interview people as they leave the polling station and ask them how they voted. Typically, additional information is also collected, covering such topics as age and the nature of current employment. This information, taken together allows the 'pollsters' to generate a socio-economic profile of the interviewed voters, which is then matched to their political preferences. This information is not only used to predict the outcome of that particular election campaign, but can then be employed to target similar groups at the next election, in an attempt to predict that result through tracing any noticeable shifts in political allegiances. Further, by knowing how all the parliamentary constituencies voted last time, you might then select those constituencies which best reflect particular elements within the national voting pattern, and use these to undertake more detailed opinion surveys in the run up to the next election. You could then test what impact the political parties' attitude to key issues appear to be having on the voters, as further means of predicting the election outcome. Such an approach could be readily employed, for example, in undertaking staff assessment of organisational change. An initial survey of all staff could be used to highlight what they considered to be the key changes needed to improve working practices, and this could then be fed into the re-organisation process. Following its implementation, smaller focused discussion sessions could then assess whether the actual changes properly addressed their concerns, and had improved working practices.

Snowball or reputational sampling

Snowball sampling involves purposely selecting one respondent as a starting point, and then asking them to recommend other suitable respondents. Suppose you wanted to interview those who had been influential in determining childcare policy, in particular ways, over the last 25 years. It would be difficult to identify all the relevant actors, but if you happened to know one person who was considered to be an influential decision-maker you could start by interviewing them. As part of the interview you would then ask them for a recommendation as to who should be interviewed next. By repeating this approach, over time, a number of the key players in this policy area could be included in your interviews. The value of snowball sampling is as a means of identifying interviewees whose characteristics are not obvious from any other source. It is particularly useful in identifying respondents in historical research.

There is also some benefit in using this approach, as a means of overcoming resistance to participating in a survey. If the person to be interviewed has effectively been introduced, or recommended there is a greater chance that they will participate. It is, therefore, a valuable tool when embarking on a study of individuals who may be wary of 'outsiders'. Examples of this approach have been used in trying to gain data on the care needs of certain minority ethnic groups, or people with special needs. Studying the experiences of women and children in a Women's Aid Refuge would undoubtedly require the adoption of such an approach. The big problem, of course, with snowballing is that the sample is based on personal contacts and reputation: it is entirely possible that in making their recommendations respondents might, consciously or unconsciously, ignore other important actors and consequently bias might be introduced. Using snowballing to locate so-called community leaders may only give voice to one strand of opinion within a community that has many distinct and separate voices.

Making choices

The most commonly asked questions about sampling must be, first, which is the best sampling method to use and, secondly, how large should the actual sample be? There is no straightforward answer to either question. The decision on which method to use will be very much influenced by a variety of considerations – the research goals, the nature and size of the population in question and, not least, the resources available to carry out the study. Naturally, you will want to adopt the best approach, the one which you think will produce the most representative sample and the fewest errors. Yet, the practical constraints on the decisions which often have to be made often mean that the sampling method used is a compromise somewhere between the desirable and the possible.

As for sample size, the basic point to remember is that accuracy increases with size. Suppose the research was considering the income of tenants in a small sheltered housing complex. There are 50 tenants whose incomes range from £5,000–£50,000 per annum, with the mean income for the population being (say) £18,000. If just five tenants were sampled at random, you might well get a figure significantly higher or lower than the true mean; just by the luck of the draw. If, on the other hand, you were to survey 40 tenants the anomalies would tend to be ironed-out. Consequently, the estimated mean would be closer to the true mean for the population. In other words, the larger the sample size, the closer the sample estimate will be to the true figure for the population. Also, the larger and more varied the population, the larger the sample will have to be.

Statistical sampling

As a general rule many researchers would suggest that where statistical analysis is being contemplated the sample size should be not less than 30 cases, but the upper limit depends on the characteristics of the population in question. Use can be made of statistical techniques to determine the appropriate sample size. The object here is to be able to make generalisations about a population, within a known and acceptable margin of error. Critically, there should be no significant difference between the sample and the population on any important characteristics. In determining sample size by statistical means, two important considerations need to be addressed; namely sampling error and your confidence in the representativeness of the selected sample. In qualitative research, finding out what people think about the world they live in, is a prime focus. The more representative the sample, the more the researcher is likely to find out about the population as a whole – aspects about life that they agree and parts that are more contentious. This is what gives research the capacity to comment critically on a whole variety of interactions in a way that transcends simple reportage.

Sampling error

Sampling error is a function of the sample selection process. There are two types of sampling error, namely systematic error, or bias, and random error. It is unlikely that the characteristics of any sample will be identical to those of the population from which it is drawn. Small differences will always exist, but your aim should always be to make sure that any such difference is minimised. Systematic error typically occurs as a result of the following: the selection process was not random, meaning that the selection of respondents, or cases was not made from a list covering the entire population. Or was it that the non-respondents, those refusing to take part in the survey, were not a cross section of the population? Random error is a direct function of the sample size, with the larger the sample minimising the impact of such random errors. Random error is also far more likely where there is a variable that varies widely within a population. The incidence of dyslexia provides a useful example of such randomness within a population, as is the prevalence of HIV infection, or dementia. Sampling error overall, namely the difference between the population as a whole and the selected sample can be reduced by drawing a larger sample. In this context it is always important to consider the potential rate of non-respondents and increase your sample accordingly. The final factor to take into account relates back to the type of analysis you intend to subject the data to. The critical consideration here is how many cases do you need in your smallest sub-group to make your analysis plausible?

Confidence level

Confidence in the representativeness of the sample is expressed in terms of the probability of error. Typically, confidence levels of between 95–99 per cent are chosen. If you chose a level of 95 per cent, for example, what you are saying is that you are confident that the sample and the population characteristics will be the same 95 per cent of the time. That, of course, also means that there is a five per cent, or a 1 in 20 chance that they will be different.

Formulae for determining sample size are available in many research methods textbooks (see for example Fowler, 1988; Nachmias and Nachmias, 1996). These formulae make use of statistical procedures that are beyond the scope of this book. However, anyone with a basic understanding of statistics will have no difficulty in determining sample sizes using such a formula.

To illustrate this simply, suppose you wanted to draw a sample for a survey from a population comprising of say 10,000 individual cases. The required sample size could be determined by following the formula given in Nachmias and Nachmias (1996: 198–9). This formula is derived from the equation for standard error thus:

$$SE = s/\sqrt{n}$$

where

SE = standard error
n = sample size
s = standard deviation

Inverting the formula the calculation would then look like this:

$$n = s^2/(SE)^2$$

This leaves parts of the calculation unknown, namely the standard deviation, which is the amount of variation around the mean, and the standard error. As it is impossible to know accurately these figures, without collecting the data, some estimate has to be made. This might be achieved by using a pilot study, or alternatively by making use of the results of previous studies, for example material drawn from a related local or national survey. In this case if a random sample is to be drawn from a population of 10,000 we might settle for an $SE = 0.16$ and $s^2 = 0.20$, as Nachmias and Nachmias (1996) do in their example. The sample size would be calculated as follows:

$$n = 0.20/0.00026 = 769$$

If this estimated sample size is considered too great a proportion of the population, a correction can be used. In this case the final sample size is calculated by:

$$n' = n/1 + (n/N)$$

where N = population size (in this case 10,000)

$$n' = 769/1 + 769/(10,000) = 714$$

In this case, therefore, a random sample of 714 cases should be representative of the 10,000 population, given the limits that have been set.

In practice, however, decisions on sample size are usually far more complex, particularly where more than one variable is being considered. Resource constraints also have to be taken into account. So what you often have to settle for is whatever degree of accuracy is practicable. Statistical formulae such as that used here, may provide a useful guide to appropriate sample size, but they still need to be treated with care as there always remains an element of guesswork, particularly in estimating standard deviation and standard error.

One other factor to be taken into account when deciding upon the final sample size is non-response. If, as above, you want a sample of 714 people to complete a postal questionnaire, but you estimated that 20–25 per cent will not reply, you would need to select a sample of some 900 in order to improve the chances of reaching that original 714 target. Again this illustrates the degree of subjectivity that is required when conducting this type of exercise. Unfortunately, there is no simple statistical formula that can provide the ideal sample size.

Interviews

Introduction

Interviews and questionnaires are two of the most widely used research tools in social welfare research. The distinction between them is somewhat arbitrary. A questionnaire is, in essence, a highly structured interview that requires respondents to answer a pre-determined set of questions. Interviews on the other hand are generally less structured, allowing the questioner an opportunity to more fully explore of a particular topic with the respondent. Such interviews allow you to record and explore the personal attitudes and feelings about the topic in question, whether that be their views on services for young offenders, or the value of a recent organisational change. As such, interviews are the core tool employed in qualitative work. That said, questionnaires can contain a significant number of open-ended questions, allowing respondents to express their opinions in their own words. Whether you opt to use an interview or a questionnaire very much depends on the nature of the research question being pursued. While this chapter focuses upon interviews, Chapter 8 considers the use of questionnaires.

Interviews have much in common with questionnaires. Both require careful planning, the development of properly considered questions and meticulous organisation in their execution are necessary to achieve a successful outcome. Interviews, properly conducted can yield a wealth of information, which can provide any study with depth and colour, elements often missed when using a questionnaire. Fundamentally, an interview is a way of generating a conversation. It is this dialogue which provides the interviewer with data that reflects, '*peoples experiences, opinions, aspirations, attitudes and feelings*' (May, 1997: 109). To illustrate this point, first consider the following questionnaire question.

Q.1

Please indicate, in rank order, the centres in which you would prefer to work. Your first preference should be ranked 1; 2 denotes your second choice, and so on with the least favoured area being indicated by the number 5 or 6.

Broomhill ☐
Eastgate ☐
Ryegate ☐
Greenwood ☐
Tunstall ☐
Other (please specify) . . . .

This question is fine, as far as it goes, but it doesn't provide an opportunity to explore the attitudes that inform the staff members' preferences. If that is what the study is focusing on, then consideration should also be given to using some sort of interview instead of, or in addition to a questionnaire. The alternative is ask people to respond to some pre-conceived notion of why they might want to work in one place, rather than another. The researcher will inevitably shape the presented questions, rather than the respondents' themselves. So, by comparison the questionnaire is likely to produce responses that fail to adequately reflect respondent views. The big advantage of using an interview in such circumstances is that the respondents are free to express themselves and their opinions in their own way. The researcher, through using an interview, provides a framework – more or less loosely constructed – within which the respondent can answer and elaborate on the various questions. It allows opportunities for them to go on to discuss the various issues that they feel are relevant to the topic under consideration. It is this flexibility which distinguishes an interview from the typical questionnaire. Interviewers have the opportunity to probe the responses, drawing out more fully the feelings and beliefs that help shape the respondents' attitudes.

Interviews can also be useful when exploring the possible parameters of a previously under researched area. They are often used to scope out a study, that is, to establish issues and parameters as part of the initial research design stage. Such small-scale interviews may highlight issues or approaches that were not considered by the researchers, and should help in framing the questions for a larger scale survey, perhaps using a questionnaire. Similarly a small number of carefully selected interviews can also be used to expand on the data and issues revealed by other research tools.

Interviews do have a very major downside, and that is their capacity to generate large quantities of information. It is, therefore, crucial to ensure that any interview work is carefully thought through prior to going into the field. This chapter aids that process by discussing the various types of interview and detailing the basic approaches to interviewing method. Later sections then focus on interview techniques, considers the critical problem of bias, the possible effects the interviewer has on the data, and how best to record information. Certain logistical issues, which need to be considered before opting to pursue the interview as a research tool, are also discussed. The chapter concludes by noting the advantages and disadvantages of this particular research method.

Types of interview

Having decided to use interviews as a means to collect data, you then have to decide which the most appropriate type is for your purposes. There is a clear continuum in relation to interviewing; at one end the highly structured interview, and at the other, the open unstructured interview. Between the two is a range of semi-structured options. For a more comprehensive discussion of interview types see May (1997), Spradley (1979) and Fielding (1993).

Structured interview

The structured interview is designed to be a basic research instrument. The core principle here is that each respondent is taken through the same sequence of events; they are all asked the same questions in the same order. This procedure is intended to limit any variation in the way questions are asked and, as a result, minimises the possibility of bias being introduced. By adopting this approach you can limit the possibility of a series of different interviews being held with different people covering the same topic.

The advantages of adopting this structured format lie in the ease of analysis and replicability. The downside is that much of the individuality and uniqueness of a conversation, spontaneity and flexibility – the hallmarks of a dialogue – are lost. In essence, such an approach very much mirrors the questionnaire format. Some probing of responses is possible, but this tends to be limited by the pre-conceptions of the researcher, rather than those of the respondent. That said, for those who are new to conducting interviews, such a structured approach provides additional security. It is also a useful format to employ where there are a number of different interviewers involved. A typical question taken from a tightly structured interview schedule would be as follows.

Q.2

How would you describe your view on the use of CCTV in your neighbourhood?

It is a much needed tool to help reduce anti-social behaviour ☐
It will not achieve anything that cannot be achieved already ☐
It represents an infringement of civil rights ☐
Other (record in full) . . . .

Unstructured interview

Unstructured or informal interviews depend on establishing a rapport between the interviewer and respondent, so that the interaction produces a natural flow of conversation. Indeed the respondent may be left with the impression that the interview was simply an interesting and stimulating conversation. However, from the interviewer's perspective this was a conversation that had a very clear purpose. The interview questions posed were generated from the flow of the discussion, with the clear intention of creating an open atmosphere that encouraged the respondent to answer with considerable latitude. Unstructured interviews also give the interviewer greater flexibility in that they can, at any time, alter their line of questioning in response to the differing situations that can emerge from individual responses. In relation to Question 2 above, within an unstructured interview session the respondents would be asked for their views on CCTV and the interviewer would then carefully pose each of the above questions and explore their responses. They might also be asked their views on other possible responses, as a means of understanding the range of opinions the interviewee holds on this particular topic and related issues such as crime prevention and safe neighbourhoods.

Informal interview techniques are typically used in participant observation or ethnographic research. They may also be employed in the early stages of a research project to generate the necessary background material, which is then used to develop other research tools. When thinking through what research instruments would be most helpful to a particular study it can be extremely helpful to first explore the topic by conducting a set of interviews with people directly involved in the subject area.

All interviews are designed to elicit information. However, getting the required information using the unstructured format demands considerable skill. The term unstructured interview should never be misconstrued to imply that the method represents a soft option. As with any interview or questionnaire it requires careful planning and execution. The interviewer must be confident with the subject area and be capable of pursuing a variety of related lines of questioning, while always keeping to the core research question in view. Interviewers, therefore, have to combine considerable inter-personal skills, a level of empathy and a sound knowledge of the topic in question.

Another issue associated with employing unstructured interviews is that they are open to the charge of bias, due to what is termed 'interviewer response effect'. The problem of bias is, of course, common to all interview methods and will be considered more fully later. That said, bias is especially relevant when unstructured interviews are being used. The amount of material generated by such interviews can also create data management, as well as data analysis and interpretation problems. While new software has been developed to assist with qualitative analysis, it is still time consuming, challenging and involves the researcher carefully processing all the responses generated. Given the very flexibility of the technique in accommodating not only different people, but also different situations, the resulting data set may be very difficult to analyse and interpret for patterns and trends. Only by building up experience and expertise can you hope to meet the challenges presented by this particular interview technique.

Semi-structured interview

Most interview methods not surprisingly take the compromise position, between these two extremes. The semi-structured or guided interview allows the respondent to talk about aspects of the topic that are relevant to them. But it does so within a looser framework, one that is intended to ensure that all the issues, thought to be important by the researcher, are properly covered. In essence, it's a compromise that draws from both the checklist of the structured interview and the flexibility of the unstructured format. As a consequence, it makes the analysis of data more manageable, while retaining the opportunity to be flexible and open in certain lines of questioning.

An interview schedule is used to guide and to focus the interview session, but this should not be viewed as a script. The semi-structured interview requires that the interviewer employs their skill and judgement to adapt the wording of the basic questions that need to be covered, as well as being adaptable in question sequencing, to the demands posed by each individual interview situation. The schedule helps keep the interview focused and provides a degree of continuity across a set of related interviews. It should not do so, however, at the cost of interrupting the flow of the conversation. An example of an interview schedule, for training evaluation purposes, is reproduced below. In this instance, social services staff, who had responsibility for organising and managing student placements, were the target groups.

Group interviews

Interviews are normally assumed to be a face-to-face interaction between two people, the interviewer and the interviewee. Group interviews, however, offer another potentially valuable source of information, and can provide data not only about the research topic per se, but also about the group norms and any associated dynamics which may have a relevance to the particular set of issues under investigation. Group interviews can,

---

1. **What has the trainee achieved during the placement period?**
   (Probe: Tasks accomplished; specific duties and responsibilities)

2. **How did the trainee perform in relation to non-task related work functions?**
   (Probe: Attitude towards work; interpersonal skills)

3. **What particular benefits did you feel the trainee gained from this practice placement experience?**
   (Probe: Strengths evident of the trainee; capacity to take initiative; expanded understanding of issues in a non-classroom context)

4. **What particular benefits did you feel the host organisation gained from this practice placement experience?**
   (Probe: Quality of work undertaken by trainee; exposing existing staff to new ideas and approaches)

5. **What problems did you have to address in hosting this placement?**
   (Probe: Internal co-ordination issues; lack of staff flexibility; liaison with the trainees institution)

Figure 7.1: Interview guide for placement evaluation

therefore, provide a distinct and different insight into an issue, one that may not have been revealed through a series of individual interviews. How people react in groups, and how the actions and opinions of individuals are affected by the way the group interacts, may be highly relevant to researching certain issues within the social welfare field. The dynamics of an organisation when faced with dealing with a new challenge is one case in point. Group interviews can also provide a means of exploring a topic where each group member brings with them a range of varied experiences. As a consequence, group interviews can be a useful means of helping to define the parameters for undertaking a study. A useful illustration of this is provided by Armstrong, Hill and Seeker's (1998; 2000) work on young people perceptions of mental illness, where use was made of both semi-structured interviews and focus groups.

Group interviews also have the added advantage of offering a relatively low-cost means of increasing the sample size in a qualitative study through the mechanism of focus groups. Focus groups are commonly employed within the commercial sector to provide feedback on product development and proposed marketing strategies. Recently, the focus group has been extensively employed to gain user feedback on a variety of services offered within the social welfare field, as well as in other public policy areas. As Krueger points out:

> *Focus groups are typically composed of six to ten people, but the size can range from as few as four to as many as twelve. The size is conditioned by two factors: it must be small enough for everyone to have an opportunity to share insights and yet large enough to provide diversity of perceptions.*
>
> (Krueger, 1994: 17).

Interviewing groups of people, of course, brings its own problems. Group interviews can be difficult to control with the resultant data or information being hard to record and analyse. An interview schedule, or checklist, is therefore essential to keeping the group focused on the research topic. Above all, to undertake a successful group interview the interviewer needs to possess considerable skills in facilitating and moderating group discussions. A variety of techniques, such as getting people to fill in individual response sheets, prior to discussion each core issue, then using these to structure the subsequent group discussion, not only helps establish a managed order within that discussion but also provides a useful record of each individuals initial views. If you conduct a similar exercise after the discussion you could see whether the weight of particular arguments changed people's views. There are also important considerations relating to the weight you give to the views of particular participants. This all means that the interviewers' group work skills have to be well honed. It may also be worth having co-workers involved in running the group interview, or at least have a facilitator, plus a rapporteur to record all the responses.

Table 7.1 provides a summary of the main characteristics of each of the four basic types of interview method. It is important to remember, however, that these do not represent a definitive list of the available options. It is possible that you adopt an interview strategy that makes use of a number of interview types. You might decide to start off using a structured format to collect information on what were perceived to be the core issues and then move onto a semi-structured or unstructured format to explore these issues in greater depth. Which interview style you choose to employ depends on the particular needs of the research study. Unstructured interviews might be useful for preliminary work, but it is probably better to impose some sort of structure later on, otherwise you may quickly find yourself drowning in a sea of information, with no time left to properly analyse and interpret this mass of material. Worse still, you might end up having no clear idea just how to make sense of the collected data. Chapter 13 provides some key pointers in what you require to do when undertaking the qualitative analysis.

Interview techniques

Any interviewer, no matter the type of interview they are conducting, needs to posses a skill in asking the questions. They also need to know when and how best to probe the responses. It also takes time and experience to learn how to guide any interview session so that it starts to flow more like a conversation. There are, as a consequence, a number of significant training issues involved in using this type of exercise.

Initially, it is worth asking the question: who would be the best interviewer for these particular respondents? The answer you come up with may help you select somebody by age, gender, race, attitudes', social status and background. France (2000) utilised eight young people, aged between 15 and 21, from a variety of different social and economic backgrounds, to act as 'peer interviewers' in a research study which explored the transition of young people into adulthood.

So how do you conduct an interview? There is no simple answer to that question. The best interviews tend to occur when conducted in a comfortable, relaxed manner. This not only implies that the location for the interview should be familiar to the respondent, but that the interview session should not be perceived to be threatening. Respondents are also more likely to confide in you if they feel fully involved in the research process. It is, therefore, crucial to try to ensure that they feel valued for what they have to contribute, and are not just being viewed by the interviewer as an information source. Finally, it is important that they feel confident that what they have to say will be treated both seriously and professionally.

How the ideal situation is best achieved depends upon the specific situation, but there are some general points that should be borne in mind when conducting any interview:

Provide a short introduction

Start by introducing yourself and explaining the purpose of the interview session. Briefly explain to the respondent why they have been chosen for interview and assure them of the confidential nature of the interview, if this is appropriate. Normally you would have

Table 7.1: Main characteristics of four main interview types

Type of interview	Characteristics	Advantages	Disadvantages
Structured	Structured schedule specifies, in advance; the nature of the topics and the issues to be covered; the exact sequence as well as the wording of the questions. All respondents are asked the same questions in the same order.	Interviewees answer the same questions, thus increases the comparability of responses. Simplifies the organisation and analysis of data. Reduces bias.	Limited flexibility and standardised wording can appear mechanical and may inhibit responses. Some questions might be irrelevant to, or inappropriate for certain respondents. The structure can introduce a bias right from the start.
Unstructured	Questions emerge out of the natural flow of the conversation; there is no attempt to determine the sequence or exact wording of questions.	Introduces flexibility, in that the interviewer can respond to the interviewees and the situation. Interviewees are free to express themselves in their own words. Sensitive and personal information can be obtained, when used with care.	As data is less structured, comparison across interviews is more challenging. Data management, analysis and interpretation can also be more difficult. The quality of the collected data relies more heavily upon the skill of the interviewer.
Semi-structured	Scheduled outlines give notice of the general topics to be covered. The interviewer is then free to ask about other issues – which emerge during the course of the interview – or probe responses as and when appropriate.	Retains some of the openness and informality of the unstructured approach, while allowing for comparisons to be made across the 'core' questions.	As the interviewer selects which issues to follow up this may increase the possibility of bias and limit the potential comparability of interviews.
Group	Provides data not only about the research topic *per se*, but also about group norms and any associated dynamics.	Useful tool when trying to establish the parameters of a study.	Can be difficult to control and therefore should not be conducted by a novice researcher. There are also limitations in comparing the data generated.

been in contact with the interviewee prior to the interview, either by phone or better still by letter. Either way you will be re-iterating and re-enforcing the key points made in the earlier communication.

Always try to impress upon the respondent the importance both of the research and of their active participation. People are more likely to co-operate if they feel that the subject is both important and relevant to them. Then tell the interviewee how long the interview will last; and ensure that you keep to the specified time. The introduction should always be brief and to the point.

An introduction to an interview on client satisfaction, for example, might look like this:

> *My name is Douglas Robertson and I work for the adult literacy services section of the community education department. I am conducting interviews with clients to find out how they feel about the adult literacy services provided by the Council. Your name was one of those selected at random for inclusion in this study. If I can get a good idea of what clients think about the current literary service provided by the department then, hopefully, this might help to improve their quality in the future. It is important, therefore, that we get the views from as wide a cross-section of clients as possible. We should, therefore, be grateful if you would agree to take part in this survey by answering a few questions. The interview will take about 15 minutes. All of the answers you give will be treated in complete confidence, and your name will not be used without your permission.*

Interview one-to-one

Except in the case of group interviews, it is best to conduct all interviews with just yourself and the interviewee present. That is, however, not always possible especially when conducting interviews in people's homes or in open plan offices. The presence of other people can be distracting and inhibiting for the interviewee. It can also be a potential source of bias. Imagine, for example, being interviewed about job satisfaction with your line manager sitting over the desk. No employee would feel comfortable with this situation and any responses would be affected. So try and arrange a room prior to the interview, where you can be alone with the interviewee.

Be sensitive

It is important to be sensitive to how the interview may be affecting the interviewee. It is obviously important to get the wording right before starting the interview, but it may help to rephrase some questions as you go, or to change the ordering of questions in response to the individual needs of the interviewee. It is critical that you do not alter the meaning or focus of the questions. Similarly, if the respondent has difficulty in understanding or hearing the questions, you will have to speak more slowly or loudly.

Listen

The main aim of any interview is to get the respondent's point of view. The interviewer's job is to facilitate this process. It should certainly not be a means for the interviewer to present their own particular views. Use your ideas on the topic as a means to encourage a response, but excessive contributions are bad practice. The more the interviewer talks, the less the respondent does. At the very least this will affect the quality of the data and may bias the findings by leading the respondent to agree with the values or opinions of the interviewer. Occasionally interviewees will try to use the interviewers specialist knowledge, especially when they are being asked about issues or are confronted with terms they are not familiar with. The danger here is that the interviewee's take their cue from these responses. This might also suggest that the questions are not as well refined for the audience as they should be.

Avoid interruptions

Try to arrange a time and place for the interview where you are not likely to be interrupted. If the interview is taking place in your office make sure that all phone calls are re-directed, or disconnect the phone and ensure that colleagues know not to interrupt during the interview session. If the session takes place in the interviewee's home try to ensure the same conditions, although minimising interruptions might prove more difficult. Trying to get the undivided attention of the interviewee is the crucial consideration here.

Use visual aids

Visual rather than verbal aids can be helpful in trying to clarify ideas or questions. The most commonly used aid is the flash card. For example, respondents are shown a card that has a range of possible answers, statements or even photos printed on it. Interviewees are asked to respond in ways that they feel best expresses their views. Much care is needed when designing visual aids because what you perceive to be easily understand drawings or diagrams may produce a blank response from an untrained eye. This issue is considered more fully in Chapter 14 when discussing the use and misuse of visual aids in research presentations.

Presentation

By adhering to the above points the interview session should convey the impression of being well thought through and professionally carried out. Creating the right impression is crucial, especially when carrying out the less structured interview sessions. If the proper introduction and procedure are not employed the interviewee could start to think that the session has not been clearly thought through and is a waste of their time.

Special needs and sensitivities are particularly important in social welfare research settings. Levels of literacy, English, verbal reasoning and cultural understanding may vary considerably. Developing an appropriate interview method is, therefore, crucial.

Causes of bias

As all interviews are a subjective exercise they run the risk of introducing bias. The most obvious source of trouble emanates from the interview schedule itself. As was noted earlier, ambiguous wording and a poor structure can result in unreliable or distorted data. It is crucial that you clearly convey the questions to the interviewee in a manner that is equally clear to both parties.

There are other factors at play during the course of an interview that can also lead to bias creeping in, but again these may not be obvious to the researcher. The interviewer, for example, may well hold strong opinions on the topic being considered and these may, intentionally or unintentionally, be introduced during the interview, and thus influence the respondent answers. The use of particular words or phrases can create a particular reaction, as can non-verbal expressions of approval or disapproval. An interview is in essence a social interaction and to be successful it requires a certain rapport between interview and interviewee. Such rapport can, however, also lead to bias. Borg sums up the main causes of what he calls the 'response effect':

> *Eagerness of the respondent to please the interviewer, a vague antagonism that sometimes arises between interviewer and respondent, or the tendency of the interviewer to seek out answers that support his preconceived notions are but a few of the factors that may contribute to biasing of data obtained from the interview.*
>
> (Borg, 1981: 87).

How can you eliminate such bias? The short answer is that you can never totally eliminate the possibility of bias. What you can do, however, is be alert to the possibility of bias and be prepared to deal with it. The issue of bias was touched upon in Chapter 1, where the notion of 'value free' research was discussed. Always be alert to the fact that you will have your own views on the research topic, and try and ensure these are not transmitted to those participating in the study. Once you have considered the evidence, operated reflexivity and then undertaken appropriate analysis, then you can write this up in the final report. Influencing the data to substantiate your views is poor research. So be alert throughout an interview for any signs that you might inadvertently lead the respondent to agree with your views by the way in which you ask the questions, or by your manner when recording their response. Indeed, the matter of how you record the responses is an integral part of the research process. If possible, use more than one interviewer on the project, since it is easier to pick up on bias. As was mentioned in the previous chapter, it is also good practice to randomise your interview sample so that any such bias can be dissipated.

Recording and verification

The data collected through conducting interviews is essentially words – quotations which may as a result of interpretation reveal what interviewees' think, feel, or do in the specific situations which they have been asked to talk about. The goal of interviewing is to try and get the interviewee to fully articulate their views so that you can better understand these experiences. Recording the actual words used by interviewees is, therefore, critical to the success of the project. The views of the interviewees cannot be represented accurately, using verbatim quotations, unless you have carefully recorded their original words in the first place.

Exactly how you record the interview will depend upon a variety of factors. If you are using a highly structured format, one that requires the circling or ticking of categories from a checklist, for example, then recording is a straightforward exercise. Standard responses are ticked and any additional comments or observations are noted on the sheet. In the case of the less structured interviews, however, the recording of responses is more of a challenge. One way is to take brief notes as the interview progresses, perhaps using the interview schedule as a guide, and then expand upon these notes shortly after the interview has been concluded. It is possible, with practice, to produce an accurate record of the interview in this way. Having short-hand skills would help here, but that is very much a dying art.

Taking lengthy verbatim notes of what is being said, however, can disrupt the flow of the interview. So if the respondent agrees, another approach is to audio record the interview. Introducing an audio recorder into an interview context, without prior warning, can be unnerving for an interviewee. It may make them clam up, and only provide you with limited responses. Others will have no difficulty with the presence of such equipment. Recording a focus group interview has its own technical and logistical difficulties.

Audio recording offers many advantages, such as providing a crosscheck on the accuracy of your notes, helps clarify any uncertainties the notes throw up and guarantees that any quotations used in the final report are verbatim. It certainly does not eliminate the need for accurate note taking. Such notes are useful in understanding the context in which certain responses were generated, and as such are an invaluable aid to the subsequent analysis and interpretation of the collected data. Using an audio recorder also allows the Interviewer to be more aware of the needs of the interviewee. By not focusing unduly on trying to take a comprehensive set of notes they can be more alert to the various signals that emerge in an interview session and these can add greater comprehension and understanding to the study. We re-visit some of the technical aspects of recording interviews and other interactions in Chapter 12.

If you have sufficient time and/or secretarial resources it is best to produce a full transcript of the interviews and use this as the basis for subsequent analysis. This allows you to read through the interviews carefully and start to draw out the key patterns in these responses. In addition, the latest qualitative analysis software that assists in this task is designed to be compatible with the main word processing packages. These packages then sort the interview data by the key words and/or phrases you select for analysis purposes. You do need to be very clear, however, about just how much work such an approach involves and consider, at the planning and design stage, whether or not such detailed analysis is needed. Solid note taking may be all that you require, given the particular demands of the study. Another consideration is that with the advent of relatively inexpensive, high quality, digital audio recorders, you can very quickly locate and label key excerpts from the interview. These can then be accessed and transcribed within the appropriate topic blocks. This new technology may also reduce the time involved processing entire interview sessions and also improves the reliability and quality of subsequent qualitative analysis.

Special considerations

Interviews can provide very high quality information, but they do so at a price. Interviews are labour-intensive, in terms of design, implementation and subsequent analysis. As a rule of thumb, an hour-long interview might take seven hours to transcribe, and even longer to analyse and interpret in detail. Add to this problems associated with arranging interview appointments, dealing with call-offs, postponements, return visits as well as the logistic of getting to and from the interviews. Working full-time, you might expect to complete no more than four hour-long interviews on a good day, although even this is considered optimistic by some seasoned researchers.

Finally, given that resources are always tight, it may be that the eventual number of interviews you can conduct as part of the study might have to be quite small. While interviews can never hope to provide complete coverage of all possible views when the interview numbers are small, the problem of representativeness becomes that bit more acute. A similar situation arises if you meet with a significant level of non-responses. As is mentioned throughout this book, such possibilities always need to be clearly thought through at the planning stage, and any necessary contingency plans put in place. As with any research technique, only if you can properly justify its use, and have the logistics to ensure it can be adequately carried out, should it be employed. It may well be that other methods would be better in meeting your specific research demands

Strengths and weaknesses

As a means of collecting certain sorts of information, interviews have a great deal to recommend them. Interviews are:

- A useful means of eliciting answers that are explanatory rather than descriptive, given the capacity to probe or explore the responses.

- Capable of exploring relatively personal matters, in a non-threatening manner if the work is well planned and professionally executed.
- Flexible in terms of questions and the ordering of questions.
- Convenient for the interviewee as they can work at their own pace.
- A useful means to compare different responses if designed in a structured way.

As with all research methods, however, there is also a downside. Interviews are:

- Not an efficient or cost-effective means of collecting information from large numbers of people.
- Very time-consuming in terms of development, design, execution and subsequent analysis.
- Relatively expensive, given the time involved in carrying out such work and the fact that a skilled interviewer/researcher is required.
- Unable to offer the same degree of anonymity that is possible with questionnaires.
- Difficult to analyse particularly where no clear structure has been employed.

CHAPTER 8

Questionnaires

CHAPTER OBJECTIVES

This chapter is designed to ensure that you:
- **Understand when it is appropriate to use questionnaires.**
- **Can construct a questionnaire to address your research topic.**
- **Understand the differences between the various types of questions commonly used in questionnaires.**
- **Are able to consider all steps necessary to properly administer a questionnaire survey.**

Introduction

Questionnaires are perhaps the best known of all available survey methods in social research. It is also the case that their strengths and limitations are not always fully appreciated by those who use them. There is a tendency to assume that if its research, then we must have a questionnaire. This is not a practice you should follow. Questionnaires have their value in particular research contexts, but they are not the only survey method or tool. Other research instruments can often better address your specific research requirements, as the following chapters in this section will illustrate.

Everyone is familiar with the questionnaire, from an opinion pollster on the street with a clipboard, to the glossy magazine survey invariably entitled '*Does your sex life shape up?*', the male health MOT, or even by the angst created, every decade, through filling in the National Census. Reasons for the over use of questionnaires are not hard to find. They can offer a quick, relatively cost-effective and efficient means of gathering a broad range of information, directly from people about their feelings, attitudes, beliefs and personal circumstances, as well as their social and economic situation. It should be noted, however, that the quality of information derived from such questionnaires is dependent upon the type and actual size of survey, how the questions are posed and the care taken in its execution. Although questionnaires are a well-used research tools, they need to be treated with caution. Care must be taken at every stage of their design and utilisation if they are to yield truly meaningful and useful information.

Within the social welfare field, both client and social surveys are widely used as a means to gather information, which informs day-to-day operations, as noted in Chapter

1. This material can provide an insight into how current services are functioning, or are perceived to be functioning by staff and clients alike, which can assist in monitoring operational efficiency. Such questionnaires can also provide the basic information necessary for policy planning exercises. With the recent growth of 'Supporting People' funding, both client and service provider surveys would provide one means through which social services departments could gain insights into how well the new funding arrangements are working. The above tasks have direct operational and strategic objectives, but the same information can also provide public relations material useful for resource funding or legislative reform debates. It can also provide an information base that could inform future training programmes for new staff, and help develop 'best practice' initiatives.

This chapter considers some of the main issues involved in questionnaire design, highlighting both the strengths and weaknesses of this data-collection tool. It also details the care necessary in conducting any questionnaire survey in the field. Once the questionnaire has been used, you then have to analyse and interpret the information collected. As with research design, having a clear idea of what you are seeking to find can help you focus the survey and minimise the need for much unnecessary analysis. Again a fuller discussion of analysis and interpretation of data is provided in Chapter 13. The planning of the research question and the research process are described in Chapter 1.

Types of questionnaire

Having decided on the basic objectives of the proposed research, consideration needs to be given to the most appropriate type of questionnaire to be employed. There are four basic questionnaire methods:

- the postal survey
- the telephone survey
- computer-based surveys
- the face-to-face interview

The final choice will be influenced by a number of factors, namely the specific nature of the topics to be explored, the type of respondent to be interviewed, access to available resources – essentially time and finance – and considerations about data accuracy.

Postal surveys are relatively cheap, don't involve interviewers and can accommodate a large sample size more readily. However, on the downside they generally produce very low response rates. The issue of response rates is considered more fully later in the chapter. Such low response rates can undermine the reliability of the sample, as those who reply may not be representative of the research population, as was discussed in Chapter 6. Another weakness with this type of survey is that it is not particularly suited to complex questions. Questions posed in a postal survey need to be simple since they are for self-completion. Complex questions or questions that then lead onto a series of related follow-on questions are typically left to face-to-face interviews, where the interviewer can offer assistance. On the plus side, the anonymity usually offered by postal questionnaires when dealing with sensitive issues can be useful.

Telephone surveys require the use of trained interviewers and also incur telephone charges. As was noted in a previous chapter those without access to a telephone, or who are ex-directory or solely use a mobile may be excluded by such a survey and this is likely to introduce a marked bias in the results. These limitations may not be as relevant in some research contexts. Telephone surveying of social services departments or a specific range of projects or initiatives would not be affected by these concerns, whereas client or basic population surveys would. In both cases, confidentiality issues would have to be carefully considered. In a telephone survey you need to try and identify who it is you are speaking to, because failure to do so can introduce another type of bias. Children answering for parents or a junior member of staff posing as a manager would distort the findings of the survey. While the short and well focused telephone survey can deliver a high response rate, the best results tend to come from a pre-contact, as opposed to a 'cold calling' approach, particularly where such an interview method could be viewed as intrusive. The main disadvantages are that such interviews have to be short, lasting no longer than twenty minutes.

Increasingly, computer-based questionnaires are being designed either for self-completion or for direct inputting by interviewers. The concept of actively seeking consumer views is certainly not new, but has now become central to the various Best Value initiatives introduced for the public sector by New Labour. Recent research findings indicate that service users, and in particular young people, are more willing to participate in a well-designed, interactive questionnaire survey using a computer software programme (Dotchin, Davies and Muhlemann, 1995). The speedy response time and familiarity with the computer screen, coupled with the avoidance of dealing directly with adult interviewers and 'social workers' appears to underpin the success of this survey medium. In terms of cost, it is hard to compare these surveys on a like by like basis with other types of questionnaire. The advantages appear that they are easy to duplicate and transfer to new locations, and can be readily modified. But for some people, particularly older client groups they are likely to be viewed as being intimidating. Since they can be used as a building block towards constructing future questionnaires, lower operating costs, plus the various spin-off uses may offset initial development costs.

Face-to-face surveys are the most expensive type of questionnaires to conduct, given the labour and travel costs involved. As noted above, face-to-face interviews can offer support, helping to clarify any misunderstandings that arise from the questions. As a result, they can be used to tackle more complex issues that demand a series of related questions to be posed. This introduces its own set of problems, in that while the researcher may understand the purpose of the questions, the person responding and even the person conducting the survey may be less clear. To overcome these issues such interviewers require careful training, because without it they can introduce their own bias by either consciously or unconsciously steering the respondent in one particular direction or another.

Where possible, when using any questionnaire method, a covering letter should be sent to all selected respondents, bearing in mind literacy and language issues, explaining the purpose of the research. This letter should also stress why their participation is important, outline any permissions that may need to be obtained, such as from employers, and indicate what use will be made of the subsequent results. In the case of a face-to-face survey, the letter should clearly indicate when exactly the survey will take place. With postal surveys, a deadline should be set for the return of the completed questionnaire. Two weeks is seen as about the right length of time, but state a precise date. It is also usual to guarantee confidentiality or anonymity, but be sure that you have the systems in place to honour such a undertaking. Don't promise what you cannot deliver, especially in relation to anonymity. The letter should be brief and friendly, but businesslike in tone. In other instances it may be more appropriate to get an article about the survey published in the local newspaper, or to have a special newsletter distributed to the selected residents. It is also worth briefing all those who might be contacted by those affected by the survey, especially the relevant social services department staff and the local police. In this way any rumours about the survey can be dispelled at an early stage, before they gain momentum.

Asking questions

The questions posed in any questionnaire survey should directly relate to the objectives set for the research. If you were using a questionnaire to assist in the planning of adequate care support for disabled children within a particular locality, over a ten year period, questions about the nature of the disability, household age and make-up would be critical, as would those on income levels and benefit dependence. The nature of the child's current housing might also have a bearing, as would any future housing preferences and the involvement of the child in determining their own care and support package, as they get older.

In most cases you only have one chance to put your questions. Questions must therefore be constructed in a way that ensures clear and unambiguous interpretation. Respondents must understand clearly what they are being asked. The questions must also focus solely on the core aims of the study. It is often too easy to include additional questions, which although of general interest, are not relevant to the task in hand.

Care and attention should also be paid both to the use of language and to the wording of items. Think carefully about your target audience and construct the questionnaire using language that is as simple as possible, yet still conveys the meaning of the question. Similarly do not ask questions which fall beyond the respondent's knowledge or ability to answer. Asking clients their views on 'operational efficiency' or 're-presentation rates' will merely produce a blank look. Further, a community worker may be reasonably expected to know about the day-to-day operation of the detached youth project, but may not be conversant with the local authority's social inclusion policy that funds this initiative. If specific information is required you will need to identify the staff members who are able to provide comment and invite them to be respondents. Another approach often used is to give those being interviewed advance notice of the topic areas that the questionnaire will cover, so that the respondents become familiar with the necessary information. Clearly if the survey is designed to test the technical competence of staff working in a particular area, this would not be a helpful approach.

> *A good questionnaire has to be designed specifically to suit the study's aims and the nature of its respondents. It needs ... to be clear, unambiguous and uniformly workable. Its design must minimise potential errors from respondents, interviewers and coders. And, since people's participation in surveys is voluntary, a questionnaire has to help in engaging their interest, encouraging their co-operation, and eliciting answers as close as possible to the truth.*
>
> (Honville and Jowell et al., 1987: 27).

Taking the time to think about the wording of questions, at this stage, will help avoid a lot of hard work and frustration later on, when it comes to analyse the collected information. A useful rule is that, at all times, ask yourself why am I asking that particular question? Will it be understood, and does it produce the information needed by this study? If the answer is no, then omit the question. How you make sense of a response is the critical consideration within this context. If you fail to define clearly and precisely what you mean, the differences between respondents may reflect differences of interpretation, rather than differences in experience. So always ensure that a question does not contain any words, expressions, or technical terms that might be confusing, or have a different meaning for different respondents. Consider, for example, the following question taken from a client appraisal questionnaire on a new day care facility:

Q.1

Do you find the new facility satisfactory?

Yes	☐
No	☐
Don't Know	☐

The answer generated here would be meaningless, because the term 'satisfactory' has no end of interpretations: what is satisfactory to one person is unsatisfactory to another. To get an answer to this question a more detailed set of questions would need to be posed.

Just as crucial is the need to avoid prejudicial language and that has unconscious sexist or racist assumptions. Just how easily questionnaire designers fall into this trap is illustrated by the following question from one survey:

Q.2

Do you agree or disagree with the following statements?

It is generally better to have a man at the head of a department composed of both men and women employees.

Yes ☐

No ☐

It is acceptable for women to hold important political offices in State and National Governments.

Yes ☐

No ☐

(Eichler, 1988: 43–4).

Both these questions, in effect, ask respondents to measure women against an assumed norm, namely, that men head up departments. In this case respondents could only agree or disagree with the statements. They could not, for example, express a preference for a woman head of department. Similarly, using the term 'Christian Name (s)' rather than 'First Name (s)' can also be considered offensive to members of other religious groups.

Also you need to be careful when asking questions which rely upon someone's memory; people are often better at remembering what has happened to them, rather than when. For example, one way to pose this question would be:

Q.3

If you have received assistance from staff working in this office, in the last year, please provide details of the month and year of your last visit.

XX Month. 200X Year.

But is the level of detail demanded by this question really necessary for your purposes? If not, it might be better to provide respondents with a list of options to tick. This alternative approach would ask:

Q.4

In the last year when did you last receive a visit from staff in this office?

(Tick the appropriate box)

In the last six weeks ☐

In the last six to twelve weeks ☐

In the last twelve to eighteen weeks ☐

More than eighteen weeks ☐

In this way you ensure that the most recent visitors, if those are the group you are specifically interested in can be highlighted.

Any list of options should be exhaustive, in that all possible answers are covered. This is often achieved by introducing an 'Other' category, perhaps with an additional 'Please specify' request. It is also important to ensure that each item contains just one question. Do not ask double-barrelled questions where the respondent's answer could fit more than one category. For example:

Q.5

Do you think the Council should cut spending on pre-school education, to make savings on staffing costs?

Yes   ☐
No   ☐
Don't know   ☐

Even the most professional researchers can consciously or unconsciously construct a question that invites the respondent to agree with their personal views, or prejudices. Posing leading questions encourages biased replies and negates the whole research exercise. Questions must, therefore, always be designed in such a way that respondents do not feel that their answers are incorrect, or that the response will meet with disapproval or that the question is intrinsically biased. To illustrate this point, any respondent might feel pressured to answer 'yes' to a question couched in the following terms:

Q.6

Do you disapprove of the proposals for probationary tenancies for young people?

Yes   ☐
No   ☐
Don't know   ☐

Whereas the following question construction might elicit a better range of views:

Q.7

Which phrase most closely approximates with your views of the proposal for probationary tenancies for young people?

They are a much-needed tool to reduce anti-social behaviour   ☐
They will not achieve anything that cannot be achieved already   ☐
They represent an infringement on the civil rights of tenants   ☐
Other (please specify)   . . . .

The exception to using biased questions is when the researcher specifically wants to test the strength of their respondent's views on a particular set of statements. In such instances, use is made of a Likert scale question, a technique which provides a measure of the strength of that opinion. A fuller discussion of this tool will be provided later in this chapter.

How exactly you construct sensitive questions and where they should be located in a questionnaire is another issue that needs proper consideration. As with any question posed in a questionnaire, but more so with questions on sensitive subjects, it is important to ensure that you get the information you need, and need the information you get. Again ethical considerations need to be carefully thought through in this context, given the potential to cause offence or upset to those being interviewed. Four useful questions to consider, in relation to asking sensitive questions are:

- Do I really need to ask the question at all?
- Just what level of detail do I really require?
- How should I word the question?
- Where should this question or questions be positioned within the questionnaire?

Many researchers prefer to place potentially sensitive issues near the end of the questionnaire, so that, should the respondent decline to answer such questions, you at least have all the information from the earlier sections. If sensitive or personal questions come early on they may refuse to participate at all. Always bear in mind that the introduction of a sensitive question may terminate the interview. Another avenue is to try and develop a more appropriate or acceptable way of asking such questions. Asking respondents to tick categories or place themselves within bands often diffuses the impact of potentially sensitive issues. For example, when asked about income a respondent might be happier to tick a box within a broad income banding, rather than state their actual gross annual salary. While this does not provide accurate data it might satisfy your particular requirements. If you fail to get the information you need, or choose to drop certain questions, bear in mind there may be other data sources which could shed light on your topic of interest. Generalised income information for particular groups within the population, could be generated from the Family Household Survey. With the advances in information technology unemployment levels and benefit take up within particular neighbourhoods may be made available from the local Department of Work and Pensions.

Question types

When selecting question types there are a number of choices to make. Do you, for example, write the question as a statement? To glean information on the quality of the service provided to clients do you pose the statement: 'Project staff are usually helpful when dealing with enquiries' and then ask the respondent to select from a closed response menu? Or do you set a question, such as: 'How helpful are project staff when dealing with your enquiries?' In this case you could use an open-ended format to record the actual individual response. Statements tend to be seen as less threatening, since they are usually phrased in a general, non-personal way. The problem here is that you are asking respondents to react to somebody else's idea of the service, rather than allowing them to directly answer the question in their own words. In qualitative studies it is critical to articulate the respondent's own voice, and then interpret these expressed views. The approach adopted will depend upon the sort of information you want to glean. Also bear in mind that using both styles of question, within the same questionnaire, can be a good way of breaking the monotony created by relying solely upon questions or statements. Changing the rhythm or flow of a questionnaire is a useful technique, especially in the case of surveys that take some time to complete.

Open-ended or closed Items

Questionnaire items which use an open-ended format allow respondents to answer questions, or respond to statements, in their own words:

Q.8

How helpful are project staff when dealing with your enquiries?

Write Response . . . .

The advantage here is that the respondent is allowed a greater freedom of expression: they can say what they feel without being encumbered by the researcher's idea of what are appropriate response categories. Limiting response categories can act as a source of bias, which can be avoided by using open-ended items. The respondent can expand and/or qualify their answers, as they feel necessary. By adopting this method of question construction, it is possible to gain more insight into individual's real level of satisfaction.

The difficulties with using open-ended format questions come when you are trying to analyse and interpret the data. Their very flexibility can make coding for quantitative analysis – preparing the information for computer data analysis – both difficult and time consuming. Further, because respondents use their own words, these responses then have to be interpreted and classified. If not carefully handled such qualitative analysis can give rise to misinterpretation and misclassification.

If the survey does not require robust qualitative information, use can be made of the alternative 'closed', or 'forced choice' question format. In this instance, the respondent is faced with a number of alternative answers to the question or statement posed, and is asked to select the response that comes closest to how they feel. For example, Q.8 above could be presented in a closed format:

Q.9

How helpful are project staff at dealing with your enquiries?

Very helpful   ☐
Helpful   ☐
Neither helpful or unhelpful   ☐
Unhelpful   ☐
Very unhelpful   ☐
No opinion   ☐

Closed items are quicker to answer and easier to code than their open-ended alternatives. They are also more reliable, given all respondents are asked to react to the same set of options. The respondents also do not have to be articulate. On the other hand, they can give a misleading impression by forcing respondents to choose from what they may consider a limited range of options. They may also be annoyed that there is no opportunity for them to qualify their responses. As was noted in the chapter on measurement there is always a danger that the researcher attempts to create categories that do not equate with peoples understanding of their world.

Closed format items come in a variety of guises, with the most common categories being the single-answer list, the multiple-answer list, category, rank order, numeric, grid, Likert type and semantic differential.

Single answer list

As the name suggests, a single answer list involves the respondent choosing one answer from a given list of options. The response categories, as in all types of closed item, must be mutually exclusive; that is, the respondent's answer should fit one and only one category. They must also be exhaustive, in that the available categories should cover all the possible options. The usual way to ensure that closed items are exhaustive is to provide a catch all category such as 'Other' or 'Don't know'. A typical single answer list item would be:

Q.10

How would you describe your current employment status?

[Please tick the appropriate box]

Employed full-time	☐
Employed part-time	☐
Full-time student	☐
Unemployed	☐
Retired	☐
On invalidity allowance	☐
Other (please specify)	. . . .

The problem here is that full-time students now typically have a part-time job, whereas in the past this was less common. It is also common to allow the respondent to provide additional information when they select the 'Other' category. In the above example, 'Please specify', invites the respondent to write in details, which if a distinct pattern of responses emerge, allows them to be coded at a later date.

Multiple responses

To deal with the issue of getting more than one response to a question, a different format is employed. If, for instance, you wanted to build up a profile of staff expertise within particular areas, you might opt for a multiple response question such as:

Q.11

How many of the following courses, held over the last six months, have you attended?

[Please tick one or more boxes as appropriate]

Group working   ☐

One to one working   ☐

Health and safety   ☐

Leadership   ☐

Listening to others   ☐

Dealing with stress   ☐

Introduction to counselling   ☐

Category

When personal information is needed in a survey it is often better to provide categories of responses because these appear less personal and specific. As was noted above, information about age and income is commonly elicited using broad categories or bands. It is also important to ensure that your banding categories do not overlap.

Q.12

What is your age?

[Please tick the appropriate box]

Under 16   ☐

16–20   ☐

21–25   ☐

26–30   ☐

31–35   ☐

36–40   ☐

Over 40   ☐

Q.13

Which of these categories best reflects your household's gross annual income?

[Please tick the appropriate box]

Below £10,000   ☐

£10,000–15,000   ☐

£15,001–20,000   ☐

£20,001–25,000 ☐
£25,001–30,000 ☐
Above £30,000 ☐

The disadvantage with such banding exercises is that they may mask the information you really require. In neighbourhood deprivation surveys, more often than not, you need to access finer grain information than is provided by the above income-banding question.

Rank order

The rank order response format is similar to the multiple response questions. The difference is that the respondents are asked not only to make a choice, but provide relative judgements by putting their preferences in rank order. Suppose, for example, a new healthy living centre was being planned with several possible locations available to site this development. It may be useful to find out from potential users of the facility which location would best suit them. To gather such information, use could be made of a rank order question, such as:

Q.14

Please indicate, in rank order, the five areas in which you would prefer to see the new Healthy Living Centre. Your top preference should be ranked 1; 2 denotes your second choice, and so on, while the place you would least like to see this development should be recorded using the number 5.

Broomhill ☐
Eastgate Estate ☐
Foleys Farm ☐
Greenwood Gardens ☐
Princes Park ☐
Other (please specify) . . . .

It is important not to ask people to make too many ranking decisions. When asked to express more than about five preferences, the task becomes too difficult and respondents may start to allocate ranks on an arbitrary basis. This negates the potential usefulness of the information

Quantity

If the required response is a numeric value, giving the amount of some characteristic such as age, number of children, the cost of participating, or the time taken to travel to a local service, it can be expressed either as a quantity, or numeric response. This reduces the need for lists. The actual data categories can then be determined at a later stage when the pattern of responses is considered. For example:

Q.15

What is the approximate distance (in kilometres) from your home to the rehabilitation centre?

[Please enter your answer in the boxes provided]

☐   ☐   Km.

Grid

Grid response formats can be used where it is both possible, and appropriate, to ask a series of related questions at the same time. Users of a drugs counselling service could be asked to comment on the agency using a grid or table, such as:

Q.16

How would you rate the quality of the service provided by the drugs counselling project?

	Service provided				
Quality of service	**Appointment/ Waiting time**	**Opening times**	**Staff flexibility**	**Advice service**	**Programme**
Very good	☐	☐	☐	☐	☐
Good	☐	☐	☐	☐	☐
Average	☐	☐	☐	☐	☐
Poor	☐	☐	☐	☐	☐
Very poor	☐	☐	☐	☐	☐

Likert scale

The Likert scale is a means to test the strength of attitudes to a given set of statements on a particular topic. Respondents are asked to indicate on a scale, the strength of their agreement or disagreement with each statement. The statements should be equally divided between those that indicate a positive attitude towards the issue and those that reflect a more negative attitude. Unlike other questionnaire items, the statements used in Likert type scales are intended to solicit attitude scores and, therefore, can be biased. The following example attempts to explore attitudes towards new methods used in deciding upon:

Q.17

The introduction of the new management arrangements has improved the quality of service delivered to clients.

[Please consider the above statement carefully and then tick the box which comes closest to your opinion.]

Strongly Agree	☐
Agree	☐
Undecided	☐
Disagree	☐
Disagree Strongly	☐

Attitude scales are useful tools, but it is important to understand that respondents may still impute different levels of meaning to their choice, which can result in quantitative analysis blurring the intentionally of the respondents.

Semantic differential

Here again the respondents are asked to react to a series of concepts or statements. In the case of the semantic differential, however, the extremes of the scale are labelled with opposing adjectives, such as good or bad, rich or poor. Respondents indicate the strength of their feeling on a scale between these two extremes. A seven-point scale is generally used, but other ranges of numbers might be more applicable.

Q.18

How would you describe your job as a community worker?

[The following adjectives represent extreme views. Please ring the number which comes closest to how you feel about your job.]

Satisfying	1	2	3	4	5	6	7	Unsatisfying
Interesting	1	2	3	4	5	6	7	Boring
Demanding	1	2	3	4	5	6	7	Undemanding
Responsible	1	2	3	4	5	6	7	Menial
Varied	1	2	3	4	5	6	7	Repetitive

Layout and design

The layout adopted in any questionnaire is an important consideration. Not only should the document look professional, but good layout is also an essential element for the smooth running of any questionnaire. As people will be put off by a poorly presented questionnaire it is crucial that paper copies should be well designed and properly printed. Having access to standard word processing packages as well as desk top publishing (DTP) software should ensure that good quality design and presentation is achieved.

While there are no hard and fast rules about questionnaire design there are a number of points that need to be considered. Firstly, it is important to leave plenty of white space around each question. Questionnaires should never look cramped, as this can confuse either respondent or interviewer. Saving on paper cost can be a false economy if respondents don't understand the layout of questions. Secondly, any instructions to the respondent, or interviewer, should be clear, especially when use is made of contingency questions. These are questions which state that if you answered yes here, move on to question 6 and do not answer any of the intervening questions. Use should, therefore, be made of different typefaces, emboldening or colour to distinguish questions from instructions (for instance, normal black typeface for the questions, red italicised type for the interviewers' instructions). Thirdly, if computer analysis is to be used, the general convention is that the right hand column should be left solely for data coding purposes. Actual response boxes should be towards the right-hand side of the page, as this helps the respondent in completing the questionnaire, and helps with any subsequent coding of results. A clear separation, on the right hand side of the page between response and coding boxes is, therefore, required as in Q.19 below. Often the coding section of the page is shaded, or printed in a different colour. To get a better feel for layout and design issues look at a range of questionnaires, such as the Census and any previous surveys conducted by your organisation.

Q.19

How would you describe your job as a social worker?

[The following adjectives represent extreme views. Please consider each set of adjectives carefully and then place a circle around the number which comes closest to how you feel about your job.]

Satisfying	1	2	3	4	5	6	7	Unsatisfying	☐
Interesting	1	2	3	4	5	6	7	Boring	☐
Demanding	1	2	3	4	5	6	7	Undemanding	☐
Responsible	1	2	3	4	5	6	7	Menial	☐
Varied	1	2	3	4	5	6	7	Repetitive	☐

Questionnaire design is not merely an issue of visual design, in layout terms, but also involves the ordering of questions. A useful convention is to start with closed questions leaving any open items until later. The initial questions set the tone for the questionnaire. Begin with straightforward questions, those that are non-controversial and easy to answer. Questions of a sensitive or personal nature, as was discussed previously should generally be left until nearer the end. It is also a useful practice to end sections within the questionnaire with an open question, so that if the point they want to make has not been accommodated, they can record their views as further comments. It is always good practice to allow respondents an opportunity to bring in their own experiences or points of view.

As we have already mentioned, with the advent of laptop computers it is now common for the questionnaire surveys to be completed electronically, without the use of a paper survey form. This has many advantages. First the respondent is not faced with a large complex questionnaire, so the actual length of the survey is hidden. Questionnaire software packages also allow contingency questions to be automated, so you jump onto the next relevant question. From the researcher's point of view this approach also has the

overcoming potential distrust. This is less of an issue if you are conducting a survey within organisations or projects in which you are well known. As mentioned earlier, informing those who are to be surveyed either by letter or via a newsletter is essential no matter who you are surveying.

Response rates

Given the care taken in designing, piloting and administering the questionnaire it is natural that the researcher wants to receive as many completed replies as possible. Yet, not everyone will complete the questionnaire. Non-response can be a serious problem, especially in the case of postal questionnaires. The possibility that those who choose not to reply, are different from those who do, can seriously undermine the representativeness of the survey, as was discussed in Chapter 6 on sampling. So what then is a good response rate? As a general rule 'the more the merrier', but it really comes down to a question of trying to ensure you achieve your defined sample. As noted in Chapter 6 there is a procedure to determine an ideal sample size for your study, and you should try your best to achieve that requirement. If you think there is likely to be a noticeable non-response rate then you will need to draw a larger sample so the non-completion rate does not undermine the surveys representativeness.

So how then do you improve the response rate? In the case of postal surveys the initial inclusion of a stamped or pre-paid self-addressed envelope is a useful aid to encouraging a response. Alternatively, if the geographical coverage for such a survey is small, the questionnaire could be delivered by hand, thus allowing the opportunity to introduce the survey, and make arrangements to pick it up at a convenient time. Such an approach is employed by the Census. In the case of most postal surveys, once the specified date has been exceeded, a reminder or follow-up, is sent to those who have not returned the questionnaire. The reminder should be brief and to the point, and it often helps to enclose another copy of the questionnaire. Sometimes a second or even third reminder may have to be sent, but there is a diminishing return to such an exercise, as costs increase while responses decline.

In the case of face-to-face interviews response rates can be improved by ensuring adequate training of the interviewers. Calling at the most convenient time is also crucial. Calling on a winter's evening does not produce a good response, particularly with elderly residents. Calling on Sunday mornings, and during public or trade holidays will also produce a poor response. In this context, it is also important to set in place a return call back procedure. Again there is an issue of diminishing returns, in that the more return calls, the higher the cost, yet responses are invariably more difficult to generate.

If you plan to operate a follow-up system it is necessary to have some means of identifying the respondents. Questionnaires can be numbered, for example, so that non-respondents can be identified and reminders sent. However, if you have guaranteed respondents anonymity then, of course, you cannot follow-up non-respondents. Decide at the planning stage if a follow-up is to be used, or if anonymity is so important that you are prepared to accept a lower response rate. Consideration might also be given to other methods of encouraging people to respond such as offering incentives. Incentives can range from copies of the final report to money, or the chance to win a prize such as a portable television. You need to consider whether you have the resources to offer such incentives and whether they are appropriate to the research group being studied. For example, it would not be appropriate to offer a television set to homeless people.

Strengths and weaknesses

As a means of collecting certain sorts of information, questionnaires have a great deal to recommend them. Questionnaires are:

- An efficient means of collecting information from large numbers of people and/or over a wide geographical area.
- Relatively inexpensive, especially where they can be administered without the direct support of an interviewer/researcher.
- Convenient for respondents who can work at their own pace.
- Able to offer a degree of anonymity that is not possible with other research methods.
- If designed in a standardised and structured way, able to improve the reliability of the information collected.
- Easy to analyse using computer-based statistical packages.

As with all research methods, however, there is also a downside. Questionnaires are:

- Essentially superficial, in that they elicit answers that are primarily descriptive, rather than explanatory, since there is no capacity to probe or explore the provided answers.
- Not particularly flexible in terms of questions and response categories.
- Likely to yield poor response rates, especially in the case of postal surveys.
- Very time consuming, in terms of development, design, execution and analysis.
- Also unpredictable, in that while a questionnaire may be targeted to a particular person there can be no guarantee that they will have answered the questions, and that they did so unaided.

A final thought

While questionnaires offer a means of quantifying opinions and attitudes, they will be subject to interpretation and analysis that may be erroneous. Take the example of a survey exploring the incidence of racism. This might show a comparatively high percentage of white males who display negative attitudes towards members of other ethnic groups. That does not, however, mean that being white and male causes racist attitudes, it only shows there is a correlation. The issue of analysing survey results will be explored in greater detail in Chapter 12.

Observational Methods

Introduction

Is a glass containing water to the half way mark half filled or half empty? It could be either: it all depends what your purpose is. My purpose is to persuade you to look at a common everyday phenomenon – deviance – and see it in a different light.

(Box, 1971: vi–vii).

Observation may seem to be amongst the easiest, most natural of research methods: it is after all something that we do, to a lesser or greater degree, all the time. In research, it takes careful thought, rigorous planning and lots of patience to use observational methods successfully. The investment, however, can be very worthwhile since observational techniques can give access to aspects of behaviour, or events that may be difficult to obtain in any other way. You can interview social workers about how they relate to clients, for example, and then follow this up with a postal questionnaire to canvass client views about how they see the relationship; but can you be certain that the views expressed reflect what actually happens? Without being there, directly observing events as they happen, it's impossible to be sure.

Observational methods have a long history in social science research, and they have been widely used in social welfare contexts. This chapter, therefore, examines the role that observation might play in social welfare research. You will learn something about the direct observation of everyday life using both structured and participant observation. The advantages and disadvantages of intruding into, or getting involved in the phenomenon being observed, will also be discussed.

Observer or participant?

Participant observation is an approach by which the researcher enters into, and becomes part of, the actual events being studied. It was probably first used in social and cultural anthropology where the researcher was an ethnographer, and moved out of the academy or armchair and into the real worlds and lives of non-western peoples. The researcher attempts to experience the events in the same way as those involved do. This was termed, by Lacey (1971), an exponent of this approach, as learning '*to live in and understand the new world*'. Lacey's classic study detailed the experiences of the staff and students in Hightown Grammar and it still provides a good example of how to undertake participant observation (Lacey, 1971). This study demanded a great deal of commitment on the part of Lacey, in terms of time and effort, but resulted in an interesting and informative picture of everyday life in a secondary school. Similar studies have been conducted in other organisations and social settings including the military, the police, prisons, drug takers and young offenders.

Observational method presents a number of challenges to the researcher. When you directly observe an event, can you be totally confident about your interpretation of that event? Can you, as an outsider, understand the full meaning that may lie behind different people's actions? Further, does your presence as an observer not affect the situation that you are trying to study? Is it not the case that people behave differently when they realise they are being observed? Does what is termed the 'observer effect' become more marked when you are observing your colleagues in a workplace setting, where you are in some sense a participant in the events being observed? While such familiarity may not breed contempt, it could affect your objectivity and the behaviour of those being studied. This in turn poses a question: should we as researchers always be seeking objectivity? Indeed, many researchers who use participant observation methods would concur with Lofland (1984: 12), when he describes the process as, '*. . . a many sided and relatively long term relationship with human association in its natural setting*'.

One obvious way to counter 'observer effect' would be for you to distance yourself from the group being observed. You could adopt an approach that allows you systematically to record events, without playing any active part in them. You could, for example, choose to view events covertly, by using a one-way mirror or closed circuit television. This is often termed the naturalistic approach, where the phenomenon being studied is left to its 'natural state' without interference from the researcher. But wouldn't such detachment make it impossible for you to relate to the events and to understand the meaning of the behaviour of those involved? If you accept this perspective, you might then opt for structured observation, which while still being a qualitative method, draws on some quantitative approaches to event recording.

Whichever style of observation you adopt, the structured approach, the naturalistic model or the participant observer, you must always bear in mind that your job is firstly to observe and record events, and then, secondly, to analyse and interpret these events. It is important to remember you are an observer first, and a participant second. While that is easy to say, when working out in the field, it is not always an easy task to accomplish. Some researchers even argue that it is neither feasible nor desirable, since their involvement allows them to be reflexive about the changing scenario being studied and their changing knowledge base. For instance, Williamson and Butler (1995, 77) in their research with young people stressed the need for researchers to accept that young people would assess themselves in terms of '. . . *"maverick" qualities, of which humour was a central part. Being a "good laugh" was a critical attribute'*. Being able to understand, or react to that understanding would be crucial for a researcher involved in youth work.

Structured observation

Structured, or systematic, observation is a process in which you first decide what it is you want to study. Then you set about developing some form of framework for recording, coding and making your observations. The range of information recorded using this framework is then subjected to your analysis and from that your interpretation of the observed events emerges. So let's consider the questions to be addressed at each stage:

1. **What is it you want to observe?**
   The answer to this question will depend on your specific interests, and on the actual research questions you are pursuing within the study. Perhaps the most important point to realise, at the outset, is that you cannot observe everything. This may seem a rather obvious point to make, but you must be clear about what it is you are looking for before you begin to observe. If you are not clear about what you want to observe then you can find yourself swamped with so many images and potentially interesting observations that you might end-up recording nothing. However, in many social welfare situations, it is often the unexpected interactions and occurrences which provide the richest vein of research material, so predicting what is 'out there' is equally problematic.
2. **How do you record the observations?**
   Once you have decided what to look at, the next step is to devise a framework, typically some form of checklist, for recording your observations. Suppose you are researching the decision-making process within a voluntary organisation. Given committee meetings are the key decision-making forum, it would seem appropriate to observe a series of these meetings. The recording framework drawn up for this purpose could be a simple matrix in which each member of the committee is identified by a letter and the activities and behaviours you want to record are coded using the numbers one to twelve. Each relevant committee meeting agenda could then be examined, and the key decision items selected for observational recording. When each of the selected items comes up for discussion you would then observe and record what

was happening, using the relevant member and activity codes. So, during the discussion on the future funding application if the chair (a) provides information to the committee members you would record 6 in the appropriate cell. Similarly, when committee member (c) asks for information during the discussion on changing the staff work patterns a 9 is recorded in that cell. Where a committee member says nothing during the discussion of a selected item their recording cell would left blank. You would also have the opportunity to record any notes about the discussion, either as the debate unfolds, or after it was concluded. These notes will help later in your analysis of the actual decision-making process.

This sort of observational technique, illustrated in Table 9.1, provides one perspective on the decision-making processes of that committee. It does not provide a detailed account of the meeting. It will also not tell you how much time was spent on this, or that topic, or on the process of sharing information, as opposed to making decisions. What you get, however, is a sense of the dynamics of the meeting, and who are the key decision takers on the committee. You should be able to isolate out which members take a more active part in committee meetings, rather than just detail those who talk more than others. It also provides some evidence of the processes leading up to these decisions being made. Sociologists term this, as giving a construction of reality. This construct will undoubtedly enable some conclusions to be drawn. But bear in mind these conclusions are only one reality, and at the same time they may tell you more about the recorder, than the subjects. This is because relying on narrative recording places great emphasis upon the recorders value judgements about what has taken place. Other strategies may be employed, however, to reach firmer conclusions.

Depending on the nature of what it is you want to observe, you may need to design your own recording and coding frame. If you are interested in interaction, for example, there are a great many systems available 'off the peg' which you might use. Perhaps the best known of these is Bales' Interactive Process Analysis (IPA) system. The categories employed in Table 9.1 were taken from Bales (1970). This system is based on analytical categories that reflect verbal, non-verbal and extra linguistic interactions within groups. The number sequence employed is simply for coding purposes, and implies no rank order. Further the phrase 'seems friendly' is not quantitatively better than 'seems unfriendly'.

Coding in this structured way involves you in both recording and interpreting the meaning of an event and the associated behaviour at the same time. Clearly this can be difficult, since you have to decide not only that behaviour has occurred, but also what meaning to attach to it. What criteria would you use to decide that, for example, a particular behaviour was 'unfriendly', as opposed to being indicative of 'tension'? This problem becomes more acute where a number of researchers/observers are being used. In such cases you must agree on the interpretation of behaviours at the outset, otherwise

Table 9.1: Bales' interactive process analysis system

Committee member	Observation Period							
	1	2	3	4	5	6	7	8
A (chair)	6	4	—	5	6	6	8	6
B	3	4	7	12	3	4	3	3
C	2	2	9	5	5	6	—	2
D	—	3	4	5	7	7	—	7
E	11	1	7	7	11	3	3	3

Codes

Positive Actions	1. Seems friendly	Questions	7. Asks for suggestions
	2. Dramatises		8. Asks for opinions
	3. Agrees		9. Asks for information
Answers			
	4. Gives suggestion	Negative Actions	10. Disagrees
	5. Gives opinion		11. Shows tension
	6. Gives information		12. Seems unfriendly

Source: Bales, 1970.

the varied recording and coding of the events may invalidate the entire exercise. Video and audio recording, if allowed, might also be considered in structured observation. This allows you to replay events, and then, in the case of video, view what is happening again and again. A little more detail is offered later in this chapter in the section entitled 'Taking Notes', and in Chapter 12 on Information Communication Technology.

The actions of staff members in the group may be monitored in relation to various interactions and reactions. These may be individual, or representative of shared group feelings. More accurate recording may be needed to note the activities of each individual member of the group. The criteria employed might include involvement, commitment, attendance, types of relationships, activities engaged in, and any changes in circumstance, which effectively alter group behaviour. Again these criteria can be very difficult to test accurately. However, if carefully thought out, methods may be drawn up which can help lead the recording process to be of use in evaluation and assessment of individual and group performance (Dearling, 1979). Group performance can be recorded in a way that considers content, quantity and quality.

Naturalistic paradigm

Not all researchers are happy with a structured, rather quantitative approach to observational method. They prefer to use what is termed a naturalistic approach, which they consider more in keeping with qualitative research. As was noted previously in Chapter 5, qualitative research is based on certain epistemological assumptions –

assumptions about the nature of knowledge – that are in opposition to those of quantitative research. Put simply, quantitative research tends to assume that knowledge is concrete, tangible and objective: social 'facts' are akin to the facts in the natural sciences. In qualitative research, on the other hand, social reality is viewed as being more ambiguous and subjective. As was mentioned earlier, which side of the debate you fall on does not inevitably determine the sorts of research methods you will adopt. Nevertheless, how you choose to answer these two questions: what are we trying to learn about? and what is the best way to understand it? will very much influence your choice of research design. If you are inclined to support the more subjective viewpoint, then your research design is more likely to be influenced by the naturalistic or participant observation methodologies. Matza (1969) an advocate of the naturalistic paradigm argued that the quantitative tradition, conceives people as objects and use:

> ... *methods that probe human behaviour without concerning themselves with the meaning of behaviour, [and] cannot be regarded as naturalist ... because they have molested in advance the phenomenon to be studied. Naturalism ... claims fidelity to the empirical world.*

> (Matza, 1969: 8).

Naturalistic approaches are obviously not participant observation. Yet both are concerned with events that were not created or maintained purely for research purposes. Together, they constitute key qualitative research tools.

Observation and involvement

The first consideration in planning a study using observational methods is to consider your own role as the researcher. The main question is, to what extent do you participate in, as opposed to merely observe the activities or events being studied? At the one extreme, you could adopt the role of 'complete observer'; the detached, objective recorder of events. As an unobtrusive spectator, the complete observer has no involvement with the subjects and no responsibility for the events being observed. At the other end of the continuum there is the 'complete participant', who by contrast is intimately involved as an integral part of the group and, therefore, involved in shaping the events which are being investigated. Those being observed may even be unaware of the identity of either researcher.

So, suppose you were interested in studying the day-to-day experiences of homeless people. One approach might be to interview a range of homeless people. While this would produce qualitative information, you could feel that it will not provide data that accurately reflects the deprivations involved in this lifestyle, because those interviewed may have grown immune to certain aspects of their daily lives. To overcome this problem you might opt to become the 'complete observer'; recording the day-to-day events, while remaining detached from the individuals concerned. Information gathered in this way would be limited, especially if your declared intention was to see the world as those who are homeless experience it. The other approach would be to become totally immersed in the world of the homeless, as the 'complete participant', replicating what George Orwell did in the 1930s when researching for his famous novel *Down and Out in Paris and London*. This novel clearly documented the difficulties inherent in adopting such an approach, not the least of which are the major ethical issues involved. Jeremy Sandford, the author of *Cathy Come Home* (1967) which when filmed for television, led to the establishment of the homelessness organisation, Shelter, followed Orwell's lead by researching and writing *Down and Out in Britain* (1971). Describing his experiences he said, '*For a time I descended into the bilges of our society*' (Sandford, 1971: 9).

Neither the role of 'complete observer' or 'participant' is entirely satisfactory, yet each has its plus points. As the 'complete observer' you might get nearer to the perspective of a homeless person, given you view and record their situation. Yet, while your detachment ensures a degree of objectivity, you might never get close enough to the lifestyle and the values of homeless people to properly understand and, therefore, articulate their point of view. That perspective would certainly be more to the fore, if you adopted the role of 'complete participant', but then living the life of a homeless person for a defined period will never provide a full or truthful insight. It does, however, have the potential to produce better quality data than solely relying upon more distant observation.

Participant observation

The development of stakeholder participation in welfare services has been paralleled by the adoption of models of participatory research. This is not solely about using participatory observation models of research, rather it has led to a range of processes encompassing genuine tools to help both individuals and communities learn about 'their' lives and experiences. It should equally be about participation by stakeholders in the shaping and undertaking of research. The reality of this can take a number of forms, but it includes managers and staff members:

- Collecting data from their workplace interactions.
- Proactively involving users in research processes.
- Reflecting upon and analysing research findings, using focus groups and other means of collectively sharing information.
- Writing up data for professional presentations in training arenas and the professional media.

This range is now sometimes referred to as participatory learning and action (Pretty, 1995) and was initially developed in a number of developing, or majority world countries.

Participatory observation in its research context initially seems straightforward, but it is inherently difficult for researchers to work in unfamiliar and possibly threatening situations, especially when working with a range of people whose behaviour and attitudes may be antipathetic to the researcher. The need for detailed record-keeping and a flexible approach towards a variety of people and social situations are a necessity when undertaking this type of research. At its best, the approach reveals a fascinating and complex set of social relationships and understandings. As May (1997: 139) puts it, '*In "doing" ethnography, engagement is used to an advantage*'.

Adopting the role of participant can run the risk of 'going native' and in the process losing sight of the research goals. Over-identifying with the subjects of the study, to the extent that the needs of the study become secondary to those of the subjects is a common problem. Delamont (1992) provides an interesting discussion of the problems and issues associated with going native. Hobbs (1988) in his study of working class relations with the police in the East End of London provides an amusing insight into the problems that 'going native' can throw up. As his research work necessitated a certain amount of 'socialising':

> . . . *for the most part I spoke, acted, drank and generally behaved as though I was not doing research. Indeed, I often had to remind myself that I was not in a pub to enjoy myself, but to conduct an academic inquiry and repeatedly woke up the following morning with an incredible hangover facing the dilemma of whether to throw it up or write it up.*

(Hobbs, 1988: 6).

Inevitably, the very presence of the researcher will have an effect on the research situation, and this changes or distorts it in some way, no matter how carefully the researcher has tried to be non-intrusive. This is where you need to carefully reflect on exactly what your impact will be, and where this is considered problematic, set in place strategies to ameliorate these influences. The same point was also touched upon in the previous discussion on interview techniques.

Finding a setting

The issues associated with sampling in studies involving participant observation are more concerned with setting, than with the more usual issues of representativeness. Sampling methods within this context do not, therefore, necessarily follow the basic rules set out in Chapter 6. As was noted previously in undertaking a study of homelessness, random sampling may not be possible. Rather, to gain an understanding of the homeless experiences, locating both men and women through an opportunistic sample may be the best solution. That way you can decide on the group of people you want to study and then look for locations, or settings where they are most likely to be found. For a discussion of sampling issues in relation to studying homeless groups, see Kemp et al. (1993).

Snowball sampling, as discussed earlier, is a opportunistic technique widely used in identifying appropriate settings and individuals to study. The process often involves the use of key informants, people who have expert knowledge of the area and/or group you want to observe. Or, they may be the first respondents you talk to, who then network you with other appropriate research participants. These key informants can help you gain access to these groups, a critical consideration when trying to conduct successful participant observation. If you want to learn about how people manage and interpret their everyday lives, you will also have to develop some sort of rapport with them. The bottom line is they have got to trust you. That is not something your key informants can help you with.

How you negotiate access is often an important part of establishing such rapport. For example, in seeking to conduct some observation work within a social services office, you might think it appropriate to negotiate access through senior management, in the first instance. That might not guarantee the co-operation of those you want to observe, far less their trust. Their initial reaction to your request might be to suspect that your research is part of some management re-organisation strategy. As a researcher you need to be aware of potential concerns, and devise an access strategy that acknowledges the different levels of power and decision-making, and also ensures the access needed is agreed to the satisfaction of all parties. Negotiating access should never be viewed simply as a practical, administrative problem. The process of gaining access is part and parcel of the research process, and can on occasions reveal a great deal about the nature of the organisation, or group you seek to study.

Taking notes

Having found your setting, you now face the problem of how to record your observations. Researchers now have a staggering array of techniques, from using simple written checklists and recording forms through to audio recorders, camcorders and laptop computers. The recording equipment used in participant observation studies, however, tends to be limited to pen and paper, or perhaps an audio recorder if the setting allows. Memory is also important in certain situations, especially when covert observation is being employed. It is, however, important to bear in mind that memory can be fallible for all sorts of reasons, not least for the reasons cited by Hobbs (1988), noted above.

Almost every participant,or observer undertaking fieldwork keeps some kind of notes. How and when you record information will vary from researcher to researcher and will be influenced by the practicalities of the setting. This description of taking field notes in a study of educational practice is fairly typical:

> *My field notes fell into three main categories. On large note cards I recorded material that was primarily observational in nature. Observations of classroom activities were recorded chronologically and classified under class name. Observations that were about particular students or Mrs Lewis were also kept chronologically, but were classified under the student's or teacher's name.*

> *On loose-leaf size paper I kept typed accounts of each interview. These accounts were about ten pages in length, single spaced and were classified under the student's, graduate's or teacher's name ...*

(Valli, 1986: 227, quoted in Delamont, 1992: 61).

How you choose to record the various sorts of information will very much depend on the actual nature of your study. The important consideration is that you are thorough and consistent in your approach. You will know what it is you want to record and why, so you need to note everything that might be relevant. Your field notes should also include all decisions made in the course of the study, and any insights you gleaned that might be useful in subsequently interpreting the data. Lofland and Lofland (1984) offer useful advice on keeping field-notes.

A useful illustration of the value of note taking is provided by Lindstein's ethnographic study of children of alcoholic parents in Sweden (Lindstein, 1996). In this work he used a triangulation recording method with each of the three researchers involved in the study keeping individual observational recordings in a dedicated group journal, in addition to his own research journal. The aim was to achieve a very detailed understanding of how children reacted to life within a dysfunctional family. Through a number of sessions with the children, the researchers built up a detailed record of their behaviour, attitudes and views on life. A particular focus was whether they viewed their families as 'problems', and what it would be like to live within an 'ideal' family.

Lindstein noted that this method produced very different observations of the same interaction. '*Often we had noticed quite different things and we asked different questions in connection with what each of us had to relate*' (Lindstein, 1996: 70). Lindstein, thus showed that having different recordings from people with very different views of what they were observing, taken together, formed a much more 'holistic' picture of the events that occurred during the research. Further, he contended that this method of multiple observations produced qualitative research information which provides a '*... study of human expressions of lived life in whole contexts of meaning where totality and the partial pictures of the phenomena interact*' (Lindstein, 1996: 74).

Interpretation and generalisation

There are a number of criticisms that can be made of participant observation and of qualitative methods in general. The two most important concern the problems of interpretation and generalisability.

Interpretation

While acknowledging the idea that looking at events through the eyes of those most directly involved is an integral and appealing aspect of qualitative methods, it is also highly problematic. To what extent is it really possible for you to isolate out the 'real world' of your subjects? Can you really view and interpret events from their point of view? All information, no matter how it is collected, will be mediated to some extent by the values and mores held by the researcher. Again this is where reflection comes in. When using observational methods this problem is exacerbated by the fact that the technique is dependent upon the selection and observational skills of the researcher. It is entirely possible that the researcher will choose to include or exclude information because it fits or does not fit with their preconceived notion of the situation. Given the limitations of case selection, and the lack of transparency of the data collection instrument, such studies can be more open to a charge of bias. Where the researcher goes 'native' such a charge is hard to deny.

However, here is a brief checklist which researchers should consider in relation to how well they are performing their own particular research tasks, based on work by May (1997: 145–7):

- Time: the length of time spent in the field.
- Pace or setting: the nature and effect of the social setting.
- Social circumstances: the variety of different settings observed.
- Language: the language of the culture of the subjects.
- Intimacy: the greater the intimacy, the greater likelihood of an in-depth knowledge base.
- Social consensus (or otherwise): the homogeneity of the group being studied.

Generalisability

The observations made using this technique may be relatively small scale and limited to a small number of settings. This means that they are always vulnerable to the charge that the findings are too specific and, therefore, not generalisable; that they lack external validity. To some extent this problem can be addressed by combining methods – using triangulation – to view the event from a range of different vantage points. Many qualitative researchers would, however, simply reject this criticism given they consider notions of generalisation to be both unacceptable and irrelevant. Denzin, articulates this well when noting that:

> *The interpretivist rejects generalisation as a goal and never aims to draw randomly selected samples of human experience. For the interpretivist every instance of social interaction ... must be seen as carrying its own logic, sense of order, structure and meaning.*

> (Denzin, 1983: 133–4).

Participant observation, in that it is part of the interpretivist tradition, is concerned with engaging and trying to understand the 'sense of order, structure and meaning', sometimes referred to as the 'social construction of reality' (Berger and Luckmann, 1967). As such it should not be viewed as an easy research option. To conduct such work properly, a great deal of thought and hard work needs to be expended, not only in collecting the data, but also by carefully analysing what you have found. This issue will be considered in greater detail in Chapter 13. Observational method, despite its critics, does have the potential to offer new and interesting insights into many areas of social activity. And when used in conjunction with other methods can contribute to a far more rounded and considered study of many of the diverse locations in which social welfare activity occurs.

CHAPTER 10

Case Study Contexts

CHAPTER OBJECTIVES

This chapter is designed to ensure that you:

- Appreciate the various types of case studies that can be utilised when undertaking social welfare research.
- Understand both the value and practical difficulties involved in using case studies.
- Are alert to the limitations of working with case studies.

Introduction

'Case study' is an umbrella term for a range of ways in which actual research can be structured. It is not, in itself, a research method. Rather, the full range of research methods detailed in Chapters 3 to 9 can all be employed within a case study format. What case studies have in common is the researcher's decision to focus the inquiry around either a single instance, or set of instances (Adelman et al., 1977). Put another way, the case study is an idiosyncratic combination of elements, or events (Mitchell, 1983). That is both its inherent strength and obvious weakness within any research setting.

At its simplest, a case study merely provides the unit, or focus for further systematic analysis or investigation, as defined by the researcher. This can be a description of one or two cases or events, detailing what happens within a particular timeframe. It therefore provides a snapshot of the case, or an event, occurring at a particular point in time. At its most complex, however, case studies can be used to test experimental research within a natural setting, by controlling the influence of particular selected elements (Hakim, 1987). Case studies can, therefore, depending on how they are selected or constructed, act as a microscope or provide a spotlight. Their value depends entirely upon how well the researcher utilising them selects the focus (Hakim, 1987).

Within the social sciences, case studies are employed to allow for the fine-tuned exploration of a complex set of interrelationships. Within the social welfare field, case studies have proved particularly useful as a means of monitoring and evaluating a wide variety of policy and practice initiatives, or developments. Case studies are commonly used in evaluation studies to allow an examination to be made of a particular process of change. For such evaluative studies to be of value, it is important that they generate information from before and after the introduction of the intervention under examination.

Ensuring that there is relevant contextual material, which sets the case study within its defined context, is also important. So if you wanted your study to trace the changes that emerged from altering the services delivered to support disabled children and their families it would be critical to detail what this change meant to the lives of the various participants. In setting the study in context it would be important to detail the role played by all participants in the intervention, both before and after the service was changed. Then you would need to detail what the various parameters of the intervention were, and then why it was felt necessary to alter their focus. Only then would you be able, through the case study, to detail how the process and outcome of this change affected all participants. Through adopting this focus, you should be able to increase your understanding not only of the specific change, but how that change impacts differentially on those who participate in the intervention. This sort of case study enhances our understanding of causality and the effects of particular actions and interventions.

Evaluating the case study approach

The concept of recording 'cases' in medical and welfare settings is a familiar one. Casework is regarded as an everyday investigative tool in social work and counselling settings. The case notes then form the record of the interactions between the social worker and the client. In particular, they are used as a means of assessing changing needs, the effectiveness of interventions and for logging changes in the client's life. The case study approach in many ways is a natural extension of working practices common within health and social work agencies.

A case study approach in social welfare research is often employed because it provides an individual researcher with a scale of research work that they can easily tackle. It allows one aspect of an issue, or a particular initiative to be studied, in some depth, over a defined period of time. This is important, given the limits imposed on all research studies, both by time and resource constraints. That is not to say case studies cannot be employed over long periods of time. Many longitudinal studies will undertake on-going case study work, or revisit case studies at defined intervals. It is the scale and, therefore, the ambition that distinguishes a case study approach from a larger, more comprehensive survey. Given this, case studies are often viewed as a logistical compromise. But that ignores their adaptability and wide applicability, which also goes a long way to explain their popularity within social welfare research. It is this very flexibility, however, that must be properly understood if they are to assist you with your specific research work.

In undertaking any case study work you should have two objectives:

- To provide a description of each case.
- Then, through comparing and contrasting these descriptions, explanation should emerge.

At their best, case studies should be descriptively valid and have a more general application. So when conducting any case study examination, you need to ensure that the various parameters of the particular case under consideration are comprehensively detailed. To achieve this goal, a variety of techniques should be employed in order to delineate the focus of the research. The second objective, namely, expanding our knowledge and understanding of the issue or project, could help in the construction of wider concepts that have applicability wider than just the cases examined. In this way, case studies can be seen to provide a means to contribute to, and engage with, wider theories. The challenge presented here is that to be truly useful a number of distinct research methods need to be employed within the individual case studies. This may sound rather abstract, but an obvious example is provided when social workers test a series of observable interventions in order to see what support they might provide, or capacity to change the damaging behaviour exhibited by a client. Devising ways of recording the various interventions, writing this information up and then evaluating the value of the interventions constitutes a simple case study.

Case studies also have the advantage of allowing the researcher the opportunity to appreciate what they are studying from the perspective of those being studied. There is never just one way of viewing the world, and case studies can facilitate these wider discourses. 'Official' interpretations of particular projects, policies or events are often at variance with those who work on them, or those whose life experience has been touched by them. Research which draws out this material, and compares and contrasts these varied interpretations, improves our understanding of the various processes that are taking place, and can inform both practice and policy in social welfare organisations. The challenge here is to write up the case study material in a manner which is clear, accessible and cuts through the mass of indigestible local, specific material and draws out the key conclusions. Being able to integrate carefully selected, robust and central examples from the local data, which help explore the key questions and issues raised by the study, is a real research skill (Hakim, 1987). This is not a case of adding local colour to a study, which undoubtedly has its own value and merit, but rather it is about improving and enhancing understanding. There is always a symbiotic relationship in the research process between description and explanation.

As with all research work, the case study approach is inherently incomplete. Schuller (1988) in making this point sees much virtue in case study work for this very reason because, contrary to first impressions, it must confront and make explicit that incompleteness. A case study can, however, be distinguished from the anecdote, on the one hand, or simple narrative on the other, by the fact that it is not randomly selected and that it does have some potential for explaining events or circumstances beyond itself.

Case studies types

Case studies can be employed in a number of ways. They can be used as a follow-up to a questionnaire survey, as a means of examining specific examples of what has occurred at a particular place and time. They can also precede a survey, highlighting issues that may require more detailed follow-on investigation. As well as being illustrative, they can also act as a proxy for a specific approach, or type of organisation. Selected case studies can be used to illustrate the merits, or demerits, of a specific approach, or can focus on a unique project or initiative that is considered to be an example of 'best practice'. Case studies, overall, offer the researcher a certain degree of creative flexibility, not only in the type of case study that can be employed, but crucially in the variety of research techniques that can be employed within the selected case study.

Case studies should not, however, be viewed as an easy option, for they certainly are not. Exactly how you go about selecting case studies is one critical consideration, as is the way you then undertake the associated research within these selected cases. Then there are issues about how you report on the findings from your case study work. Critically, does your approach to case studies allow your research to try and explain, rather than merely describe specific social phenomena?

A case study can focus on an individual, a group, an institution, a facility, a resource, an intervention or a geographic area. Outlined below are a number of examples which not only illustrate this diversity, but also outline the broad range of research methods which can be employed within these case studies. The majority of these techniques have been detailed in the preceding chapters of this block.

Table 10.1: Case study types

Type	Description
Individuals or groups	Tracing the careers, or experiences of individual people. This approach has been extensively used to illustrate the housing histories of young homeless people, the experiences of children in care and those receiving other forms of intervention. The views of minority ethnic community mothers about their post-natal care or ex-prisoners about their experiences of re-entering mainstream society provide two examples.
	A recent report by the Princes' Trust (2003) utilised a case study approach through interviews and focus groups to obtain the views of 19–25 year olds in four categories: unemployed; educational underachievers; ex-offenders; and those in or leaving care. The research focussed on how particular young people were doubly disadvantaged through their lack of qualifications, coupled with abuse of drugs and criminal records. The individual responses indicated that poor commitment to work or further education was exacerbated by their view that they were better off on benefits.
Resource or institution	Project evaluation is a core feature of social welfare case study work. Case studies can allow a detailed examination to be made of the role and impact of a particular facility or resource, such as a women's aid hostel, or a family centre. The practices adopted by similar statutory bodies when taking on new responsibilities, such as those arising from the 'Supporting People' initiative, provides further opportunities for institution-based case studies.
	A case study approach was used in both Middlesborough and North-east Lincolnshire to help evaluate the implementation of key worker services projects (Mukherjee et al., 1999).

Table 10.1: *Continued*

Type	Description
Resource or institution (*cont'd*)	Rather than offer purely evidence-based research, the findings highlighted the need for a good infrastructure to support and manage the changes. In particular, the study pointed out the need for 'time out' for staff to engage with multi agency working practices and the need for external facilitators to enable findings to be translated into lessons for practice.
Intervention	This can focus on the introduction of a specific policy initiative, such as the 'Communities That Care' initiative. France and Crow (2002) undertook a long-term evaluation of three demonstration projects that sought to trace how these communities, and the professionals supporting them, identified local risks to young people and how they sought to address these. Another example of an intervention case study is the work of Green et al., (2001) who looked at a range of different projects that mapped and tracked vulnerable young people, and shared the collected data between the various support agencies. Developing a programme in schools to help socially excluded young men be better prepared for the transition into work was monitored on a case study basis which looked at the effects of the intervention on 51, 14–15 year olds in three south London schools (Lloyd, 2002). The project appeared to be positively received by the young men, because it treated them as adults; was practically orientated; and through undergoing a rigorous competence assessment of their new skills, they received a reference.
Geographic	Often case studies are selected on the basis that they are used to represent a particular category of geographic area, such as rural or urban, or semi urban or semi rural. These are sometimes referred to as exemplars. Combe (2002) selected six contrasting geographic case studies in her study of young people's involvement in local government decision-making processes. Pugh (2000) looked at a wide range of agencies delivering a diverse range of services in rural areas. One of his examples detailed the operation of training for practical facilitators and users of mental health services in the rural district of Powys in Wales. Monitoring and evaluation ten one day training sessions, which involved over 130 individuals raised a number of shared concerns which included: unresponsive attitudes amongst GPs and the question of informed consent over both treatment and medication.

From the above examples it is clear that these categorisations are not mutually exclusive. Individual, group and institution could, in certain instances, be interchangeable. While this illustrates the flexibility of case studies, it also aptly illustrates that any categorisation is, at best, arbitrary. What is critical is what you intend to get from applying a case study frame to your research.

Case studies are also commonly applied as a means to engage in comparative analysis. When data from similar situations in different locations or countries are compared, common themes and patterns can be identified, leading to the generation of hypotheses and the development of theory. The examination of themes and patterns is common to all uses of case studies, but is especially important where the research design demands comparative analysis of the cases. There are, however, limitations to the comparative capacity of case studies. Again this comes back to the problem of the specific being used to highlight what may be a general pattern. In cross-national comparisons the effects of national policy environments can limit the capacity to generalise. That said, it may be that the same issues arise, but what differs is the way they are addressed. Comparisons within the one national context are generally more useful, but care has to be taken in how you express the links between the separate case studies and what you feel this reveals about the wider pattern. Harloe and Martens (1984) provide a useful discussion of the practical problems associated with international comparative housing research. The following chapter considers the whole issue of comparative research in greater detail.

Case study selection

It is important to always remember that each case study is unique. Any case study, no matter the type, will display both common and unique features. So can any case study ever be seen to illustrate more than just itself? Do the unique features not detract from it being seen as a exemplar for the other cases that share its common features? In some instances a case study is selected precisely because it illustrates something that is quite unique. It may, for example, represent a specific point of view, or a particular approach. In other instances, case studies are selected to illustrate the experience of operating within a specific environment. But can they ever be anything but unique? Case studies are always unique, but the researcher can select them as being illustrative of wider patterns. The term 'illustrative' is used in preference to 'representative', because no case study should be described as being 'representative' of a specific type.

What case studies can often provide is a detailed snapshot of a piece of social welfare practice. In turn, this can be compared and contrasted by other managers and practitioners with their own experience. Although it won't necessarily produce 'blueprints' or 'template', it can provide ideas and models that can be adapted and adopted to work in a variety of settings. Any discussion should focus primarily upon what the case study itself, has revealed. Great care must be taken when trying to extrapolate the case study findings into the wider context. That is not to say it cannot be done, but rather care needs to be taken when making links between the case study evidence and any perceived wider pattern. In a study of local authority care management practice, for example, a rural case study area may have been selected. If that rural local authority had a well-run social services department with exemplary care management systems, could this situation be taken to be indicative of the situation for all rural authorities? Clearly not, because the case study could have been selected on the basis that it illustrated 'good practice' in a well-managed authority. So there are clear limits to how the descriptive material derived from case study contexts can then help develop explanations that are transferable.

So the purpose for which the case study is to be put, determines the way in which it is selected. The case study's purpose, in respect of the research question being pursued, directly influences the selection criteria. Researchers, therefore, always need to make explicit the reasons that lie behind their particular selection decision. This allows the reader to consider and, where necessary, challenge the basis of selection. It may be that, in turn, this leads them to reject the research conclusions.

It should also be borne in mind that, given the researcher selects the area for study, decides upon what data to collect and determines which material should be presented in the final report, it is difficult to cross-check the data generated. Case studies can either consciously or unconsciously, lead to distortion and bias. While this is certainly not a problem unique to case study based research, it is more obvious. To avoid such criticism it is crucial that you are explicit about the approach adopted, explain why certain decisions were taken during the course of the study, and are clear about their potential implications.

Type, quality and range of data

While documentary work, observation and interviews are the most commonly used methods within case studies, no method is excluded. Typically both qualitative and quantitative approaches are combined to generate the range of information required to illustrate the various points or issues under consideration. It is not uncommon, in social welfare research for a comprehensive survey to be followed up by selected interviews. Case studies can often involve detailed documentary studies, given such material is often essential in setting the context for the case under consideration. If the case studies are geographically based then this context setting work is enhanced by quantitative analysis, drawing from the Census and any other useful spatially based data held by the local authority. It is common for certain social welfare data sets to be held on such a geographic basis, given the marked advances in Geographic Information Systems (GIS) over recent years. The capacity to generate both past and present socio-economic information has clear advantages within any analysis. In relation to data collection within a case study context, the guiding principle should be nothing is ruled out and nothing is ruled in.

Accessing the best information available is the key to good case study work (Bromley, 1986). Emphasis does, as in all research contexts, need to be placed on the words 'best' and 'available'. The preceding chapters, within this part of the book, should have helped you appreciate just what is meant by these terms. Each chapter should also have made it clear that what is best is not always available. Available time and resources usually result in some sort of compromise which does affect the quality of the final research work. The crucial point is that, at all times, quality should be the key objective in respect of data collection.

Some practical issues

In a typical, limited funded research study, a large-scale survey may have to be reduced down to just eight case studies. This final selection is, in turn, a compromise, in that each of the cases must try to cover a range of issues which the larger survey would have touched upon. Then having selected and justified this selection, the use of a case study method can throw up a few practical issues.

When selecting any case, you will have an impact upon what it is you are researching, as was discussed in relation to observational method in the previous chapter. For example, in the study of elderly care management practice the imminent arrival of a researcher may result in the staff 'brushing-up' of the administrative systems that are to be examined. Those involved in executing the day-to-day work may undergo individual or organised training to ensure that they are all up to scratch. The researcher will always have an influence upon those being studied. While there is little that can be done about this, you do need to be aware of it. That said, solid interviewing technique can, on occasions, highlight inconsistencies and discrepancies in practices, thus breaking down such preparation. As was discussed earlier, the best way to get round this is to ensure access to a range of data sources, so that you can cross-check information, thus highlighting any discrepancies that arise.

There are other practical problems associated with organising your research within a case study context, which Schuller, (1988) detailed as follows. These examples were developed from his long experience of conducting such work:

- You go in and get nothing because access issues were not thought through properly, or previous assumptions or guarantees come to nothing.
- You go in but can only get so far, because it proves to be a lot harder and more time-consuming to access the required data than had been assumed. This may create tensions with others involved in the case study.
- You go in and get the material, but it is sensitive and easily attributable to one specific case and is therefore hard to use. An example of this is where income data from a particular geographic case study highlights the fact that a number of residents could be engaged in defrauding the benefit system.
- You go in and get so much information it proves hard to keep a clear focus on the research topic at hand. The case study throws up a host of new ideas and this makes you re-think the basic assumptions of the study.

Again, none of these issues are unique to case study based research, but are equally applicable within any research context. It is important to be aware of these potential problems, and try to plan out the research method in a way that avoids such pitfalls. Yet, all the meticulous research planning in the world will not be capable of predicting the problems that can, and do arise in conducting case study work.

So the advantages of case studies are that:

- They allow for in-depth focusing on shifting relationships.
- They can capture the complexities of the situation.
- They allow a focus on the local understandings and a sense of participation in the case.

- They can produce readable narrative data that brings research to life and is true to the concerns and meanings under scrutiny.
- They can help generate data that assists in the development of a more general hypothesis and theory.
- They can provide examples of good, best or even worst practice in a range of social welfare contexts.

The disadvantages of case studies are that:

- They can be an unwarranted intrusion into the affairs of others.
- They are very much bound by situation, and a particular point in time.
- They require the careful collection of high quality data which takes time and much effort.
- They may be so particular and unique that they fail to provide replicable practice, or management learning material.
- The researcher can become so immersed in the case that subsequent data analysis can become difficult.

As has been outlined above, the purpose of adopting a case study approach should be more than just providing the means to add colour and authenticity to a study. A case study, if properly conducted, is much more than just a story about, or a description of, a particular event or state. It should also be capable of providing more than generalisations. To take a case study beyond these limited outcomes, as with all research, evidence has to be collected in a systematic manner. Only through the methodical planning of data collection can you hope, at a later stage, to reveal whether there is a relationship between the variables.

Case studies are too often criticised as being 'soft subjectivity'. Yet, what should be clear from this chapter is that adopting a case study approach is no soft option. It has its own rigour and should be judged in its own terms. To get around these criticisms you will need to ensure a range of data collection methods are employed, and where possible a triangulation of this data is achieved. It is always crucial to get different perspectives on any event or phenomena. Finally, as noted elsewhere in the book, it is often advisable, where possible, to try and engage more than one researcher when gathering information on the case. Different people will draw out, or are alert, to different aspects operating within the case. Clearly, when conducting a small-scale project this may not be feasible, but it is worth considering when conducting, or commissioning a larger scale study. Overall, a successful case study should provide, '*the reader with a three-dimensional picture and will illustrate relationships, micro-political issues and patterns of influence in a particular context*' (Bell, 1993: 9).

CHAPTER 11

Comparative Research

CHAPTER OBJECTIVES

This chapter is designed to ensure that you:
- **Appreciate the relevance of cross-national and other cross-cultural approaches to social welfare research;**
- **Appreciate the very specific nature of 'comparative' research methods;**
- **Are aware of some of the controversies surrounding the use of comparative methods.**

Introduction

Comparative research is increasingly being seen as being a major aid in the development of appropriate policy and practice responses to particular social issues or problems. As Clasen (1999) notes, policy makers and practitioners frequently use cross-national experience to inform their decision-making. Alongside this, improvements in information communication technology (ICT) now make it easier to access detailed information on alternative policy approaches and associated practical examples. There is also a growing desire, or pressure, for a certain degree of policy harmonisation across Europe, partly in response to EU membership. Further, with regional government becoming a more significant political entity throughout Europe, there is a desire to compare and contrast policy development and practice approaches at this sub-national level. Governments increasingly, therefore, look to other countries or regions across the world for new ways of addressing specific, yet universal, problems such as social security, criminal justice, child welfare, heath care and elderly care arrangements. In Europe, the different fiscal and legal arrangements, within these legislative entities, ensure growing panoply of approaches, albeit within an increasingly more standardised policy framework.

In a sense, much of the research discussed to date has a comparative dimension. Projects operating in similar settings are often compared, while different approaches in different parts of the country are also examined to try and discover what constitutes 'good practice'. There has also been the long-standing practice of using comparative research to explore variations in both the policies and practices pursued between England and Wales and Scotland. Interestingly Northern Ireland rarely features in this type of study. What is relatively new is the burgeoning of trans-national comparisons between different

European states, or Britain and the wider world. For instance, much of the current Government's social security reforms such as 'Welfare to Work' and the 'New Deal' display a strong American antecedence. There are also long-standing and strong links in social welfare policy and practice between Australia, Canada and New Zealand. Within social welfare, comparative research has been used to answer the following questions:

- Which policies and programmes work, which don't, and why?
- What are the lessons to be learned from shared practitioner experiences of common social welfare issues?
- What is the cost and value of different programmes and their associated policy regimes?
- What differences exist in relation to socio-cultural behaviour, and how does this impact upon welfare support systems and their operation within different locations?
- Why are social, cultural and institutional settings important in assessing and comparing international data?

Linguistic and cultural conflicts

Such cross-national lessons are, however, often based on only a superficial understanding of the policies and programmes being considered. Too often little attention is paid to the critical legal, social and cultural considerations that underpin the particular social strategies of individual countries (Ball, Harloe and Martins, 1988; Blickman, 1998; Kemeny and Lowe, 1998; Robertson and Rosenberry, 2001). In reality, there is a far wider range of conditions, which help contribute to the success, or failure of a particular policy or practice approach. While lessons can be drawn from cross-national experience, it is critical to appreciate and respond to the different legal, political, social, economic and cultural contexts. It is also critical that the problems being addressed are directly comparable (Doling, 1997). As a result, valid lessons from cross-national experience can only be drawn on the basis of a systematic application of knowledge about the particular problem under investigation, coupled to an appreciation of how specific national policies and institutions operate (Heidenheimer, 1990). Only by adhering strictly to these requirements is it valid to draw lessons from one jurisdiction and apply them in another.

Hantrais (1996) makes a very pertinent observation when commenting that one of the major problems confronting would-be comparative researchers, is that:

> ... *relatively few social scientists feel that they are well equipped to conduct studies that seek to cross national boundaries, or to work in international teams. This reluctance may be explained not only by a lack of knowledge or understanding of different cultures but also by insufficient awareness of research traditions and processes operating in different national contexts.*

Almost embedded in the very use of the term: 'comparative research', there is a linguistic conflict between the everyday use of the term, and the more specific (but sometimes still conflicting or contradictory) use of the terminology in the research world. At a basic level, any information that compares and contrasts the functioning of different systems or behaviour could be described as a form of comparative research. But clearly that is not enough to give it status as useful and accurate grounded research. Cross-cultural or system comparisons, whether within one country or between countries, are obviously only of value if they accurately reflect, analyse and interpret not only the subject under consideration, but the different environments in which it operates. This is the aim of various European wide research programmes and observatories, currently monitoring the responses of European member states to 'problem' areas such as social security, drug dependency and homelessness.

World-wide comparisons are also undertaken which pose even greater research challenges. A good example of this is the massive United Nations study, The Human Development Report (United Nations Development Program, 2000). The primary purpose of this report is '. . . *to assess the state of human development across the globe and provide a critical analysis*' (UNDP, 2000: 141). Later on the same page of the report it states that despite '*the considerable efforts of the international organizations to collect process and disseminate social and economic statistics and to standardize definitions and data collection methods, many problems remain in the coverage, consistency and comparability of data across countries and over time*' (UNDP, 2000: 141).

The usefulness of comparative studies can be further challenged by subtle differences in the meaning of what should, at face value, be broadly similar definitions. This often results in what were assumed to be like-for-like data sets proving to be incomparable, or at least not directly comparable. A useful illustration of this is provided by the term co-operative. Within the UK, co-operative is associated with one of the three pillars of the early Socialist Movement, namely the Trade Unions, the Labour Party and the Co-operative movement. When the same term is employed within former Eastern Block nations it had a directly opposite meaning. Housing co-operatives in Poland were, for example, initially State controlled and then operated independently (Clapham et al., 1996). Rather than being a left of centre philosophy, co-ops in Poland were deemed to be almost right-wing self-help organisations. Within the American context, co-op means micro or grass roots capitalism (Birchall, 1997). Given this variation in the basic meaning of the term, direct comparisons of housing or food co-operatives across different countries can be rendered meaningless.

Comparing the prevalence levels of reported child abuse between countries provides another illustration of the same problem. Within certain countries it is typical for all child abuse cases to be recorded, with an incident being re-registered when a criminal conviction was secured. Yet in other countries registration only occurs once a conviction has occurred, so any direct comparison of these two data sets would not be very helpful.

The role of participation in combating social exclusion has been subject of a recent four-country research study. Stevens found that their research was dogged by, '*a persistent feature in calls for increased participation is the lack of clarity about what the term is meant to mean'* (Stevens et al., 2003: 85). So, perversely, while all four countries studied wanted more participation, the study also revealed varying degrees of willingness by those with power to give it up to socially excluded people, engaged in local decision-making. Participation, as a concept, was understood in four distinct and different ways.

Another example comes from research carried out under the Targeted Socio-Economic Research Programme in Europe. Baptista and Perista (1999), working from Lisbon, found that when comparing poverty data for Portugal within the UK, conflicting definitions for different categories of people were constantly being thrown up. As a result, the data was not directly, or even accurately comparable. In Portugal, for example, the 'single parent' category includes any single parent with children still living at home, even well into adulthood. This was not the case with UK statistics. As was noted earlier in this book, official data sets often derive from the welfare policies that they are designed to inform, and as such are very much socially and culturally constructed. Engaging in comparative quantitative research would, therefore, require a degree of cultural knowledge and an acceptance of some degree of compromise. Such considerations and qualifications need to be clearly articulated to any potential users of both the statistics and the resulting analysis. This, in turn, may severely limit the potential value of the comparative study.

In the remainder of this chapter, examples of how comparative research has been used to explore certain social welfare questions is discussed, with a view to illustrating both the benefits and the nature of the problems that can be thrown up. By being alert to the limitations of comparative research, and being explicit about them in any work undertaken, should ensure that false conclusions are minimised.

Uses for comparative research

Comparative research has evolved within a number of academic disciplines associated with social welfare matters. These include sociology, anthropology, economics, and cultural studies, as well as in the field of geography, social policy and political studies. For this very reason, it embraces a rather ill-defined set of methodologies, most of which rely on the research methods already described in this book: sampling, measurement, documentary study, observation, interviews, questionnaires and all associated subsequent analysis. At the heart of comparative research lies a presumption that we can learn from, and make informed decisions based on studying behaviour in one location and comparing it with what happens somewhere else. For instance, in the field of criminology, the UK has increasingly over the years, 'borrowed' programmes such as 'zero-tolerance' policing, the appointment of a 'drugs czar' and the piloting of drugs courts from the United States (Eley et al., 2002). Within England, the development of family group conferences has its roots in New Zealand child law practice. At the same time, many countries including Belgium and France have extensively studied the Scottish Children's Panel system (Hallett and Hazel, 1998).

What is open to question, however, is the appropriateness of these policy imports, or practice 'exemplars' to another country. This has been particularly true in the case of health programmes and reforms which have, on occasion, been taken from developed industrial countries and re-applied, quite inappropriately, in developing, or majority world countries (Gonzalez-Block, 1998). What he emphasises is that any 'exemplar' must be seen within its entire cultural context, and that while it is possible to benefit from shared learning, when it comes to imitating, these must be seen in terms of whether it is '... *worth importing? Can it be adapted? and is it politically feasible?*' (Gonzalez-Block, 1998: 11). Gonzalez-Block then used this method to evaluate the pros and cons of the United States seeking to imitate the Canadian health system. His view was that while the Canadian system was more equitable and cheaper, the 'individualistic creed of life' in the United States made it difficult to conceive of the Canadian model being imported on a state-wide scale.

At the intra-national level it is far easier for research programmes to be focused on comparisons between the ways people, or systems are operating within similar legal or administrative arrangements. We say this because it is reasonable to assume that researchers will already understand the language of the country they are operating within, and will probably also understand many of the laws, administrative procedures and cultural systems which underpin much of the social phenomena they are wanting to study. At a cross-national level, it is far harder to achieve this basic level of understanding for two or more countries. Inevitably, in the case of the UK, this can lead to criticism that the resulting research is Anglo-centred, even at the level of comparisons between England, Scotland, Wales and Ireland. Certainly, comparative research is inevitably 'culturally situated' and has to be read with caution because of this. Webster's comments on television reportage of 'news' have much relevance in this context:

> ... *the news we receive is a version of events, one shaped by journalists' contacts, and availability, moral values, political dispositions and access to news-makers. Yet, if we can readily demonstrate that television news is not 'reality' but a construction of it, then how is it possible that people can suggest that beyond the signs is a 'true' situation?*

> (Webster, 1995: 178).

In France, for example, the cultural framework, which emanates from the philosophy of Rousseau, sees the State, the family and child having the same ultimate goal in relation to child welfare. In the UK it would be common to see the State, family and child in conflict. As a result, child welfare legislation is very different because the basis of policy derives from a totally different philosophical stream. Laws relating to family and marriage within Europe also reflect a distinct religious heritage, with southern Europe reflecting Catholic 'family welfare' principles, while those of northern Europe have a distinctly Protestant outlook, in which the state takes on from the welfare provided by the church.

France, due to its revolutionary and associated secular heritage displays a distinct approach of its own. This might mean that a UK based comparative study of family law and its consequences for social welfare provision would be well advised to look at Holland, Denmark or Sweden, rather than France, Spain or Italy. That said, a comparison with Spain might help draw out the importance of this religious cultural heritage in shaping the nature of one's own welfare provision.

Applied comparative research

In social work, there have been moves, through EU educational exchange programmes, such as Erasmus and Socrates, to enable students to undertake professional training in other countries within the European Union. Interestingly, because this has demanded that university staff and managers in the field travel more to supervise students from abroad; it has led to an increased awareness of different practice, policies, legislation and procedures. One such exchange programme, which focused on the ethical dimensions of the 'personal' and the 'professional' lives of social welfare workers, involved students from fifteen educational institutions across Europe. They were drawn from a range of social professions including social pedagogy, youth work, community education and special education. Banks and Williams (1999), who wrote up the findings of this exchange programme, started their report with the words of one Danish student, '*why professionals are afraid of getting too involved and when is it too much?*' The methodology employed for this comparative research involved each of the 57 students, from twelve different countries working through seven separate case studies. One of the seven case studies, which was drawn up by a Dutch teacher, is reproduced immediately below.

A LONELY CHILD

Hans is a 10 year old boy living in a child protection home located in a small village. He lives in a 'group' with seven other children. It is almost Christmas and all the other children have been allowed to go home to celebrate with family and friends. Hans cannot go home because he is not welcome there. His father has just run away and his mother does not care about him. It is Christmas evening and Wilhelm is the social care worker on duty in the home. Wilhelm and the child are alone in the institution, sitting together next to the Christmas tree. The Christmas tree is already losing its needles – the counsellors in the home jokingly call it an 'acid rain' tree. Wilhelm is thinking about the situation. Even with the music on, it is very silent. Even candy, cake and drinks do not help create a festive atmosphere. Clearly this burden is heavy for Hans. Wilhelm thinks of his own Christmas tree at home: his pride and joy, green and full. What should Wilhelm do?

1. What are the ethical issues involved in this case?
2. How do you think they arose?

---

3. Would this case present a dilemma for you if you were the full time worker involved?

4. On the basis of the information you have here, how would you act if you were the worker?

5. What reasons would you give for deciding to act in this way?

6. What kinds of ethical problems might arise as a result of your decision?

(Banks and Williams, 1999: 53).

Without offering the full findings of the research, Banks and Williams (1999) were able to perceive distinct differences in the level of 'professionalisation' of the service in the twelve different countries. A total of 41 of the 59 student respondents suggested that they would take Hans, either to their home (22) or at least somewhere else. Many of the Scandinavian students suggested taking Hans home, which may relate to the fact that, '*some of the Swedish literature on ethics argues against a separation between personal and professional.*' (Banks and Williams, 1999: 57) French students were more in favour of going outside, which again might reflect their culture where more activities are available over the Christmas session, when compared to many other countries. But the English students responded differently. They were very aware of government guidelines on such matters, and most thought staying in the institution was the only proper option available. One Durham based student stated '*anything else would be unprofessional and putting myself at risk*' (Banks and Williams, 1999: 56–57).

Whilst this research example of professional ethics training for students is relatively small-scale, many cross-national research projects focus on comparing systems which operate in different countries using large scale data sets. Ruxton's (1996) study *Children in Europe* is one of the most useful and comprehensive. Funded by, amongst others, the European Commission, this substantial volume brought together both statistical information and a comprehensive descriptive analysis of child welfare systems across all the member states. For instance, he provides a historical, statistical and descriptive analysis of the developments and current policies across Europe concerning 'adoption', seen as one of the most controversial areas of child care (Ruxton, 1996, 347–371). In his opinion '. . . *adoption has again come to be primarily seen as being about providing permanent homes for a wide range of disadvantaged children, rather than as a source of babies for infertile couples*' (Ruxton, 1996: 347).

Rupert Hughes, in his foreword to *Protecting Children: Messages from Europe* by Hetherington et al. (1997: iii) offers a rallying call in favour of comparative such trans-national research. '*Countries differ widely in their social, cultural and legal situations and values and at first sight it might seem too difficult to undertake anything other than the most superficial comparison of the societies and particularly of something like the child protection system which I think is greatly affected by these variables.*' However this book shows that this is a mistaken view and that it is possible to draw insights out of other systems with which to compare one's own approach. The aim of this study, by

Hetherington et al. (1997), was to compare what social work practitioners would do in one particular child protection case. In their methodology, the researchers said that they aimed to '. . . *discover what they would do, why they would do it, what the legal constraints and possibilities were, and the theoretical and conceptual basis of their thinking.*' (Hetherington et al., 1997, 43).

The other strand to this research was aimed at sharing the findings, and feeding them back with all the participants through a series of seminars and videos. The resulting book records the findings, stating that the study was able to offer a means of using '*practitioners' experience for its primary data*', (Hetherington et al., 1997: 52). It then goes on to suggest that the distance between the researchers and the researched was largely 'dissolved' through the practitioners sharing, through a process of reflexivity, the results from the comparative research exercise. They even contend that, '*In summary, this is a concept of research as intervention, as policy change, rather than research as transmission or as an aid to the technical fix for a malfunctioning machine.*' (Hetherington et al., 1997: 53). Their work strongly advocated the relatively new emphasis on the, '. . . *shift in orientation towards a more interpretative, culture-bound approach means that linguistic and cultural factors, together with differences in research traditions and administrative structures cannot be ignored*' (Hantrais, 1996: 3).

When comparative research encapsulates this 'interpretative' dimension we are able to understand and appreciate how the cultural 'bag and baggage' of a particular society or nation shapes the way in which policy and practice responses are constructed. This understanding is critical for future research progress in many social welfare areas. It is important to amass both 'hard' and 'soft' data using the variety of methods described throughout this book. By revealing the cultural underpinnings, which shape policies and practices in other countries, we stand a better chance of appreciating just what ensures they will function in our country.

Benefits and problems

As we have already seen in this chapter, comparative research in common with case studies, does not represent a distinct type of research. Rather it is another means by which research can be structured. It does, however, offer certain benefits and insights to social welfare researchers, practitioners and policy makers. Among the benefits are that it:

- Can provide new insights, solutions and ideas which can inform existing policy and practice.
- Can encourage cross-national integration of policy and practice.
- Can create new information resources to assist policy makers and practitioners.
- Can enhance our understanding of the role played by the underlying socio-cultural influences on human, societal and organisation behaviour.

The problems, are that as an approach it:

- Can lead to over simplification and generalisation of the policies and practices pursued in other countries.
- Can come forward with inappropriate transference models either between countries or intra-nationally.
- Can attempt to compare what is often non-comparable.
- Can underplay the importance of different socio-cultural influences such as languages, history, politics and legal traditions.

CHAPTER 12

Information Communication Technology

CHAPTER OBJECTIVES

This chapter is designed to ensure that you:

- Appreciate the various opportunities where information communication technology and the Internet can offer social welfare researchers.
- Understand the importance of planning the use of computers and the Internet right at the start of any project.
- Understand the limitations, the ethics of, and potential problems that can arise from using information communication technology.

Introduction

He coveted the files, staplers, erasers, coloured inks and gadgets whose functions remained a teasing mystery, thinking that if only he could afford to equip himself with all this apparatus his thesis would write itself: he would be automated.

(Lodge, 1981: 70).

If you substitute information communication technology (ICT) for the paraphernalia of the 1960s office, then anyone who has ever been involved in undertaking, or writing up a research study will both understand, and identify with, Adam Appleby's desire for automation. What Adam was looking for was the means to organise and speed up the research process. Increasingly, that is exactly what the recent advances in ICT would appear to offer. In the last decade, massive advances have been made in the quality and capacity of computer equipment (the hardware) and the programmes that the hardware runs (the software). Then there is the advent of the Internet through the World Wide Web (www). Software packages are now available to help with almost every aspect of the research process – literature searches, library access, obtaining official statistics and research findings, as was noted in Chapter 3, have all become readily available through ICT. There are also software packages that assist with specific research instruments, data collection, data management, accessing or finding respondents, as well as the eventual data analysis. Well-known software packages also help greatly with both the writing-up and presentation of the resulting study. So the only real task you are left to do is the thinking. But thinking is the core activity demanded of the research process, and it cannot be automated.

This chapter provides a brief insight into the world of computers and ICT, focusing on the various ways in which computer applications and the Internet can make the tasks of the researcher that much easier. On the plus side, the chapter illustrates how ICT offers new opportunities for collecting and then manipulating information, which in the past would have been considered far too complex and/or too time-consuming to consider. In doing so, ICT helps provide new solutions to age-old data collection and processing problems. It also opens up an entirely new means of reaching, and sharing information with, the specialist research community, and with individuals and communities that are to be the focus of the research. On the down side, ICT also gives rise to a new range of new issues and problems. The chapter therefore concludes with a brief 'health warning' about the use and abuse of ICT. It also raises some particularly vexing questions about research ethics, a vital consideration for all those engaged in any form of 'people-focused' research.

This chapter provides but a brief overview. It cannot detail all the information necessary when deciding what software, or hardware should be employed to meet your particular research needs. In the ever innovating world of ICT, with hardware, software and the Internet changing continuously, coming to any clear decision about particular applications and uses almost demands its very own strategy. Given the complex range of subjects and applications across the social welfare field it is important you fully appreciate the specialist 'nooks and crannies' that exist within your particular field of interest.

Using ICT in research

Research, in essence, is knowing what you want to ask, of whom, and then knowing exactly what you want to do with those findings. Once you have sorted out the conceptual and theoretical issues, a process greatly aided by your literature review, the research process can be greatly speeded-up and enhanced by the sensible application of ICT. How best to make use of this technology depends upon the nature of the research project, the type of analysis to be employed, the resources available to you, and critically, your own level of competence with the technology. Thinking about the role and function of ICT as it applies to your own specific research task, right from the start, is good practice. Trying to find your way around a software application or plunging into the potential black hole of the Internet, with the final deadline for the project looming large, is unfortunately, all too common.

Within most workplaces basic keyboard skills have now become an essential prerequisite for the majority of jobs, even if their application is limited to basic word-processing or data entry. The skills required to operate the software packages useful to the researcher often demanded a great deal more training and, therefore, you need to build in the time needed to acquire such skills within the original research proposal.

Likewise, and of ever increasing importance, are the practical skills needed to use the Internet as a basic research tool to access both information and data. Understanding the scope and limitations of the various ICT applications is also very useful for those involved in commissioning and managing commissioned research work.

Literature searches

The application of ICT in literature searches was explored, in some detail within Chapter 3, so there is little point repeating it here. The important point to reiterate, however, is that in using the range of literature search software systems you need to be clear about which aspects of your topic you wish to explore. As these systems all operate by the use of keywords, it is crucial that a good deal of thought goes into defining the parameters of the research question, prior to embarking upon a search. This reinforces the earlier discussion, in Chapter 1, about spending time honing down your specific research question, to a level where the keywords easily emerge.

Different 'search engines' such as Altavista™, Google™, Jeeves™ and Yahoo™ and their associated directories, scour through all available Web sites on the Net, each employing slightly different methods in setting the parameters for any search. It is the connections between the keywords that accounts for these crucial differences. For instance, in a Boolean™ search for material about the youth drug scene you do not need to add in the word 'and' – the search will look for all phrases containing either, 'youth' or 'drugs'. Putting single or double quotes around keywords can link them together, so that only the complete phrase is isolated in the search of Web sites. Inclusion of a + sign between words has a similar effect within some search engines. So it is important that you find out about the system conventions employed by your particular search engine, and assess whether it is adequate, or whether by switching to another engine, more useful information might be accessed.

Bear in mind that if you 'Surf the Web' as a means of undertaking a basic literature search, you will access a rich and varied set of potential sources of information. Articles of varying provenance will be discovered; this means some will be properly researched papers, while others could merely be the random thoughts of someone with an interest in that subject. You will, therefore, need to try and assess the worth of the article, something that conventional publishing outlets achieve through their peer review system. Such searches will also throw up abstracts, information on research centres and their past and present work, and sometimes even entire library records.

If it is a topical issue, then a host of different publications and sources will emerge. The basic problem here is that this mass of related information, which can be quickly accessed, demands time to process it for your own particular needs. Each and every site that looks 'interesting' has to be clicked on, downloaded to your screen and then carefully searched through. While recent advances in broadband technology dramatically speed up the information transfer process, making it almost instantaneous, clearly the more sites you access, the greater the workload involved in checking out the site and assessing the usefulness of available data. This again reinforces the need to carefully construct your search strategy, so that you identify the sites that are most likely to produce good information. Further, when utilising an Internet search, ensure you 'bookmark' the useful sites in your 'favourites' box immediately you decide they are of value. Such favourites can then be subsequently organised in a way that suits you, to ensure a more extensive re-visit. Adopting a systematic approach to all data search operations is critical.

Databases such as FileMakerPro™ on Apple Mac, or Access™ or DBase™ on IBM compatible PCs provides a useful means of managing your particular information needs, whether these are constructing bibliographical details or holding the associated notes which you have taken from these sources. Information stored in this fashion can be easily retrieved, instantly updated and then interrogated again using keywords, in the same way as employed in library catalogue searches. Having read through a range of relevant references, the careful incorporation of appropriate keywords can ensure you quickly reassemble this material in an order which best suits your particular purposes. The 'Find' command in most word processors also offers a speedy way of searching through notes in order to construct a basic index. For those of you who are active researchers, or who have an information function to perform within your organisation, the adoption of such systems can make what was once the time-consuming and laborious task of data retrieval relatively straightforward. Jones (1999) provides a useful introduction to the various issues that can arise when using the Internet as a basic research tool.

Internet research

In 1998 the journal *Social Work in Europe* embarked on assembling articles for a special issue on drugs in Europe (Dearling, 1998). The journal quickly discovered it was short of potential contributors who could cover specific specialist areas, such as harm reduction, treatment, education, policing and punishment programmes. Using the search engine Google™ various combination of the above words were used, such as drugs + europe + harm + minimisation. Then a check was conducted of specialist sites such as the Trimbos Institute in Utrecht, The Netherlands *http://www.trimbos.nl* and the European Monitoring Centre for Drugs and Drugs Addiction (EMCDA) based in Lisbon, Portugal *http://www.emcdda.org*. Messages were also left about the special issue of the journal on these and other sites throughout Europe.

Almost all the special issue contributors emerged from this web based search process. Jepson (1998), contributed a section about the normalisation of the Christiania community in Copenhagen; Skefton (1998) provided a piece about the work their organisation had done on raves and parties to encourage 'safe dancing', as part of a harm minimisation when dealing with recreational drug use. Other contributors highlighted various policy and practice responses devised by government and welfare agencies right across Europe, including a very detailed account of German drug enforcement practices. Via the use of email a network, encompassing a variety of agencies and individuals, working together produced 30,000 words on current European drugs work. Employing an Internet search engine provided the means of identifying possible sources of information, and subsequent targeted requests, allowed the requirements of the journal to be satisfied. The Journal's publishing conventions then assures that the resulting articles all conform to a standardised format.

Word processing

The advantages of any word processing package are their ease of use, the ability to make corrections (whether for spelling or grammar) with the minimum of fuss, and the capacity to re-order text through the use of 'cut and paste' facilities. This does not of course absolve the writer from the need to carefully proof read all written work, given that spell-checkers can only identify misspelt words. As such, they cannot detect words which, though spelt correctly, are wrongly used: two, too and to are all perfectly acceptable so far as a spell-checker is concerned. Also bear in mind spell-checkers may default to English-American as opposed to English-UK, resulting in odd spelling suggestions. Always check the default settings of such software packages. Grammar checkers work on similar principles. While these can sharpen up your writing style, by forcing you to break down lengthy sentences and help correct basic grammatical faults, they are an aid rather than a substitute for good writing. There are also many instances of the researcher being careless with their use of upper and lower case, titling conventions and the use on acronyms. What is critical here is to adopt a standardised application of style conventions and ensure a consistency of application.

The basic word processing package is also a simple, but versatile research tool. Specifically designed to produce and revise written text, the word processor has many uses in a variety of research tasks. The most obvious use of word processing is in revising drafts of the final report. It can also be used to take, then edit back field notes. Transcribing interview material is another common application. Word processors are also a very useful tool when designing specific data collection instruments. As noted above they can also be used to undertake very basic qualitative analysis through the use of the word-search facility.

Word-processing skills are not too difficult to pick up. Microsoft Word®, the dominant word-processing package on most PCs, contains a 'teach yourself' course as part of the basic software. Word-processing courses are also available in most parts of the country. Once you have grasped the basics, only use and practice will expand both your knowledge and skills. To progress on from two-finger typing use should be made of a basic typing 'tutor' programme, such as Mavis Beacon®, which is readily available on disk.

While word-processing packages can help with most basic aspects of research, other related applications have been developed to address certain more specific tasks.

The first of these involves the use of text recognition scanning software programmes such as Textbridge™. These enable users to scan in large amounts of text from anything that is typed, or word-processed, whether from a book, a magazine or a fax. Once scanned in these new text files can then be manipulated using your standard word-processing software. Improvements in this technology have meant a significant reduction in the number of text errors and ever faster scanning. As a result, ten pages of text can be imputed and corrected in about 20 minutes.

The second development in this area has been in relation to speech recognition programmes such as DragonSpeak™. The present generation of programmes work, but they take a long time for the programme to accurately recognise your individual speech pattern and specialist vocabulary. Current users of such packages report that the frustration level is still high. That said, given the advances made to get the systems up to this level, it will not be long before a user-friendly and accurate system is on the market, and typing may then become a thing of the past.

Again it is also imperative that you develop good habits when using the word processor. Naming and saving your files in a coherent manner is important, as is backing up files to a floppy disc, CD-ROM or a network back up facility. With the increasing use of graphics, files have become much larger and, as a consequence, more vulnerable. Computers can and do 'crash', and no one wants to lose hours, if not days of precious work. So, take time to learn how to set up the auto-save function in your word-processing package and, in addition, adopt robust file management practices.

Layout and design

While basic word-processing packages can be used for designing most research instruments such as letters of introduction, questionnaires, interview guides, data collection sheets or observation schedules, desktop publishing and graphics software such as PageMaker™, Photoshop™, QuarkXpress™ and In-design™ can introduce the 'professional touch'. However, developing a competent skill level using such packages requires both time and a certain amount of design expertise, as well as an up to date computer with plenty of memory. Gaining an appreciation of what will work and what does not, in relation to graphic design, is something that benefits from specialist training.

Other specialist software is now available which allows you to set up a questionnaire, enter the data and then analyse the results all within the one single package. While these packages do not require the use of paper, they do need careful management to minimise any potential for data loss, given you operate with no hard copy. One example is QuestionMark™, which can be used on either Apple Mac or on a PC, while another, Survey System™ is solely PC dedicated. It is also now possible to scan in forms and questionnaires using programmes such as PagisPro™. As was discussed previously, in Chapter 8, good design and layout helps greatly in achieving a questionnaire that works.

Collecting and recording information

This is one aspect of research where more traditional collecting and recording methods are much in evidence. Laptop computers are currently being used to record data directly in the field and some software packages now make it possible to run tests in-situ. Interviews, as discussed in Chapter 7, may be transcribed using a computer, but the initial recording of the data will usually be in note form, or via an audio tape device. The recent advances in digital recording can provide a data set that can be easily edited and re-ordered in a way that minimises the transcription process. With the potential for developments in speech recognition software it might not be long before interviews can be automatically transcribed into text.

Once the information has been collected, the task of getting it into a manageable format is greatly helped by the use of ICT. Data from hard copy questionnaires, for example, can be keyed directly into a format that the analysis package can handle. If you have the necessary funds, it is worth considering employing a commercial firm to carry out what can be a time-consuming chore. Bear in mind, however, that data entry needs to be accurate. Cost cutting in relation to basic data preparation can result in many hours trying to remedy non-random data entry errors. This task is gradually becoming easier via the use of machine-readable instruments, or optical scanners. At present, however, the technology is not entirely a substitute to basic accurate data entry through the use of a keyboard.

Storing and accessing information

In the past, storing research data involved holding large amounts of paper records in loose folders within bulky filing cabinets. Today, a computer diskette can store more information than that which is held in an average sized book, while the hard drive on even the most modest desktop computer is now capable of storing the equivalent of millions of pages of data. Zip drives, CD-ROMs and tape streamers are three other formats for storing large data and graphics files, and the advent of CD-RW, allows for the re-writing of files to a CD up to a million times. At the time of writing, 800 megabyte CDs and even larger DVDs are available, but in the near future cheap, efficient storage systems of many gigabytes capacity should become standard. Further, whereas once computers held only numbers or text, graphical material, photographs, audio and video clips can now be stored and managed relatively easily using software packages such as Photoshop™, PageMaker™, Easy CD Creator™, and software/hardware combinations such as Pinnacle™, editing suite.

As storage has become easier, so too has accessing the data from a hard drive or another storage system. Files can be opened, closed, copied, created, deleted, or amended without difficulty. Information can be managed, organised and re-organised, which is especially useful for qualitative analysis. As has already been mentioned, this further reinforces the need to be systematic in how you work, and ensure backup copies of all data are created at regular intervals. With the adoption of good housekeeping practices the problem of lost or misplaced data can be minimised, but never completely eliminated.

Analysing data

Computer-based analysis is especially useful in relation to the production of basic statistics. Spreadsheet packages such as Lotus 123^{TM} and Excel^{TM} allow you to manipulate numbers, carry out a range of calculations, including basic statistics, and then to present the results through a variety of tables and graphical displays. The great advantage of a spreadsheet lies in its ability to store and then update information. Further, given its capacity to consistently amend data, using specified formulae, spreadsheets have proved to be a versatile means of constructing databases. By creating your own spreadsheets to hold official statistics the analytical capacity of such information is thus further enhanced.

As the range of statistical tests available on a spreadsheet package is limited, for more detailed analysis you will need to invest in a more dedicated statistical software. Such packages allow you not only the capacity to work with larger data sets, but can also subject the data to a broader range of statistical tests. Statistics packages have been around, first on mainframe computer systems, and then on PCs, for a very long time. The names of the leading packages – such as SPSSx^{TM}, Minitab^{TM} and Statsy^{TM} – may be familiar to most people involved in research, even if the packages themselves remain something of a mystery. The range and complexity of these packages cannot be dealt with here, but Bryman and Cramer (1990) provide a useful guide to quantitative analysis, while Kinnear and Gray (1999) wrote the SPSS operating bible. Gayle's chapter on quantitative data analysis in Burton (2000) also provides a helpful overview of SPSS and its basic statistical outputs.

More recently, packages have been developed that, it is claimed, take the tedium out of even qualitative analysis. Technology can now help with many of the time-consuming, but necessary tasks associated with qualitative work, such as data selection, categorisation and indexing through title, location and data type. In the past, this would have been done by hand, using index cards to record and manage information; and of course some researchers still choose to organise their material in this way. Transcribing interviews, note keeping, and basic analysis, as noted above, can be tackled using a word processor. Anything more complex, however, might best be left to dedicated software specially designed for qualitative work such as HyperQual^{TM}, Hypersoft^{TM} or NUD.IST^{TM}. There are significant differences in what is offered by these various programmes and you need to think carefully which, if any, would be most useful for your purposes. In this regard, Tesch (1990) offers a useful guide to what is available in the field, while Miles and Huberman (1994) provide a useful source book. Other texts that deals specifically with NUD.IST are Stroh (2000) and Gahan and Hannibal (1998). To keep completely up to date, a quick surf on the Internet is likely to provide information on new tools, discussion about the use of old favourites and user suggestions to deal with common problems.

Integrated packages

Report writing is where the word processing package really comes into its own. Now a number of integrated packages are available which combine word-processing, a spreadsheet, a database, a presentations package and HTML for Web design, to make the whole process of analysing data and presenting the results even easier. Microsoft Works™ and Microsoft Office™, for example, are integrated packages for Apple Macs and PCs that allow the user to copy information between various software applications in a straightforward manner. Suppose, for example, you were carrying out a small-scale client satisfaction survey for a social services organisation. Using a spreadsheet you could analyse the results from a questionnaire and then display the findings both in a tabular and graphic form. These tables and graphics, bar charts, pie charts or frequency diagrams could then be imported into the appropriate place within the research report being prepared using the word processing facility. If, in addition, you had stored the results of your literature search on the database facility, you could then import the relevant information into the reference section of the final report. When it then came to presenting your findings you could select the key information from the report and import it to produce Power Point™ slides. From this you could then use HTML to put the Power Point™ presentation and an Acrobat Writer™ PDF file of the research paper onto a Web page. Such presentational issues are discussed in greater detail in Chapter 14.

A health warning

If all this sounds too good to be true, then that's just about right. While computers offer a world of automation and ease, there is a downside. Computers can be very quick at processing routine tasks and, therefore, they allow you the capacity to explore a question from a variety of different perspectives by re-running the analysis in any number of ways. Where once this would have involved many days work, much of which was spent waiting for the result of the actual computation, these tasks can now be accomplished in a matter of minutes. Graphics can be worked and reworked until you get exactly the arrangement you want, at the exact size which will fit the page or file space using a gif, tiff or jpeg image. But such flexibility has its limitations and dangers, particularly where the analysis and interpretation of data is concerned. There is a need to clearly calculate what exactly you are trying to achieve and try not to get overly enthralled by the technology. It would, therefore, be appropriate to provide a few words of warning:

Don't let the technology drive the research. A computer programme will only offer a limited choice in analysing data and that may not necessarily include the particular approach that you would wish to pursue, or that which is most appropriate for the data.

You leave such choices to the computer at your peril. A statistical package will produce a correlation, for example, quickly and relatively easily, but it cannot tell you whether that correlation is either meaningful, or relevant to the research question.

Don't try to do too much. While a computer has little difficulty in handling large volumes of data, the question arises, can you? If you have too much information, will you have the time needed to prepare the data for analysis and will you have time to get any real 'feel' for the data? Without some understanding of the nature of the data, you may overlook certain important issues or relationships. There may also be a tendency to accept too easily, possibly misleading statistics.

Don't trawl through data. The speed and power of computer programmes can encourage a mechanistic approach to analysis. Trawling for data and quantification for its own sake, without reference to either theory, or the research question being investigated, should be avoided at all costs. There is always the danger that the technology becomes an end in itself, rather than the means to an end.

Remember the adage 'garbage in, garbage out'. If there are problems then these are likely to lie with you, rather than with the technology. As a researcher your job is to both interpret and to understand, not simply to be technically proficient. Research should always be more about thought, than application. To achieve this end, as a researcher, you must spend time thinking through the key research issues and then assessing what role ICT can play in exploring the various relationships that have been considered. You need to recognise not only the advantages, but also the limitations of ICT.

More information is not more knowledge. Bear in mind the World Wide Web, like the web constructed by a spider is a multi-faceted and complicated structure. It can lead an inexperienced researcher into many loops, complications and tangles. More information is not the same as more knowledge. Depending upon the nature of your research, web sites need to be evaluated in terms of their objectivity, quality and information accuracy. Knowing the credentials of a particular site is critical, as is an appreciation of the citation systems it employs, should you wish to go back to original sources. It may be necessary to verify information and in the very direst of circumstances, check the legality of the site itself. Finally, there are also increasing dangers of viruses infecting the researcher's computer – so take care to use protection software.

Data Protection Act

If you are thinking about using computers in any aspect of your research, it will be necessary to familiarise yourself with the requirements of the Data Protection Act, 1998. This Act requires that all personal data, namely information which relates to identifiable persons and which is automatically processed, must be officially registered. The registration requirement covers personal data stored, or processed for research purposes, whether on your employer's computer or on your own machine.

It should also be noted that the Act places a responsibility on you to ensure that those using the data other than yourself, your so-called 'servants and agents', conform to the requirements of the Act, in exactly the same way as yourself, as the registered Data User. This makes you responsible, for passing on the relevant guidance of the Data Protection Act. You therefore need to ensure that the holding, use and disclosure of any personal data, for which you are responsible, is in accordance with all the requirements of the Act. Broadly speaking, the use of personal data for research should conform to the following principles:

- You should not construct or maintain computer files of personal data, for research purposes, without the express permission of the relevant authority.
- You should be aware of the requirements of the Data Protection Act, 1998, and of the appropriate level of security arrangements which attach to the particular set of personal data you hold.
- The use of personal data should be limited to the minimum consistent with the achievement of the research objectives. Wherever possible data should be de-personalised so that it is impossible to identify the individual subjects.

For further details about the Act and how it applies to your particular research interests, contact either your employer or your institution's Data Protection Officer, if they indeed have one. Central to the Data Protection Act is the issue of confidentiality, and that is very much an ethics issue.

Ethical considerations in Web-based research

When undertaking people-focused research using Internet searches there are some important ethical considerations you need to pay due regard to. While such considerations are not new, it is just that utilising the Web for research purposes acts to exaggerate, or crystallise these issues. Critically it is the communication revolution, brought about by the Internet, and in particular the speed of information transfer to a potentially wide audience, which raises interesting and challenging ethical considerations (Jones, 1994).

Showing respect for the individuals being studied must always be your central consideration. So you need to carefully consider what impact your research might have on the individuals and/or communities who are to be the subject of your study. While this raises exactly the same question for any piece of research, there are additional considerations when use is made of Web-based information searches. These revolve round how information is collected and whether the subjects of the study are clear about how their views are to be used.

ICT also offers greater potential to both collect and generate data, without being explicit about how it will be subsequently used. Day-to-day administrative information collected about clients, using say a foyer or a rough sleepers' hostel can quite easily be reworked to produce a profile of clients, and from that individuals selected for representative case study purposes. While this example clearly raises Data Protection Act issues, these are often not properly understood, acknowledged or acted upon. It is, therefore, important to take an interest in knowing where the data you use was generated from, and whether its reuse compromises the original undertaking given about its use.

At its simplest, undertaking research through the Net involves contacting people and recording their responses to a pre-determined set of questions. Illingworth (2001) used the Internet to first contact people about infertility and IVF treatment and then conducted interviews with them via email. This particular study found that participants liked the anonymity provided by the email interviews, noting that conducting similar interviews in a clinical setting had proved problematic, given the sensitivity of the matters being discussed. So the research instrument is similar, if not quite identical to employing a postal questionnaire. The major difference is that the response is much more immediate: reply to the questions and your response is instantaneously delivered back to the researcher. That said, responding using a key board, may give people time to consider carefully their response, and this was different to the immediacy of a face-to-face interview. This difference was felt by Illingworth (2001) and others using similar techniques, such as O'Conner and Magee (2001) and Selwyn and Robson (1998), to add to the quality and depth to the resultant data.

All respondents need to know how their answers, to the questions posed by the research, will be used. As was noted in the previous discussion of ethics in Chapter 1, whether they fully appreciate what they are agreeing to is quite another matter. The researcher does, however, have a duty to convey that information as clearly as possible. Yet, electronic information can easily be copied, edited and then sent on to others and appear in places not readily expected. Posting or hyper-linking the results of a survey on, or to a special interest Web site could cause respondents some difficulties. Again while this is certainly not a new issue, it is the speed of the data transfer that throws up some interesting ethical questions. If you have offered the respondents anonymity, would the posting compromise such a guarantee? Also, was the potential for that publication format made explicit?

Another related issue is that, when accessing Web-based sources, should the subjects of research be made fully aware that they are being observed or monitored? For instance, researchers can and do make use of the bulletin boards of Web-based groupings, or 'communities of interest'. These can be either an academic-network, or a user or self-help support group, based around a particular disease, contemporary welfare issue or specialist interest. As a researcher you could advertise your study on certain sites, and ask interested parties to participate. Alternatively, you could pose as a member of a group, and post a variety of questions related to your research interest to ascertain the views of the members of that group. As with any form of participant observation, as noted earlier, in Chapter 9, the question arises as to whether you are operating under a false pretext, and are in effect entrapping your participants to become part of a study they know nothing about. The ethical issues involved here are very familiar to both observational methods, and ethnography, as is well illustrated by Hine (2000). Utilising the Web in this way does offer anonymity, and the potential to be someone you are not. But is this an ethical way to conduct your study? Or are there some research contexts, particularly in relation to sensitive issues, that justifies the adoption of this approach? Just as with observational research, would the knowledge that someone in the group is a researcher change the dynamics of the group, altering both the context and setting? It is worth noting that researchers who make use of bulletin board sources and Web based discussion groups have found it increasingly more difficult to access such groups, as a known researcher. Many groups now insist that researchers' subject themselves to a group vetting procedure. Whether that forces more researchers to adopt a more clandestine approach to gain access is unclear.

There is also an issue about how you, as a researcher, deal with information posted on such sites. Is such information effectively in the public domain, or can it still be regarded as personal, or at least personal to that group? That is not an easy question to answer. Further, can you be certain of the authenticity of any posting, either in terms of its content and authorship? Unlike academic journals there is no peer review, nor external validation of the material being posted. There is also not a lawyer acting for the publisher to ensure that their commercial interests are not compromised. That can be a double-edged sword, in that the vitality or originality of the posting, or even just this lack of formality, can provide a much richer data source. But is it always what it professes to be?

This also leads neatly into the thorny question of intellectual property rights. Just what can a researcher lift from a Web site, either to inform their knowledge base, or for direct comparative purposes? Unlike book publishing there is no equivalent to 'fair dealing', which allows for up to 350 words or 800 words cumulatively, to be taken from a single source as long as this does not constitute more than a third of the whole, and the extract is properly cited. Plagiarism, or just straightforward copying, is another major consequence of this information revolution. For example, in constructing a literature review, as a researcher you are expected to synthesise and organise the material you find, rather than 'cut and paste' someone else's efforts.

The complexity of the dilemmas surrounding the use of the Internet as a research tool needs to be broached, but whether there are easy answers to the questions posed above is doubtful. One useful source of basic ethical guidelines for would-be Net researchers is The Information Society, which posts abstracts of its internationally sourced papers on the Web *http://www.slis.indiana.edu/TIS/abstracts/*. Another useful site is the Oxford Internet Institute, which examines different aspects of how the Internet impacts upon society *http://www.oii.ox.ac.uk*.

Allen (1996), in one of the articles posted at the Institute, proposes three basic ethical pointers that should underpin any Web-based research. Firstly, protect the subject from harm as a consequence of either the research fieldwork and/or the research practices. Secondly, always endeavour to produce good social science research, and thirdly, do not unnecessarily affect the phenomenon being studied. Given the above discussion in relation to researcher anonymity such guidelines do offer a fair degree of latitude. Finally, if you wish to explore this issue further Jones (1994) and Jones (1999) provides useful introductory texts on the ways in which people have utilised the Internet for social research purposes.

Strengths and weaknesses

The advantages of information communication technology is that:

- It can greatly reduce the time involved in carrying out complex analytical, as well as routine, tasks.
- It allows for greater flexibility in testing for statistical relationships.
- The web can provide ready access to resource information, contacts and potential data.
- It can also create the space to both think through and test the significance of particular statistical relationships.
- It can improve the presentational quality of the finished research report/presentation.

Conversely, the disadvantages are that:

- ICT can be seen as a substitute for clear thought.
- The researcher can become seduced by the technology and forget that it has a specific purpose to perform, it is not the end in itself.
- You can underestimate the time required to become proficient with software packages and learning to use the Internet effectively.
- ICT requires a high degree of on-going data management to ensure information is not lost, misplaced or corrupted.
- The time taken to remedy basic data errors can prove considerable.
- ICT can exagerate and introduce new ethical issues for the researcher to address.
- The dangers of virus infection of computers linked to the internet have increased considerably.

PART THREE

Finishing Off The Project

This final part of the book considers the core research skills of analysing, theorising and presenting. When you have collected all the data you require, by whatever means, the next challenge is what exactly to do with it. How do you make sense of this mass of information, which can at this point resemble a chaotic collection of notes and numbers? Unfortunately, the data cannot speak for itself. Only you can interpret this information, and from this draw out the key findings that will underpin your research work.

All the collected data has to be organised and this is a process that is governed solely by your analytical, interpretational and presentational skills. This is where the real skill in researching lies. It is also the part of the research process which takes up a great deal of time, concentration and intellect. Unfortunately, it also coincides with the end of the research exercise, just at the point where you have least time and plenty of distractions.

This is when the study comes together, and where your assumptions are tested against the data you have collected. It is now that the gaps in the data, any weaknesses in the questions asked, or the limitations of your original working hypothesis and planning are revealed. As was pointed out in Chapter 1, you will have given some thought to data analysis and its interpretation right at the start of the study, during the initial planning stages. Now is the time when you see whether all your planning and hard work has been worthwhile. If you have all the pieces in place, then this is also the most rewarding part of the research, when you argue and develop a coherent argument, using the collected data to substantiate your claims. If you find gaps, it may be possible to fill them, if time and resources allow. If not, then you will have to acknowledge the weaknesses in your analysis.

Having worked through the analysis, the final task is to put your findings into a form that engages with those who might have an interest in this work. Presentation demands a lot more than the simple word processing of committee reports. Depending on the nature and importance of the research it could involve producing a press release, preparing a conference presentation and writing a short article on the work for a professional magazine. Each of these requires different writing and presentational skills. As was discussed in the planning stage, you need to find the best medium to ensure those that have an interest in your work know of its existence. There's little point in undertaking work which is destined only to gather dust on an office shelf.

So this final section deals with these critical 'finishing off' issues. Chapter 13 explores some of the main points in relation to data organisation, management and its analysis and interpretation, while Chapter 14 looks at report writing and the presentation of findings. This section, and the book, then concludes with a brief résumé of the key issues you need to consider when undertaking a piece of research.

CHAPTER 13

Managing, Analysing and Interpreting Data

Introduction

The data collection phase of any research exercise should provide you with a large amount of textual and numeric information; data that you hope will be both relevant and illuminating. Your specific study may have generated quantitative data, from a questionnaire. You may then have added qualitative data emanating from the associated interviews with key practitioners. The goal of research is to provide explanation. But it is clear the collected data alone, cannot provide this. Whether the data is qualitative or quantitative, it needs to be processed, a task that involves data organisation, its analysis and then, finally, its interpretation. This work is the sole responsibility of the researcher, and is the essence of research. This chapter takes you through these processing and interpretative tasks, detailing the unique features associated with quantitative and qualitative data. The limitations of basic statistical analysis are presented and, finally, the relationship between research findings and theoretical concepts is discussed. The importance of blending background reading with your collected data in ways, which may help reveal the key findings of your study, is also discussed. Finally, the findings should always be assessed with regard to their significance for practice, management, policy and theory.

Coding, data entry and data management

Given the advances in ICT software it is feasible to load your data and give the computer basic instructions to sort and then analyse this material in accordance with a standard set of analytical tests. There are standard statistical packages for numeric data, and recent software developments now mean that basic qualitative analysis is rapidly catching up. Yet, as was noted in the previous chapter, interpretation remains the researcher's responsibility. The analysis of data should reflect the thinking that you put into the study, and there are no short cuts here. It is the case that certain market research companies, as part of their service, will provide a basic analysis of any commissioned survey. However, what is provided are masses and masses of cross tabulations, and many hours of frustration in trying to isolate out the answers that specifically interest you. A far more productive strategy is to set down, right at the start, what it is you want to know. Again this reinforces the need for proper planning, right at the start of any study.

To conduct any piece of analysis proficiently, it is important that you gain a feel for the data. This is best achieved by being involved in the data collection exercise, in its entirety. On occasions this is not always possible, given this task may involve a great deal of people working in the field. If that is the case, then invest time in the coding, data entry and its subsequent management stages. Again if there is a very large data set to be processed, then you will need to contract out the coding and data entry operations. But it is important that you take a keen interest in this operation, so that you are confident with the resulting data sets. In the case of smaller data collection exercises, basic data preparation can be handled by a PC using a standard spreadsheet package. In both instances, it is the process of categorising and generating coding variables that helps you familiarise yourself with the collected information. Within qualitative analysis this is advisable, since it is a core part of the analysis work, as is detailed later in the chapter. Developing coding frames makes it easier to check the accuracy of the processed data. Mistakes will inevitably occur at all stages of data collection and its preparation, but by spending time at this stage a number of them can be easily picked up and amended prior to analysis. Finding such errors later on can be more costly, both in time and reputation. Bear in mind, no data set is ever perfect, but you should strive to undertake robust data checking and cleaning exercises. It is at this stage you require to detail all the non-responses to questions with a distinct code, so these can be noted and omitted from the overall analysis. A high level of non-responses for one question may raise concerns about the value of the answers to that particular question.

All data entry exercises begin with the creation of a code book. Each variable is assigned a unique reference code. The data is then organised by coding each and every response in line with this coding frame. This code book is nothing more than a list of all the variables to be analysed, together with their respective codes. If you are using computer analysis, some instructions, which tell the programme where these variables are to be found, should also be included. Table 13.1 is part of a code book from a local client survey. Within data analysis packages, whether for quantitative or qualitative, this coding exercise is a built-in element of the package.

Table 13.1: Extract from a client survey code book

Column	Question number	Variable label	Value label	Code
1–12		Identification ID number	ID No.	(Code exact number)
13–14	1	Gender	Male/Female	M – 1 F – 2
15–16	2	Age	Age	(Code exact number)
17	3	Day Centre	St Stephens Highridge Townsley Maddock	1

Analysing quantitative data

Having gone through this coding exercise the data is still in a raw state. It now can be organised, so it can more easily be managed. But even when you have done that, it will still tell you very little. To get hard information from your data set it is necessary to examine it from a variety of perspectives; in essence, you need to look and then interpret the distribution patterns or frequencies generated for the key variables. Producing the full range of frequencies acts as the first major data cleaning exercise, because you can quickly see where any anomalies lie. These can then be traced back to the data set and amended prior to the more robust data analysis exercises.

You should never trawl through the data in the hope that something interesting might turn up. Rather your analysis should be informed by the original theoretical concepts and by the research questions that you are seeking to answer. By applying these concepts to the data, the results can then be interpreted against the original assumptions or hypothesis.

If your data is quantitative, or has been reduced to numbers, there are a veritable host of statistical techniques that can be used for analysis purposes. This chapter can do no more than introduce one or two of the most commonly used statistical applications, namely frequency distributions, measures of central tendency and dispersion, as well as bivariate analysis. There are, however, some very useful texts available which can provide the detailed information necessary to undertake robust quantitative analysis. Rowntree (1981) provides a good introduction to basic statistics; whereas Bryman and Cramer (1990) and Gayle (2000) offer more detailed advice on generating descriptive statistics, through use of the statistical software package SPSS.

Frequency distributions

The most commonly used and the most straightforward analytic statistical tool, is the frequency distribution. It is a simple count detailing the number of cases in each category, for example, the number of males and females who were interviewed. This information can be provided either as a table or a graph. Table 13.2 below shows an example of a frequency distribution for the information accessed by a youth information centre over a one-year period. In this case women's health issues, housing matters and local sports club information were the most significant types of information requested.

Table 13.2: Frequency distribution of services accessed

Value	Frequency	Percentage
Info. on healthy eating	48	5
Info. on sexual health	125	13
Info. on housing	213	22
Info. on women's health	342	36
Info. on drugs	60	6
Info. on local sports clubs	150	16
Info. on outdoor activities	16	2
Total	954	100

Frequency distributions, however, provide you with only very limited information. So additional information must be generated in order to tell you something about the 'shape' or variability of your data. The two most common measures of variability are central tendency and dispersion.

Measures of central tendency

A measure of central tendency is simply the middle of any distribution. But its not that simple because, in statistical terms, there is not one 'best' way to define the 'average', or 'middle value' but three, the mean, median and mode, as was noted earlier in Chapter 5. The mean is the arithmetic average, that is the sum of values in a distribution, divided by the number of values. So suppose you have an age distribution, as in Table 13.3, taken from a study of homeless young people resident in a 'Stopover' project hostel. The mean in this case would be 19.0 years.

The median, another measure of central tendency, tells us where the mid-point of the distribution lies. In this age distribution, as there are 100 cases, the mid-point is 51 $((1 + 100)/2 = 50.5$, rounded up to 51). The median is the value of the 51st case, which is 18 years. This tells us that 50 per cent of the sample are aged 18 or below, and 50 per cent are 18 or above. The median is lower than the mean, because there are more people at the lower end of the distribution, than the top end.

Similar issues often arise with income distributions, where a small number of people with very large incomes raise the mean, in comparison with the median. It is not that one

**Table 13.3: Frequency distribution of 'Stopover'
project residents by age**

Value	Frequency	Percentage
16	21	21
17	16	16
18	20	20
19	5	5
20	5	5
21	5	5
22	14	14
23	14	14
Total	100	100

measure of the middle point is better than the other. But rather each, on its own, tells you something different about the 'central tendency' of the data, while the two taken together can tell you something useful about the distribution as a whole, what is often termed its skewness.

The final measure of central tendency, the mode, is simply the value that occurs most often. The mode in Table 13.3 would be 16 years. This is different from both the median and the mean and again this is because the distribution is skewed more to the younger cohort.

All three measures of central tendency attempt to do the same thing, which is to describe the 'average' value of the data, as was discussed in Chapter 5. They do so in different ways, however, and if the distribution of the data is not uniform, as in this case, they can produce different outcomes. By employing all three it is evident that a range of issues arise, such as the notable concentration of young people, below 18, and also a cluster at a higher age band. While the former may be explained by the changes in benefit entitlement for young people, the older cohort would require some other explanation.

Measures of dispersion

Whereas measures of central tendency attempt to summarise the data, measures of dispersion provide information on the amount of variation. The most obvious way of doing this is by examining the range, namely, from the lowest to the highest values in the distribution. This particular measure of dispersion is susceptible to distortion from outlying or atypical values. If you have information on employee income, for example, the range might be from less than £5,000 to more than £50,000, as detailed in Table 13.4.

Yet, the range is not particularly helpful here, since it disguises the fact that there are only a few employees in these outlining categories. The inter-quartile range would be a better measure of dispersion for it ignores the extreme values and focuses instead on the 'middle half' of the distribution; that is it discounts those values that fall within the lowest

Table 13.4: Frequency distribution of employee net income

Value	Frequency	Percentage
Under £5,000	3	7
£5–7,999	5	11
£8–12,999	10	22
£13–15,999	7	16
£16–20,999	8	18
£21–25,999	2	4
£26–30,999	8	18
£31–39,999	1	2
Over £40,000	1	2
Total	45	100

and the highest 25 per cent of the distribution. The inter-quartile range for employee income is between 25 per cent and 75 per cent of the distribution. This can sometimes give a better picture of the actual data. In calculating the inter-quartile range, of course, half of the available information is lost and this may not be appropriate, particularly if the distribution contains no extreme outlying values.

If you have interval data, the preferred measure of dispersion is the standard deviation. Standard deviation describes the difference between individual observations and the mean of all the observations. It is a sort of 'average distance from the mean for the whole distribution. Most introductory statistics texts such as Rowntree (1981) discuss how the standard deviation is derived. The actual calculation is more time-consuming than complicated, and fortunately can now be easily generated using a computer, or a scientific calculator.

Bimodal analysis

All the above measures describe the characteristics of the data in terms of one variable: they are examples of univariate statistics. As often as not, however, you will want to know something about how two variables relate to each other. Suppose you were interested in any relationship between gender or age and the information provided by the youth project, as detailed previously in Table 13.2. To achieve this end you could make use of a technique called cross tabulation, 'crosstabs' for short, to produce the following two-by-two table.

Although a much-simplified example, it helps illustrate the basic idea. In this case there is a clear difference between the information requests made by young males and young females. Information about women's health matters accounted for more than half of all the female information requests. The major information requests raised by young males

Table 13.5: Project information requests by gender

Value	Male request frequency (%)	Female request frequency (%)	Overall requests frequency (%)
Info. on healthy eating	18 (6)	30 (5)	48 (5)
Info. on sexual health	110 (35)	15 (2)	125 (13)
Info. on housing	52 (17)	161 (25)	213 (22)
Info. on women's health	5 (2)	337 (52)	342 (26)
Info. on drugs	35 (11)	25 (4)	60 (6)
Info. on local sports clubs	83 (27)	67 (10)	150 (16)
Info. on outdoor activities	9 (3)	7 (1)	16 (2)
Totals	312 (101)	642 (99)	954 (100)

were in relation to sexual health and local sports clubs. By contrasting the two sets of percentage figures you quickly build up a pattern of what are noticeably different information requests and what are similar, between the genders. It is also worth contrasting this with the overall pattern, to show just how the information delivered overall has a noticeable gender bias, which would not have been recorded had this 'crosstab' not been generated. This raises further interesting questions about why young men and women want to access such information, something the later work on the study should have attempted to draw out. In practice, any 'crosstabs' produced would be far more detailed and would usually include a correlation coefficient; a statistic used to express the relationship between the two variables.

Crosstabulations can obviously only deal with a very limited number of categories and, therefore, are not really suited to interval data such as income. You could of course re-organise the data into bands, as was done in Table 13.4, but only at the cost of losing some of the detail. One alternative mode of presentation would be to create a scattergram. This is something that is an option on most statistical software packages. The more dispersed or scattered the points are on the diagram, the weaker the relationship between the two variables. Conversely, the closer together the points, the stronger the relationship. The scattergram also includes a correlation coefficient, r^2, which is the statistical measure of the relationship between the two variables. In this case there is a low score given the lack of any clear relationship between the information request of young males and females. It should also be borne in mind that a number of the same requests may well have been made by one person. Undoubtedly how the data was collected does have a bearing on the ability to generate such analysis. In the example provided in Diagram 13.1 above, Webster (2002) compares the geographic incidence of single parent households, with areas of high unemployment. Given the strong correlation he goes on to argue that it is unemployment, more than any other factor, which leads to family break-up, and in doing so calls into question the basis on the moral panic about single parents unleashed by the Labour, and previously the Conservative government.

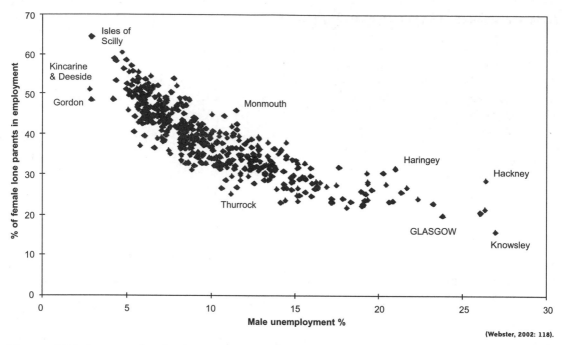

Diagram 13.1: An example of a Scattergram correlation

(Webster, 2002: 118).

Using and abusing statistics

Statistics are a powerful tool for analysing data. They are certainly widely used not only in research, but to illustrate many aspects of our daily lives. Next time you read your daily newspaper or watch a news or current affairs programme on television, note how often statistics are used to support the story. Whether the item is about law and order, homelessness, house prices, or your chances of winning the National Lottery, statistics are invariably quoted. Do you know how these figures are calculated, or exactly what they mean, or indeed if they mean anything at all? For many people the answer to these questions will have been an emphatic no. Yet statistics are a powerful and seductive, descriptive tool. Having developed an almost mystical quality it is important to bear in mind that they can be all too easily abused.

A small book, first published in 1954, should be compulsory reading for everyone who intends to use, or to come into contact with statistics. Darrell Huff's *How to Lie with Statistics* provides a humorous insight on some of the more common, '*instances of bumbling and chicanery*' to be found in the world of statistics. Take one example, which concerns the dangers of confusing correlation with causation:

> *You can make an estimate – one that is better than chance would produce – of how many children have been born to a Dutch or Danish family by counting the storks' nests on the roof of their house. In statistical terminology it would be said that a positive correlation has been found to exist between these two things. What sounds*

like a proof of an ancient myth is actually something far more valuable. It is an easily remembered reminder of a useful truth: an association between factors is not a proof that one has caused the other.

In the instance of the storks and the babies, it is not too hard to find a third factor that may be responsible for the other two. Big houses attract big, or potentially big, families; and big houses have more chimney pots on which storks may nest.

But flaws in assumptions of causality are not always so easy to spot, especially when the relationship seems to make a lot of sense or when it pleases a popular prejudice.

(Huff, 1973: 83–85).

The message is clear; always treat any statistics, all statistics, with much caution and a great deal of cynicism. As was noted in Chapter 4 on documentary techniques, you always need to think clearly and carefully about the interpretation the person producing the document is trying to convey. The same is true for statistics. Just as a document is constructed to convey a specific message, the same is true for accompanying statistics. This can become a very significant issue if your research work involves reusing secondary statistical data, in that your ambitions for the data set may differ markedly from those of people who originally constructed it. The analysis you want to do, may not be possible from the available data because that particular question was not conceived when the data was collected and originally analysed.

Analysing qualitative data

As has been shown, not all information comes in a numeric form. Text from interviews or from open-ended questionnaire items, or perhaps the mass of data generated from an observational study, also requires careful analysis. How, then, do you deal with such qualitative data? While the specific techniques of data management and analysis may be different, the problem is essentially the same, namely, how do you organise the information so that it is made amenable to future analysis. Exactly how the analysis of qualitative data is conducted often appears to be mysterious or, at least, not clearly articulated.

Some qualitative researchers still consider analysis to be an art form and insist on intuitive approaches to it. We are left with the researchers telling us of classifications and patterns drawn from a welter of field data, in ways that are irreducible or incommunicable. We do not really see how the research got from 3,600 pages of field-notes to the final conclusions, as sprinkled with vivid illustrations as they may be.

(Miles and Huberman, 1994: 2)

Content analysis

One way of addressing the problem is to quantify the data in some way. This 'content analysis' approach involves counting the frequency with which keywords or phrases associated with the main variables appear within the text. You can then present the information in the form of a frequency distribution, table or graph. It takes time to reduce qualitative information in this way, but there are sophisticated software packages such as NUDIST™, which assists you in just such a task.

To take a simple example, coding an open-ended interview question would involve reading and re-reading these individual comments, and from this develop categories for indexing this material. This technique is commonly used where 'open' items occur within an essentially closed questionnaire, or within a structured interview context. Suppose you were to ask colleagues why they decided to study for a diploma in community work. It could be framed as an open-ended question, with respondents being free to answer in their own words. Nevertheless, it should not be too difficult, reading through the range of responses to break them down into five or six key themes. You could then construct a coding sheet with these themes on one axis and the interview numbers on the other, as is illustrated in Table 13.6 below. Using this framework, you could then simply count the number of times each theme was mentioned in an interview.

Table 13.6: Community work interview content analysis coding frame

Theme	Interview number 1	2	3	4	5	6	7	8	9	10	Total
Improve promotion chances	I		I			I	I		II		6
Improve qualification		I		I							2
Financial incentive	I					I			II		4
Broaden working knowledge		I			I		II			I	5
Enhance skill base			I		I		I				3
Intellectual challenge		I					I	I	I		3
Day out of the office						I	I			I	2

The obvious difficulty in 'condensing' data in this way is that you lose something of its essential meaning and richness. Content analysis is, consequently, criticised because it cannot deliver the holistic perspective that is such a crucial part of qualitative research. Again bear in mind that these answers also reflect the particular opinions of a couple of vocal people, namely respondents 7 and 9.

Grounded theory

The grounded theory approach, developed by Glasser and Strauss (1967), takes a much more open and sceptical view of the analysis and interpretation of qualitative data.

Grounded theory proceeds not by imposing a structure on the data, as all quantitative approaches do, but by 'grounding' the categories in the data. The idea is that any structure must come directly from the data, from the concepts and categories used by respondents themselves. It is their interpretation and analysis of their experiences that is crucial: not those imposed by the researcher. Analysis from this perspective is a dynamic process of data reduction, data display, drawing conclusions and verification (Miles and Huberman, 1994). The analysis is not the end product; rather it is an integral and continuous part of the actual research process.

> *From the start of data collection, the qualitative analyst is beginning to decide what things mean – is noting regularities, patterns, explanations, possible configurations, causal flows and propositions. The competent researcher holds these conclusions lightly, maintaining openness and scepticism, but the conclusions are still there, inchoate and vague at first, then increasingly explicit and grounded ...*
>
> (Miles and Huberman, 1994: 11).

Through this process of familiarisation, reflection, conceptualisation, linking and re-evaluation, the researcher develops a 'feel' for the data and the concepts and conclusions 'grounded' therein. Qualitative analysis is not as neat and tidy as quantitative approaches. But then are quantitative analysis frameworks not constructed in a similar fashion, reflecting the researcher's expectations and understandings of the data? Qualitative analysis does not claim to have the same scientific rigour: some of the tales told of qualitative analysis sound more akin to magic than research. Nevertheless, it is a highly fruitful approach and one that has provided invaluable insights and understandings into the operation of the social welfare field.

There is an increasing literature on analysing qualitative data, and some useful texts are included in the reference section at the end of the book. Most offer practical advice on the developing use of computer software for this type of analysis. Delamont (1992) provides the following 'basic rules' checklist that should be borne in mind when working through the analysis of qualitative data:

> *Never let data accumulate without preliminary analysis.*
>
> *Index your data as you go: do not allow the data to pile up without knowing what you have collected.*
>
> *Generate themes and categories as you go along, and review them frequently. It is better to have too many categories which you recombine later than to have too few.*
>
> *Index and code your data densely: do not try to summarize them under just a few themes. Generate as many codes as you can; be 'wild' if you can.*
>
> *Sort your data into files (either physically cutting up copies, or 'cutting and pasting' in the word processor). Keep sorting and reviewing your files, in itself that can be a process of discovery.*

Every now and then stop and think. Do not go on mechanically working on the data without reflecting on where you are going and how you are getting there.

Write analytical memoranda as often as you can. Analytic memos or short notes to yourself and your supervisor in which you review what you are doing, why you are doing it, where you are going next etc.

Every time you make a decision, write it down and put it in your 'methods' file.

Try to enjoy the work. It should be an intellectually engaging and creative exercise, not a chore.

Read other people's work – for ideas, models, parallels, contrasts, metaphors, models, etc.

Read methodological literature properly and think about how it can inform your work. Do not just read it to justify what you are doing anyway!

(Delamont, 1992: 151).

It is also worth saying that most of the above advice also equally applies when conducting quantitative analysis.

Theorising: making sense of findings

It is good medicine, we think, for researchers to make their preferences clear. To know how a researcher construes the shape of the social world and aims to give us a credible account of it is to know our conversational partner – we need to know where each (researcher) is coming from. Each will have diverse views of what is real, what can be known, and how these social facts can be faithfully rendered.

(Miles and Huberman, 1994: 4).

Once the data has been reduced and analysed, by whatever means, you will want to think about what this means in a more general sense. The move from interpreting to theorising about your findings needs time and space. The relationship between theory and research has already been touched on in Chapter 1 when discussing research planning. It is only through theory that you have any notion of what to study, or how to research a particular topic. Theoretical concepts should guide all research decisions. Just as importantly, an understanding of your theoretical position – where you are coming from – helps you avoid the pitfalls of post hoc explanation; inventing a story to fit the facts after the data has been gathered and analysed.

This is not to say that you must have a particular theory in mind, or that theories cannot emerge from data that do not fit existing conceptual models. It does help, however, to be aware of your own epistemological assumptions. Some researchers believe that facts exist independent of the researcher and that all you have to do is to discover this objective reality, much in the same way as you might pick up pebbles from a beach. Others take the view that social reality is constructed and that researcher's create, rather than discover facts. Ask yourself, what your views are and how might they affect how you make sense of any research findings? Being both aware and honest, you will be less likely to ignore facts that challenge your general argument, or give too much credence to those that support your hypothesis. Again this takes you back to the earlier discussion about reflexivity, right at the very start of the book. After all, the crux of all research work, is to add to knowledge and understanding, rather than to distort it for your own ends.

CHAPTER 14

Reporting Research and Presenting Findings

This chapter is designed to ensure that you:
- **Understand the importance of good quality presentation.**
- **Appreciate the range, variety and styles of presentation necessary to address different audiences.**
- **Be aware of the various technical aspects of presentation.**

Introduction

There are at least two major problems when finishing off any piece of research. The first, covered in the previous chapter, is allowing enough time to analyse, understand and then interpret the data. The second, ensuring the results of the study are made available to the appropriate audience, is the focus of this chapter. If either of these tasks is not adequately carried out, then many of the original objectives you set for the research will not be met. This chapter deals with the various aspects of dissemination, which need to be considered in order to address the requirements of different audiences. It also provides an insight into the technical aspects of report writing and making oral presentations.

Presentational issues also have to confront the key tensions that can arise in conducting any research study. Policy makers and practitioners generally like to be presented with clear evidence and conclusions. They may also wish to have certain aspects of the research given greater prominence over other aspects. Researchers, knowing the constraints and limitations of their data, are inclined to be less dogmatic. Consequently, there is often a tension between the researcher and the policy or practitioner client. It is crucial that the researcher maintains their integrity and ensures that the research reflects their views, rather than those who have an influence on the work. In reality, within what is an increasingly politicised work area, the outcomes of any social welfare research are likely to reflect a balance of interests.

To get a feel for such tensions, and to ensure you are aware of the interests of potential research users, it can be helpful to have an advisory group. Many research commissioners now insist that such a body be established, although the title of 'steering group' may indicate an expectation of greater control over the work. Obviously, for some types of research such an approach is not feasible. Whatever the name given to the body, its function is to assist with the execution of the research through offering advice, helping to gain access to data, and in formulating the eventual conclusions. For the researcher it has the added advantage of sensitising a group of informed and potentially influential people to the various nuances of the research work. Through working with such steering or advisory groups you can gain an insight into user perceptions, which can be helpful in framing arguments when writing up. Key themes and issues from the research can be rehearsed and refined through circulating working documents and holding internal presentations. Steering group members, through their contacts, can also help with the establishment of focus groups in the field to plot material during various stages of the research project. Working with such groups can also help greatly in formulating dissemination strategies.

Presentation and dissemination

Organisations paying for research either for their own organisation, other organisations, or the general public, want the results to influence thinking. The presentation of the material and associated dissemination strategy is, therefore, of critical importance. Given this ambition, it is crucial that these issues are considered fully at the planning stage of any research project, as discussed in Chapter 1. Knowing your likely audience will have a bearing on how you focus the study. It also has an influence upon the type of research output you will produce. Having an appreciation of the likely audience largely determines the dissemination strategy.

Given the dominant policy and practice focus of so much social welfare research, presentation and dissemination issues are very important. As such, the issues and considerations are clearly more complex than those that need to be addressed by someone submitting a project on an academic course. In this instance the audience, at least initially, is likely to be no more than two people, and the presentation format will be standardised. When dealing with a larger and, therefore, more diversified audience the nature of both presentation and dissemination alter. The same material may need to be produced in a variety of formats in order to get the results and message over. That said, the principles of clarity, focus and impact should be the same, no matter the audience for the work. Those engaged in personal research endeavours should also appreciate that their work could, and on many occasions does, receive a wider airing. This chapter will provide an appreciation of the diversity of presentational options that need to be considered. We hope that this may assist researchers in the social welfare field engage with a broader range of research presentations in future.

Different forms of presentation

Different audiences require different forms of presentation. A useful example of this is provided by the major study of child protection in the UK (Hallett, 1995; Birchill, 1995).

The dissemination strategy for the results of this comprehensive study was designed to produce an impact, given its significance in terms of influencing policy and practice in this field. As a result, various presentation formats were used to disseminate the findings to as wide an audience as possible. The presentation material included:

- A main research report.
- A comprehensive bibliographic review.
- Summary or précis of the main conclusions and recommendations.
- Ministerial and government committee reports, and associated brief summaries.
- Publications in professional and academic journals.
- A one page press release summarising the main points, given the full report would be of little use to the media.
- Verbal presentations for both internal and external audiences which were provided in a variety of formats (overheads, slides, and video).

Such a range from one piece of research is exceptional, but it does act to illustrate the possibilities that are open to a researcher. It also shows that each of these different audiences demand a different type of presentation. Handing the final research report to a journalist would be of limited use, unless they were a specialist correspondent and had a specific interest in this work. Each of the above addresses a specific audience which has a specialist or general interest in the work. Each is, therefore, written and structured in a specific style. Generating a broad interest in your work by relying solely upon distributing the research report itself may not produce the desired impact.

Appreciating who the audience is has a clear bearing on the type and style of presentation. You might usefully consider the following questions:

- What relationship does the audience have to the research?
- Did parts of the audience write the brief and commission it, or will your publication be the first contact they have with the study?
- Who are the likely 'users' of this research, and how will they utilise the research 'product'?
- What is it they will want to find from your study? Users might be just a few people, or it could well be a wider, more general audience. A general audience would only be interested in the two or three main findings of the study. These could be highlighted by a short press release that comes from the summary of the report's findings.
- Would the specialist audience read the report cover to cover, or will they want to get an idea of what it is about before dipping into the parts they consider to be of relevance to their own particular interests?
- If the research hopes to influence both a professional and academic audience can both interests be accommodated within the one research 'product'?
- Are the audience experts in the field, or do they just have a general knowledge of the topic?

All this has a bearing on the type and style of presentation you adopt when writing up the study. All these questions need to be carefully considered at the planning stage. Knowing your audience and their specific requirements helps focus the research and the resulting presentational material. In some instances, such as with commissioned research, the audience, the focus of the study and the expected outputs will be clearly stated within the original brief. On other occasions you will need to think this aspect through for yourself. In the case of press releases, you have to boil the results down to just two or three main points, which can be typed on one side of A4, usually double-spaced. The old adage that any press release has to cover the who, where, why, what and when issues within the first sentence does hold true. Ensuring that the press release has a contact number, at which you can be found, will allow any interested journalist to follow up and expand the story. On the subject of press releases and dealing with the media, this is a specialist and potentially dangerous area, so advice should be sought. Most organisations will have policies for dealing with the press and larger bodies will employ their own press or media officers.

There is also a requirement on the researchers to be clear about just what they want to get over about the research. What is it that you want to convey to that particular reader? What is it you want them to understand, and how best can this be achieved? The style of writing and the way the material is presented can reveal a lot about the writer and how they conceptualise these key issues. There is undoubtedly a real skill involved in presenting material to best effect, to a variety of audiences.

The production of the research output throws up a number of constraints, or obligations that need to be considered when planning out the research study. Accommodating these issues has a knock-on effect on the actual research timescales.

For example:

- When does the final report need to be presented, and what is the standard expected?
- In order to produce a final report, to an agreed format, what timescales are involved?

Getting a typed final draft into a well designed published report, ready for distribution, can take a great deal of time if designers, typesetters and graphic artists are involved. Production timescales can be short if only a few copies are required, and you control the entire process. The minute you need a large number of copies, production moves into the hands of others and it is harder to keep control of both the time scale and eventual product. Production can also cause other presentational problems. While small production runs can accommodate colour graphics, the cost on larger runs is likely to be prohibitive. Black and white graphics are often dull, and on occasions difficult to read. But they do not necessarily have to be so. Designing your output with the eventual production standards in mind can reduce such difficulties.

The basic points to bear in mind when getting a report designed and printed are:

- Contact at least two typesetters who will need to know whether the whole work needs re-keying, or what computer software you are using, the format for the pages, typestyles and layout considerations such as the number of graphs, boxes, illustrations, tables; they will also need to be asked whether they charge for the whole job or by the page; ask about the likely time scale for providing a proof copy, corrections and a final output.

- Do you need a designer to produce art work for the cover?
- What do you require?
- Ask for quotes based on the specification you come up with.
- Determine the print run; number of pages (the extent); the page size (format); the paper and the cover card to be used, one, two or four colour printing for text and cover, and the type of binding – burst bound, perfect binding, wiro etc.; cover laminated, if required; printers may also need to liaise with the typesetter and/or designer about specifics such as tint boxes and colour separations.
- Ask for estimates from at least two printers, and ask them about turnaround time and delivery arrangements (you certainly don't want ten pallets of books arriving at your front door).
- Don't forget that someone other than yourself will probably be needed for the copy edit (before typesetting) and the proof read (after typesetting) to make sure that spelling and layout conventions are consistent and correct, and that the text has been organised in the most accessible manner.
- If your presentation requires an index, this is best done at the proofing stage, but you may have previously 'tagged' keywords for inclusion in the index.

The above list provides the basis both for a production timetable and the creation of a production budget.

Presenting research results

No matter the type of output, or product, from your research it has to be able to communicate effectively with the intended audience. In essence what you should be seeking to achieve is a conversation with that audience. To promote such a conversation, and to take on board the known requirements of your audience, you need to consider a variety of issues (Orna, 1995). The critical elements you need to highlight in carrying out this task should include:

Showing the structure of the product.

Helping readers find their way around the structure by means of 'signposts' of various kinds.

Directing attention to key points.

Telling readers what they are about to encounter, and summarising what they have just been told (previews and reviews).

Telling the 'story' of the research.

Defining terms.

Presenting relevant material from the sources we have used.

Explaining the methods used in the research.

Presenting sequences and flows of events.

Distinguishing between parts of text which perform different functions.

Presenting the results of research – both qualitative and quantitative.

(Orna, 1995: 114–5).

To accommodate the requirements listed above, you need to think carefully about writing style, structure, layout and the use of graphics in relation to both text and diagrams. The issues involved and how best to address them are well detailed in the above text. Orna (1995) provides an excellent review of presentational issues that need to be considered when trying to get the key information over to the reader. The checklist in Table 14.1, adapted from Orna (1995: 129), illustrates the range of presentational issues that need to be addressed when producing any research product.

Table 14.1: Checklist of information elements

- Headings: 'A' level, 'B' level, 'C' level and 'D' level
- Signposts: index, cross-references, displayed key paragraphs, emphasis within sentences, previews at the start of chapters, recapitulations or summaries at the end of chapters
- Narrative: sentences and paragraphs
- A list of words used indicating spelling; the use of upper and lower case and hyphenation
- Definitions
- Notes on methodology
- Flow-diagrams
- Diagrams
- Illustrations and photographs
- Tables: numeric with text, and those that contain text only
- Copies of questionnaires or interview schedules
- Lists
- Detailed text to supplement main text
- Text commentaries on graphics and tables
- Appendices

Most people have experienced ploughing through a dense and lengthy written report. By thinking through the range of issues outlined above, you will produce a research report, or publication which is accessible, through employing a clear writing style, good layout techniques and the appropriate use of supportive diagrams, tables and illustrations. As the most common output from any research work is the research report, the standard structure of this document is now considered. By focusing on the research report, in more detail, the above issues of audience focus and information components will be illustrated.

Structuring the research report

The basic structure of any research report should be as follows. Obviously, depending on the particular focus of the work this standard structure could be amended. What's important, however, is that a logical sequence is adopted. This incorporates many aspects of the checklist above:

- title with terms of reference and any specific aims and objectives
- contents page
- summary or synopsis
- method of investigation
- facts and findings (body of report)
- conclusions and discussions
- recommendations (if appropriate)
- references
- appendices (if necessary).

The summary or synopsis is very important, for it allows a reader to get a measure of the work quickly. It is also important that the method of investigation is clearly outlined, as it's this that allows the reader to assess the reliability and validity of the findings for themselves. Too often, in research studies, the actual method and approach adopted are not made explicit. If other investigators wish to check or compare your findings with a study of their own, enough information must be available to replicate the work. Hence, it is good practice to ensure that all relevant information on the type and size of the sample; method used to collect data; date and duration of survey; extent of non-response; and degree of accuracy achieved is properly detailed, either in the text, or in an appendix. Some large-scale studies often publish a separate technical report. In essence, all good research reports should provide a detailed description of the survey design. Copies of questionnaire and tabulated results should also be provided in appropriate appendices. Finally, another criticism of some research reports is that they fail to provide the tabular information from which any graphic material has been generated. This tends to be omitted on cost grounds. Yet, without this information it is often impossible to check the assumptions, or interpretations provided by the researcher. The appropriate tabular material should, therefore, also be included within an appendix.

While the research report may be the main output from a study, a number of other more targeted outputs, or products can also be generated. A solid well-considered research report, displaying a clear written presentational style and the appropriate use of visual material, can ensure such re-packaging operations are relatively straightforward, in that the groundwork for these other outputs already exists and does not need to be created.

Clear written presentation

Written text should always be broken down into clear and distinct subsections, which are provided with clear headings and sub-headings. Such 'sign posting' tells the reader where the text is leading and, therefore, what to expect next. Style and language should always be as clear and precise as possible. This can only be achieved through practice.

To aid the reader, a standardised text and layout should be employed. Use should be made of different sizes of fonts to illustrate the variations in the importance of headings. Making use of style formats on word processing packages is a useful help in this regard. Avoid mixing font styles, as this can detract from the overall appearance. While Desk Top Publishing (DTP) software packages have opened up new avenues for presentation, they have also brought with them much bad design which can be very distracting for the reader. In relation to design, always try and ensure a fair degree of white space on the page. Avoid the temptation to drop the point size of the typeface to save paper in final production.

If the document is destined for wide scale distribution, then text should be professionally typeset. The advances in word processing, as discussed in Chapter 12, should ensure a generally good reproduction standard. Typesetting from disk is now common place. That said, there are major difficulties associated with data transfer from one word processing package to another, or from word processing to the software used by the typesetter. These days, typesetters usually expect to receive reports in Word format, produced from a PC, even if they themselves are using Apple Macintosh computers. Tables and other non-standard formats need careful handling. Always check the technical requirements demanded by the production process before you set about producing the final version of the report.

Producing a synopsis

Researchers undertaking commissions for the Joseph Rowntree Foundation (JRF) are contracted to produce a four-page 'Findings' paper, which is then distributed to a wider audience in both printed form and on the Internet. This is now considered to be good practise by most research funders and the following checklist to undertake the task of producing a synopsis is loosely based on the JRFs instructions for 'Findings' authors. Producing a synopsis, for inclusion at the start of a report, also helps readers quickly grasp what the work covers, and can be used for committee report purposes.

- use only a very limited amount of jargon – professional language – or none at all;
- concentrate on describing new knowledge gained from the research
- highlight how the research contributes to any on-going professional debate
- make sure that the findings focus on any aspect and outcomes which are particularly timely

- flag up any unexpected or surprising findings
- adopt a dispassionate and factual style.

This is not a prescriptive list, but it does emphasise a number of important presentational issues, particularly important in producing short summary versions of research results. As the Joseph Rowntree Foundation themselves put it;

> *The Findings approach may dismay those who are more comfortable with the transmission of research results in a traditional, scholarly fashion. The Foundation recognises the danger of oversimplification, but believes the risk is often worth taking if the alternative is failure to get messages across to people who ought to hear them.*
>
> (JRF, 2001, 8–9)

Writing briefly, succinctly and in clear English represents a real challenge for most researchers.

Use of visual illustration

In the past, both cost and the method of reproduction acted to constrain the use of visual material within research reports. Yet, such material can provide valuable evidence to substantiate key arguments within the report. If used well, it can inform and illuminate, thereby avoiding substantial amounts of explanatory text. Graphic material also acts to lighten the overall visual impact of the report. Graphics can, however, be a distraction if they are not properly thought through and well designed. The advent of cheap and more accessible printing systems and the development of high quality graphic technology, through spreadsheets and DTP systems, should ensure a better use of graphic material.

The intended audience for the report, in large part, determines the use of a table or a diagram. Bear in mind that bar charts and other forms of graphic presentation can be very confusing to an untrained eye. To minimise such problems, always ensure that both tables and graphics:

- Are simple and unambiguous.
- Have a clear and concise title.
- Include a statement about the source of data.
- Have column and row headings that are brief and self explanatory.
- Have clearly shown units of measurement.
- Have logical changes in units of approximations.
- Have a layout that emphasises the vertical, not the horizontal.

Finally, always ensure that all graphics are clearly linked and referenced to the text, and are placed at the most appropriate place within the text. The integration of software packages means that it is now easy to place the graphics within the text, rather than adopting the previously unsatisfactory practice of placing them together at the end of a chapter, or in an appendix.

Design should always be viewed as far more than a cosmetic exercise. It is critical to reader understanding. This basic point is now more widely accepted, given the improving quality of so much research material. In particular, the JRF has set a high standard in the way it designs its research outputs. Unfortunately, there are still those who believe that design quality is an expensive irrelevance and continue to produce what are effectively typewritten reports stapled between a couple of bits of coloured card.

Making presentations

While the production of written material is the major output from any research exercise, there is often an expectation that some type of verbal presentation will also be made. This is a typical prerequisite in many research projects. When such a presentation is made at a conference, or workshop it could encourage more people to take an interest in the published material and raise the profile of associated professional issues.

Verbal presentations are different from written reports in a number of important respects. When people read reports, they can either choose to pay attention or not, because they always have the opportunity to re-read. If part of the report is unclear, they can go back over it more slowly, and attempt to puzzle it out. This is not an excuse for sloppy writing, but rather a clear illustration of the advantages of written communication. Yet, when an audience is listening to a presentation, they are denied such advantages. As they generally hear the message only once, they have to pay close attention at all times. While most presentations allow an opportunity to ask questions, often the audience fails to use it, or the time left is limited with only one or two points being taken. That said, it is clearly easier to ask questions of a speaker than a book.

Given these limitations, verbal presentations need to be clear. Prior organisation is a must. The audience, in order to understand the message, must see how the speaker gets from point A to point B, at each section within the presentation. This is no easy task, but there is a systematic way to approach it. The system detailed below will not make your presentations spellbinding, for content and personality are of considerable importance as well. It will, however, ensure that your presentations are focused on an intended audience, that the information is both clear and logically developed and that you do nothing to distract from that message. That said, practice and skill is also required to put that final polish on your presentation.

Preparation

In any presentation you need to grab the attention of the audience early on in the talk. This needs to reassure the audience that they made the right decision in coming to your presentation. In this regard, it is also critical to let the audience know about your credentials to speak on the topic. In any presentation you have about three minutes to convince the audience that you have something important to say. Fail to hit the mark, your audience's attention drifts, and in some cases actually melts away. This initial stage in the presentation can be partly eased by a good clear introduction from the person chairing the session. When asked to provide speaker's notes, don't ignore the request, or quickly scribble something in the taxi to the meeting. Instead, take time to think about what information would enhance your credibility in the eyes of that particular audience.

When thinking through your presentation, try to appreciate what your audience knows about your topic. Do they have any emotional ties to the subject? For example, speaking about anti-social neighbours at a housing conference almost guarantees a polarisation into at least two camps, representing the 'liberal' professionals or the more 'reactionary' tenants and managers. Knowing or suspecting the attitudes of an audience is, therefore, an important consideration. If you can anticipate reactions, you can act to address or defuse them as part of your presentation. This is a skill that transfers well into the organisation of meetings, where problems tend to be rife and fixed attitudes tend to be more easily predicted.

Focus down on the topic

Always check that sufficient time has been allocated for your presentation. Will questioning be permitted during the presentation, or afterwards, and how will this affect the timing of the presentation? The time allocated influences the type of presentation and its focus: a ten-minute 'filler' is vastly different from a two-hour training session.

When organising the information for any presentation, first determine the number of key points you wish to make. These should be either points of information, which you want the audience to understand, or items that support your argument. Ensure each point is distinct, and that each is similar in scope or level of importance.

Having determined the key points, you need to arrange them. As with written communication, this arrangement needs to make sense, not only to you, but also to the audience. While the topic itself may suggest a range of ways to order the main points, you need to decide the arrangement that is best. Starting with the conclusions, and then explaining how you got there is often a better approach than working your way through the contents of a research report to reach the conclusions. Normally, these key points are the basis for your visual aids.

The outline for a presentation should then follow that particular structure. It shapes the detail needed for your presentation. It is important to limit each section of the outline to one idea, using a short phrase to remind you of the specific point you want to make. Always ensure that sections do not overlap, as this will cause audience confusion. The outline should also act as a primer for your presentation notes, so that with practice your notes become redundant.

Focus on the transitions within any presentation. Transitions are the points at which the audience need to follow your train of thought. Introductions and brief summaries act as transitions, for they connect an audience to the topic and also tie the main points and sub-points together. Transitions are also needed to link the key points together. This point was also made previously in relation to written presentations.

Finally, don't overlook conclusions. It is the sharp conclusion that brings a presentation to a successful completion. Too often a presentation comes to an abrupt halt, without the audience knowing whether it had finished or just pausing to get your breath back. If you are running short of time, cut the content, never the conclusion. Presentations that do not conclude merely die.

Types of delivery

There are four possible ways to deliver a presentation, three of which exhibit their own advantages and disadvantages. The final approach, that of the impromptu presentation should never be attempted. Choose a method that makes you feel most comfortable, but always ensure it also produces an effective presentation.

Manuscript: With the manuscript method you essentially read out the paper. It has the advantage of determining the speaker's words beforehand, hence, it minimises concerns about losing the thread, or forgetting what to say next. It also has advantages for rigid time limits, given the entire presentation can be practised until it fits the allotted time. The disadvantage is that without training and practice most people cannot read out loud. Reading a manuscript also limits eye contact with the audience, allowing the audience's attention to wander. While this problem can be overcome by including 'look up' instructions in the manuscript, this does not address all the limitations of the approach.

Memorise: An alternative approach is to memorise the presentation. The advantages are exactly the same as they were for the manuscript method. In addition, memorisation is also good for eye contact with the audience. Unfortunately, the disadvantages are more serious. First, memorising text as any actor will vouch takes a great deal of time. If you find reading aloud difficult, then recitation is likely to be worse. The most serious disadvantage, however, is partial memory loss. For these reasons, memorising a presentation should be avoided.

Extemporaneous: Most speakers opt for what is called the extemporaneous method, which means making a presentation from either an outline and/or associated notes. It has all the advantages of good eye contact, naturalness of language, rhythm, pace, and voice modulation. It does require practice, because it is easy to get caught up in the occasion and either talk too long, or wander off the subject. These disadvantages notwithstanding, you should get into the habit of using the extemporaneous method of presentation delivery most, if not all, of the time.

Impromptu: The impromptu method, that is making it up as you go along, should also be avoided at all cost. You should always prepare a presentation. Those who profess impromptu skills, like the best comedians actually put in a great deal of behind the scenes practice.

Practicing the presentation

Practice is essential for ensuring a successful presentation. The objective should be a conversational delivery, and practice should refine the actual presentation. It is only with practice that you see what works and what does not. After six attempts a presentation is usually quite polished. This means you should:

- Practice out loud.
- Practice the entire presentation, not just key points.
- Practice in front of someone you trust to give you critical feedback.
- Practice in the actual presentation environment, if possible, or in one that is similar.
- Practice using the visual aids.
- Practice hand and body movement and voice modulation.

Bear in mind the stress placed on words by the speaker's voice is important, because it changes the meaning of what is being said, as well as calling attention to particular points in the presentation. Try not to mumble or run words together. This is another reason for avoiding the manuscript method, given that when reading a manuscript, you spend most of the time addressing the table or podium. Volume is also important: everyone in the room must hear you. This is one reason why you should, if possible, examine the presentation environment, before making any presentation. If you have a light voice, or poor vocal projection, you may want to consider an amplification system. In most circumstances stand up to make your presentation, because it creates a greater sense of presence and allows you to breath easier, helping to control your anxiety. When you stand up, get right up on your toes and then slowly slip down to your feet, ensuring you can easily pivot on your hips. This allows you to pivot around on your hips, without affecting your breathing. To calm the nerves, breathe in slowly through your nose and then slowly blow out through your mouth, as if trying to put out a candle. This posture and the breathing exercise will help you to relax as you begin the presentation.

The presentation environment

The actual location of the presentation needs to be carefully considered. If possible, always try to examine the venue prior to making the presentation. Is it a large auditorium, or a small seminar room? How will the audience be seated, theatre-style or around tables? If you are unhappy with the seating plan get it changed, or just roll up your sleeves and do it yourself. Such factors will influence the types of visual aids you may wish to use, as well as your freedom of movement. It may even affect the formality of your presentation.

Take a note of any potentially distracting elements, such as bright sunlight, lawn mowers running outside the window or a humming fluorescent light. Such distractions can make it difficult for you to gain the audience's attention. Most distractions can be tackled or avoided, and in the case of those you cannot do anything about, then at least you are prepared for them. It is also worth knowing what the audience will be doing before and after the presentation. The slot immediately after lunch does not always produce the most attentive audience.

Finally, clarify what arrangements have been made for you, as the speaker. Will there be a podium, a microphone, a table, an overhead projector, slide projector or PowerPoint™ facility? Do you have what you need, and are they all in working condition? You will be nervous anyway, so it is better to avoid unexpected surprises that might enhance your already heightened state of anxiety. Arriving with your presentation on disc, only to find no laptop or projector certainly does get the adrenaline racing. For a detailed review of the issues involved in organising training events or conferences see Dearling (2003). This provides information and checklists on various aspects of conducting training in social welfare settings. It also covers the wide range of training styles that can be employed, through to subsequent evaluation and monitoring of the event.

Using visual aids

Visual aids can play an important role in presentations, but style is not a substitute for content. With the advent of PowerPoint™ the visual aid has come to dominate many presentations. It is not always used to best effect, however. Visual aids should be used to highlight key presentation points. Correctly designed and used, visual aids can support, enliven and assist the audience to better understand the points you are making. If they are to do this, then they must meet certain criteria:

- They must be visible, large enough for the whole audience to see and that includes those people who invariably sit right at the back, even when front seats are spare.
- They must be clear, in that the meaning must be obvious at a glance, without recourse to explanation. Too often the flow of a presentation is marred by the speaker having to explain the overheads, in some detail.
- They must be controllable, that is easy to use at the presentation.

Good visual aids add a polish to any presentation, and to achieve that shine some basic rules should be considered.

Using words and phrases

The words and phrases should always mirror the key topic headings on which the presentation is constructed. They also need to be both short and straightforward. The trick is to make sure the audience does not have to do too much reading; for while they are reading they will not be listening to you. It is common practice for speakers to start by outlining their presentation. This approach orientates the audience to the focus you will be adopting. Given the importance of the first few minutes of any presentation, to get and hold the attention of the audience, this is a useful method to adopt.

Flipcharts

Flipcharts, or marker boards, are popular mediums for informal, small group presentations. Yet, in spite of their popularity, most people misuse them. If you are planning to provide information on a flipchart, during the course of a presentation, write it up prior to the talk and cover it. As you progress through the presentation the information can be revealed at the appropriate time. When you are ready to reveal the information it is important to prime the audience. Let them know what is coming up and why it is important, before you show it to them. Such repetition helps reinforce the key points of the presentation.

Again, writing or graphics must be clear, and neat. Detailed work, even on a large chart, is almost impossible for the audience to see. People seated some distance away from the board will not be able to see what is written. For this reason, flipcharts should be limited to fairly small presentation environments. Finally, if you need to write on the chart as part of a presentation, try to avoid turning your back on the audience. Talking as you write is a guaranteed way of distracting an audience, because they cannot see, nor hear what you say. Successful use of these charts or boards requires a little practice, for it is not as easy as it looks.

Overhead transparencies, slides and videos

Overhead transparencies are a useful means of presenting information to relatively large audiences. By adjusting the projection distance, the image can be made quite large, without a discernible loss of quality. You can overlay transparencies to add information, as the presentation progresses. Another approach is to cover part of them, only revealing the information, as it becomes appropriate to the topic. It is also possible to write directly onto them, but this is not that effective given the act of writing can be highly distracting. Also avoid placing a page of solid typed text, typically copied directly from the report, onto a transparency. The audience cannot and will not read it.

The main disadvantage of these types of visuals is the fact that they can be difficult to manipulate. They have a tendency to stick together, and if you drop them their transparent nature often makes them hard to read and therefore re-order. They are also largely restricted to black and white image, because it is hard to project in colour. To get round this problem you can opt for slides.

Slides are excellent for presenting information to large audiences. They make it possible to organise the entire presentation visually, store it in a carousel, and use it over and over again. They also allow you to introduce other images such as photographs into the presentation. The use of a remote control is another distinct advantage, in that it allows you to move about when giving the presentation. Almost all other visual systems restrict your movement. Video clips are also useful in certain contexts, illustrating a particular statement, attitude or action via a highly visual representation. You do, however, really need to know what you are doing because to produce that professional look takes both time and a certain degree of skill.

Slides and videos work best in a completely darkened room. If you, as the speaker, are not lit then the sound of a voice in the darkness can be off-putting to an audience. A warm room, the darkness and a presentation after lunch can result in many in the audience taking a nap. To get round these potential difficulties break the presentation into segments of six to ten slides, or short series of video clips. In between these segments, bring the lights up and continue with the presentation, focusing on the transitions, and finally the conclusion. This helps to provide a change of pace and avoids the rigidity, or tedium a slide or video presentation might otherwise have. As with all visual material prime the audience and then let them know what you are showing and why you are using it. Repetition acts to reinforce the key points.

PowerPoint

PowerPoint™ has almost become an obligatory means of presenting material at any meeting. In the right hands and with some degree of thought and preparation it can greatly enhance a presentation. In the hands of an enthusiast it can become the presentation. With all the visual and sound tricks, plus the host of backgrounds it is possible for the PowerPoint™ presentation to become a major distraction from the all-important message. If you take on board the points made above, in relation to other visual aids, you should be able to construct a helpful and supportive set of slides. It is again a case of not getting overly caught up with the technology. There is also a major downside with this medium, namely that to be on the safe side you will need to take your own computer equipment, and back up OHP slides just in case. For some reason, someone else's laptop, or projector always seems to fail on the day. Given the stress you are already under, you need to be confident the technology won't let you down.

As will be obvious from what has been said above, there is no one perfect visual aid for all presentations. Each approach has its advantages and disadvantages, both in their ability to present information and, perhaps more importantly, in an individual's ability to use them. Visuals can add greatly to a presentation, but equally they can detract from it, especially if the presenter is uncomfortable with its use. It is, therefore, crucial that you select visual aids that will add to your presentation; that the medium fits into the presentation environment; and, that you feel comfortable with it. Having made the choice, ensure you make time to practice so it runs smoothly.

Time and effort

Hopefully this chapter has illustrated that a great deal can be done to heighten the impact of your research. As with everything in research the potential impacts can only be realised with careful planning. It is, therefore, important to consider early on, to whom and how, the work is to be presented. Knowing your audience will help inform the most appropriate choice of presentation.

Any written presentations should demand not only good writing skills, but also high quality layout and design. Word processing and DTP packages may help, but these require skills that the researcher needs to master. Likewise making live presentations requires an equal amount of planning and skill in using the range of presentational tools, ranging from OHP slides through to PowerPoint™ and videos. If you want to do it well, you need to put in what seems a disproportionate amount of effort. A short 20 minute presentation can involve many hours if not days to ensure it runs perfectly.

A Few Final Thoughts

As in the process of planning and undertaking a research project, this book has been conceived and constructed within a fairly tight structure. The book's beginning, in the quite lengthy introduction, set down broad-brush scenarios and contexts in which social welfare research operates. This was designed to show just how wide ranging and varied social welfare research could be, and illustrate just how core basic research skills are to almost all jobs within the social welfare sector. Part One, explained the vital importance of careful and rigorous planning before going on to discuss the merits and process of contracting out research. Part Two, detailed the various tools employed in the research trade, to undertake a range of different types of research project. Finally Part Three, the *endgame*, offered useful insights into the complexities of analysis and interpretation, before going on to consider the critical task of presenting research findings to a variety of very different audiences.

Along the way, we hope that you have gained a measure of enthusiasm for the research process, in addition to picking up some useful skills and knowledge about the ways in which research, within social welfare settings, can be managed and executed. While the range of detail and diversity covered in the book cannot be easily encapsulated in a brief résumé, we would like to remind the users of the book about some of the key lessons researchers working in welfare settings should heed:

- Research should be undertaken holistically, rather than in a piecemeal manner, as a collection of unrelated stages. Taking plenty of time to engage in adequate planning and preparation cannot be emphasised enough. Get this wrong, and the likelihood is that your research outcomes will be flawed.
- We have frequently used the words 'robust', 'critical' and 'rigorous' to describe the approach you should adopt, at each stage of the research process. This remains our message, along with re-emphasising the need for you to use every opportunity to check and crosscheck each stage of your chosen method, in order to spot and correct any mistakes, or problems as they occur. If there is bias caused by the adoption of a particular approach to data collection, or handling techniques, identify them and either try to put in place strategies that address these problems, or accurately describe these issues in your final write up.
- Whether your research is using quantitative or qualitative methods, the raw material under scrutiny is likely to be real people, living their everyday lives, or trying their best to deliver social welfare services. Wherever possible, social welfare research should

seek to empower these service users and providers. With proper forethought this can be built into the design of research projects using consultation methods such as focus groups.

● Ensuring you have properly considered the range of ethical issues associated with your research work, cannot be overestimated. Take time to fully consider what impact your research will have on those being researched, as well as on those undertaking this work. Utilising new means of data collection, such as through the Internet, are fraught with potential ethical pitfalls, as well as great possibilities. Issues around confidentiality should always be clarified early on in any project. Research should help promote and encourage the provision of better services, not disenfranchise, or add another layer of damage to the lives of possibly marginalised people.

● Researchers should strenuously resist commissioners, or managers of research projects who attempt to 'buy', or influence findings and research conclusions. This is a challenge both to research professionals, and for fieldworkers, who want to engage in the research process.

● Reflexivity is a truly powerful tool in enabling researchers to critically make sense of each stage of the research process. Reflexivity raises an intriguing range of questions:
  – *Why are you doing the research?*
  – *What is it are you trying to achieve?*
  – *How do you personally perceive your various roles in the research process?*
  – *What influence are you having on those you engage with in order to undertake this work?*
  – *What do you personally feel about the subject, and how does this affect your objectivity?*
  – *What does the data tell you about the phenomenon you are studying, what have you learned?*
  – *How do you use your findings to inform your colleagues about the implications for policy, management and practice?*

Experience and reflecting on that experience is critical to the learning process and your own personal development.

Finally, its our hope that your experiences of undertaking social welfare research will be as rewarding for you, and those who you work with, as it has been for us.

Sample Research Brief

Developing a Framework for the Provision of Care in the Community Services to Black and Ethnic Minority Communities

1. Introduction

   Members of the Strategy Group wish to commission research into the development of a framework and action plan aimed at improving access to community care for identified priority client groups from the black and ethnic minority communities. The framework should also incorporate consideration of needs assessment, service design or re-design and service delivery.

2. Background

   The Community Care Plan notes that the need of black and ethnic minority communities should be addressed and prioritised for future action. In addition, the mental health framework has identified a need to improve the sensitivity and effectiveness of services to people from black and ethnic minority communities.

   In October the Social Services Department drafted a research proposal aimed at developing a framework for services for black and minority ethnic people with learning difficulties. Both agencies recognised that there was an under utilisation of services, including supported accommodation, by black and minority ethnic people with learning disabilities. The Community Care Plan identifies barriers associated with language as a major reason for a lack of awareness among black and ethnic minority communities of the services available or how they are accessed. There are also a range of cultural issues which need to be addressed in planning for the delivery of services to these communities.

3. Research Proposal

   This study focuses on four priority community care groups, namely:
   - Learning Disability
   - Elderly
   - Mental Health
   - Carers

   The study should place particular emphasis on the development of a framework for needs assessment, service design or re-design and practical operational lessons for those partners working with these four priority groups.

4. Consultancy Requirements

   The overall objective of the research should be to develop a framework and action plan for improving delivery of future, and access to existing, care in the community and related services for the selected community care client groups within black and ethnic minority communities.

Specifically the work should involve:

- Compilation of a literature review of work looking at the access to community care and related services experienced by black and ethnic minority communities. Evidence relating to recent advance in best practice should be particularly sought;
- Identification of the various prioritised client groups within black and ethnic minority communities (this should include an analysis of location and estimation of numbers);
- Establishing the current level of knowledge, awareness and views of each ethnic minority client group about relevant community care and related services;
- Recording the current uptake of services as a baseline for future monitoring and evaluation;
- Identification of critical areas of unmet need and low take up of services;
- Identification of barriers to accessing existing services;
- Reviewing examples of good practice in delivering services to black and ethnic minority communities in order to encourage take up;
- Developing a framework and action plan for improving the effectiveness of existing services to ensure a flexibility and responsiveness which is sensitive to the particular cultural and religious needs of each client group within the ethnic minority communities;
- Develop a framework for re-designed or new service provision required by individuals and groups within each of the four priority groups. The framework should incorporate needs assessment, service design and delivery (with particular reference to support at home/supported living).

5. Outputs

The principal output of the work will be a report outlining a strategic framework for improving the delivery of care in the community and related housing services to the four priority groups within the black and ethnic minority communities. The framework should provide a practical basis for changing service delivery practice where appropriate, and for prioritising any new measures. The consultant will be expected to submit ten copies of the final report. This should be accompanied by a copy of the report on computer disk, in Word format.

6. Study Management

The consultant, who will be expected to demonstrate a track record of working on black and ethnic minority research projects, will work closely with a small steering group comprised of officers drawn from relevant organisations involved in community care delivery.

The project manager for the study and the main contact person for the consultants will be Marian Black. Day to day management of the project, all methodological development, liaison reporting and presentation will be the responsibility of the consultant. The client, for the purposes of study management will be the Social Services Department.

7. Methods

Apart from an extensive desktop study, the work will involve outreach and focus group work, liaising with various black and ethnic minority groups. In addition, interviews will be conducted with users, carers and service providers.

Strong emphasis should be placed on employing best practice previously established in other related studies. In addition, consultants will be expected to make full use of current and historical data held by members of the Strategy Group.

Of particular importance to the success of the study will be the level of knowledge displayed by consultants of minority languages and black and ethnic minority culture. Consultants will be required to make appropriate arrangements for creating the conditions for effective communication with minority ethnic communities. It will also be necessary for consultants to outline to which ethics code they adhere.

8. Fees

It is anticipated that the cost of the study will not exceed £40,000 inclusive of all costs including surveys, fieldwork, analysis, draft reports, final documents, expenses and VAT. Consultants submitting proposals should use this figure as a yardstick. The fee will be paid on completion of the study or by instalments as agreed with the project manager.

9. Contractual Arrangements

The prospective research contractors will submit a detailed costed proposal, which should contain:

- Details of the proposed methodology;
- A work plan detailing phasing of the research programme and key milestones;
- The names and CV of key personnel who would comprise the study team;
- Clear specification of the individual responsibilities of the study team as well as the time input for each member;
- Clear specification of any information requirements or other input the contractor expects from members of the Strategy Group;
- Detailed fee costings, which should include and identify individual staff costs, fieldwork costs, costs relating to equipment and materials, secretarial costs, travelling and subsistence expenses and any other overhead costs and VAT.

The contract between the Social Services Department (on behalf of the Strategy Group) and the consultant will rest upon an exchange of letters. The Strategy Group will send a letter of appointment to the consultant, which will be accompanied by the terms and conditions applying to the commission. The consultants will then reply, accepting the commission in accordance with these terms and conditions, which form the contract.

10. Study Timescale

It is anticipated that the commission will be placed with the appointment contractor in December and that the project will commence thereafter. A final report should be submitted to the project steering group the following June.

Sample Research Contract

Conditions of Contract for Appointment of Consultants

Contractor's General Responsibility

1. Unless otherwise agreed in writing, the Contractor shall provide the accommodation required for the project.

2. The Contractor shall be responsible for monitoring the progress of the project and preparing a final report. or other form of output by the completion date as specified in the letter of appointment.

3. The project finance, as defined in the letter of appointment, shall be used only for the purpose specified in the letter of appointment and not for any other project or purpose.

4. The Contractor and any consultancy staff employed on the project shall ensure that they have no obligation to any other body under conditions incompatible with *the authority*'s requirements and they may not undertake any other contract which may produce, in the sole opinion of *the authority*, a conflict of interest in relation to the project. The opinion of *the authority* regarding the matter will be final.

5. Before questionnaires, or other forms may be circulated to, or telephone or interview surveys undertaken, with 25 or more commercial or business concerns, voluntary bodies, or local authorities, the Contractor shall obtain the prior written approval of *the authority*. The Contractor shall take into account the extra time required for these additional procedures. Permission is not required for surveys of individuals.

6. The authority's representatives or any person authorised by *the authority* shall be entitled to inspect and review all records and correspondence relating to the project during normal working hours, on reasonable notice given.

7. The Contractor shall submit to *the authority* progress reports (either by verbal presentation or a written report) stating the progress achieved to date at such intervals as *the authority* may specify. The authority may specify the requirement for an oral presentation of the final results by the Contractor to its Departmental Officers.

8. The Contractor is not and shall not hold himself out as being the servant or agent of *the authority* for any purpose other than those expressly conferred by this contract and shall not use *the authority*'s name in relation to the project in any press release, public information or other release of information without the prior written approval of *the authority*. It is specifically prohibited for the Contractor to use *the authority*'s name in any matter or context not directly related to the project.

9. The Contractor and any specialist staff employed on the project shall not accept any fee or any other form of remuneration whatsoever from any third party in relation to the project. The Contractor shall take all appropriate steps to ensure that neither the Contractor nor any consultant or employee is placed in a position where there may be an actual conflict or potential conflict between the financial or personal interests or such persons and the duties owed to *the authority* under the provisions of this contract. The Contractor will disclose to *the authority* full particulars of any such conflict, which may arise. The Contractor will also disclose to *the authority* any interests he/she may have in any other contracts to which *the authority* is a party.

10. The Contractor shall keep *the authority* informed immediately of any delay or anticipated delay, which may occur once the project has commenced. The Contractor shall obtain the prior written approval of *the authority* to any change in the time limits or expenditure limits.

11. The Contractor shall keep the estimates of the cost of the project under review throughout. In the event of the estimates being exceeded or likely to be exceeded, the Contractor shall notify *the authority* immediately in writing, stating any revised estimate and an explanation for the proposed increase. The limit of *the authority*'s liability shall not be exceeded without its prior written approval. For the avoidance of doubt *the authority* shall not be liable for any expenditure incurred without its prior written approval first having been obtained by the Contractor.

Equipment

12. Equipment such as computers and software as well as books and other similar material required for furtherance of the project and purchased with project funds shall be deemed to be the property of *the authority*. On satisfactory completion of the project, arrangements for disposal of the said equipment shall be agreed with *the authority*.

Research Findings

13. The copyright of all outputs, to include data and research findings, reports, information programmes and data provided, and the format in which the results are produced for the project, shall be the property of *the authority* otherwise agreed in writing by *the authority*. All information provided by *the authority*, for the purpose of the study, shall be returned to *the authority* on completion of the project.

14. The data, research findings reports, programmes and any other material related to the project shall not be communicated or reproduced, in whole or in part, by the contractor, or any party, to any third party without *the authority*'s prior written approval. The Contractor shall not communicate, with the media or any other third person, about the work carried out for the project nor publish the results of the project in any report or article without prior written consent of *the authority*, which consent shall not be unreasonably withheld.

15. The authority shall be entitled to use the outputs and the form in which results are produced in any way in which it sees fit, and to authorise or assign other such rights or uses as *the authority* in its sole discretion considers appropriate. The Contractor shall not be entitled to receive any additional payment in respect of any such use.

Staffing

16. Only persons with the appropriate qualifications, expertise, skill, care and diligence in carrying out projects of a similar size and scope and complexity to the project and capable of carrying out efficiently the duties to be undertaken by them shall be employed by the Contractor in the research team on the project.

17. The Contractor shall inform *the authority* in writing of any intended changes in the project team personnel from that specified in the Contractor's tender/proposal document.

Early Termination of Appointment

18. If any of the conditions of contract contained in these presents are not complied with, *the authority* shall be entitled to terminate the Contract. Without prejudice to the foregoing generality *the authority* reserves the right to terminate the contract if the Contractor submits on more than one occasion, material to *the authority* of a quality which does not meet its requirements, of which *the authority* shall be the sole judge. It is further specified that the following conduct (which is not exhaustive) by the Contractor shall result in the immediate termination of the contract:

    - Submission of false invoices.
    - Unauthorised publication of project findings.
    - Excessive delay in providing reports to *the authority*.
    - Use of unqualified staff on the project.
    - Non-approved use of project funds.
    - Plagiarism.
    - Bankruptcy or insolvency.

19. In the event of early termination of the Contract:
    (a) The Contractor shall be deemed to be in breach of contract and shall forthwith cease the work on the project.
    (b) The authority shall retain any sum of whatever nature due to the Contractor and shall be under no obligation to make any further payment to the Contractor. When *the authority* has assessed the cost, damage, and loss incurred as a result of the early termination of the contract, it shall be entitled to deduct the full amount of such cost, damage and loss from the total sum due to the Contractor and the payment of any balance after such deduction shall be in full and final settlement of all debt owed by *the authority* to the Contractor. In the event that such cost, damage and loss exceeds the total sum due to the Contractor, *the authority* shall be entitled to recover the difference, as a debt owed by the Contractor to *the authority*.
    (c) The authority shall not be liable for damages in respect of any loss of fees which the Contractor might have been expected to earn.
    (d) Where *the authority* is satisfied that there is evidence of misapplication of project finances by the Contractor, *the authority* shall be entitled to recover such monies from the Contractor.

20. Where *the authority* is satisfied that there is evidence of misapplication of project finances by the Contractor, but where the appointment is not terminated, *the authority* shall be entitled to deduct such monies from future payments due to the Contractor.

Breach of Contract

21. Breaches of the general conditions above or of any of the other conditions contained in these presents are material Breaches of Contract.

Disputes

22. In the event of any dispute arising between *the authority* and the Contractor the same shall be referred to mediation by either party in accordance with the mediation procedures laid down by the Law Society. In the event of the parties failing to reach agreement through mediation, other than on a matter where the decision of *the authority* under this Contract is final and conclusive, then the dispute or difference shall be referred to a single Arbiter to be mutually agreed between the parties to this Contract, or if the parties are unable to agree on the appointment of an Arbiter, chosen by the President of the Law Society for the time being. on the application of either party. The cost of referral to such mediation or arbitration shall be borne equaliy between the parties.

Governing Laws

23. These will be construed and all rights and obligations hereunder shall be regulated according to the Law of England and Wales.

Interpretation

24. In these presents, words imparting the singular shall include the plural and vice versa and words imparting the masculine shall include the feminine and vice versa.

Indemnity

25. The Contractor shall ensure that all consultants or sub-contractors or others employed on or in connection with the project are paid timeously and the Contractor shall keep *the authority* indemnified from and against all actions, proceedings, claims, losses, expenses and damages occasioned by any breach by the Contractor of any obligation, undertaking or stipulation.

Bibliography

Adelman, C. et al. (1977) Re-Thinking Case Study: Notes From The Second Cambridge Conference. *Cambridge Journal of Education*. 6: 139–50.

Allen, C. (1996) What's Wrong With The 'Golden Rule'? Conundrums of Conducting Ethical Research in Cyberspace. *Information Society*. 12: 2, 175–87.

Allen, J. (1995) *Surviving the Registration and Inspection Process*. London: Pitman Publishing.

Anderson, I. (2003) Synthesizing Homelessness Research: Trends, Lessons and Prospects. *Journal of Community and Applied Social Psychology*. 13: 197–205.

Anderson, I. and Christian, J. (2003) Causes of Homelessness in the UK: A Dynamic Analysis. *Journal of Community and Applied Psychology*. 13: 105–18.

Anderson, I. and Morgan, J. (1997) *Social Housing for Single People: A Study of Local Policy and Practice*. Stirling: University of Stirling.

Anderson, I. and Sim, D. (Eds.) (2000) *Social Exclusion and Housing: Context and Challenges*. Coventry: Chartered Institute of Housing.

Anderson, I. and Tulloch, D. (2002) *Pathways Through Homelessness: A Review of The Research Evidence*. Edinburgh: Scottish Homes.

Anderson, S. (1999) Quantitative Indicators of Crime in Scotland. in Duff, P. and Hutton, N. (Eds.) *Criminal Justice in Scotland*. Aldershot: Ashgate.

Anderson, S., Brownlie, J. and Murray, L. (2002) *Disciplining Children: Research With Parents in Scotland*. Central Research Unit Research Paper. Edinburgh: Scottish Executive.

Armstrong, C., Hill, M. and Secker, J. (1998) *Listening to Children*. London: Mental Health Foundation.

Armstrong, C., Hill, M. and Secker, J. (2000) Young Peoples Perception of Mental Illness. *Children and Society*. 11: 60–72.

Arnstein, A. with Billari, F., Mazucco, S. and Ongaro, F. (2002) Leaving Home: A Comparative Study of ECHP Data. *Journal of European Social Policy*. 12: 4, 259–75.

Audit Commission (2002) *About Housing Inspection*. London: Audit Commission.

Bales, R. (1970) *Personality and Interpersonal Behaviour*. London: Holt, Rinehart and Winston.

Ball, M., Harloe, M. and Martins, M. (1988) *Housing and Social Change in Europe and The USA*. London, Routledge.

Banks, S. and Williams, R. (1999) The Personal and The Professional: Perspectives From European Social Education Students. *Social Work in Europe*. 6: 3, 52–60.

Baptista, I. and Perista, P. (1999) Getting to Grips With Comparative Research in Social Sciences. *Social Work in Europe*. 6: 2, 47–50.

Becker, H. (1998) *Tricks of the Trade. How You Think About How You Research While Doing it*. Chicago: University of Chicago Press.

Becker, H. (1967) Whose Side Are We On? *Social Problems*. 14: 239–97.

Bell, J. (1993) *Doing Your Research Project: A Guide to First Time Researchers in Education and Social Sciences.* Buckingham: Open University Press.

Berger, P. and Luckmann, T. (1967) *The Social Construction of Reality.* London: Allen Lane.

Birchall, J. (1997) *The International Co-operative Movement.* Manchester: Manchester University Press and The International Co-operative Alliance.

Birchill, E. with Hallett, C. (1995) *Working Together in Child Protection: Report on Phase Two, A Survey of The Experiences and Perceptions of Six Key Professionals.* London: HMSO.

Bland, R. (Ed.) (1996) *Developing Services for Older People and Their Families.* London: Jessica Kingsley.

Blickman, T. (1998) *Caught in the Crossfire: Developing Countries, The UNDCP and The War on Drugs.* London: Transnational Institute and The Catholic Institute for International Relations.

Blumer, H. (1969) *Symbolic Interactionism.* New Jersey: Prentice-Hall.

Boddy, M. and Snape, D. (1995) *The Role of Research in Local Government.* Wokingham: Local Authorities Research and Intelligence Association.

Bolland, J. (2003) Hopelessness and Risk Behaviour Among Adolescents Living in High-Poverty Inner-City Neighbourhoods. *Journal of Adolescence.* 26: 2, 145–58.

Booth, C. (1889) *The Labour and Life of The People.* London: Macmillan.

Borg, W. (1981) *Applying Educational Research.* New York: Longman.

Bottomly, A. and Colman, C. (1981) *Understanding Crime Rates: The Police and Public Roles in The Production of Official Statistics.* Farnborough: Gower.

Bowes, A. and Domokos, T. (1998) Negotiating Breast-Feeding: Pakistani Women, White Women and Their Experiences in Hospital and Home. *Sociological Research Online.* 3:3, September http://www.socresonline.org.uk

Box, S. (1971) *Deviance, Reality and Society.* London: Holt, Rinehart and Winston.

Brent, J. (2001) Trouble and Tribes: Young People and Community. *Youth and Policy.* 73: 1–19.

British Standards Institution (1978) *Citing Publications by Bibliographical References.* London: BSI.

Bromley, D. (1986) *The Case Study Method in Psychology and Related Disciplines.* New York: Wiley.

Bryman, A. and Cramer, C. (1990) *Quantitative Data Analysis for Social Scientists.* London, Routledge.

Bulmer, M. (1984) *Introduction to Social Science Research Methods.* Basingstoke: Macmillan.

Centre for Policy on Ageing (1984) *Home Life: A Code of Practice for Residential Care – Report of The Working Party.* London: Centre for Policy on Ageing.

Clapham, D. et al. (Eds.) (1996) *Housing Privatisation in Eastern Europe.* Westport, Ct: Praeger.

Clark, M. and Dearling, A. (1986) *Leaving Home: A Training Manual for Workers with Young People.* Glasgow and London: Scottish IT Resource Centre and The Scots Group.

Clark, S. (2000) Talkin' 'Bout Regeneration *UK Youth.* 102: 34–5

Clasen, J. (1999) *Comparative Social Policy: Concepts, Theories and Methods.* Oxford, Oxford University Press.

Cole, I., Hickman, P. and Reid, B. (1999) *Accounting for the Uncountable: Tenant Participation in Housing Modernisation.* Coventry: Chartered Institute of Housing for the Joseph Rowntree Foundation.

Coleman, C. and Moynihan, J. (1996) *Understanding Crime Data: Haunted by the Dark Figure.* Buckingham: Open University Press.

Combe, V. (2002) *Getting Young People Involved in Local Government.* London: National Youth Agency.

Communities Scotland (2001) *Performance Standards.* Edinburgh: Communities Scotland, COSLA and SFHA.

Conners, C. and Stalker, K. (2003) *The Views and Experiences of Disabled Children and Their Siblings: A Positive Outlook.* London: Jessica Kingsley.

Crossman, R. (1976) *Diaries of a Cabinet Minister.* London: Holt, Rinehart and Winston.

Dearling, A. (1979) The Use of Recording in Intermediate Treatment. *Rapport*, May.

Dearling, A. (1998) Editorial: Drugs in Europe Special Issue. *Social Work in Europe.* 5: 2, i–ii.

Dearling, A. (2003) *Organising Successful Learning Events.* Lyme Regis: Russell House Publishing.

Dearling, A. (1997/8) Bert's Story. *Criminal Justice Matters.* 30: 30–1.

Dekel, R., Peled, E. and Spiro, S. (2003) Shelters for Houseless Youth: A Follow-Up Evaluation. *Journal of Adolescence.* 26: 2, 201–12.

Delamont, S. (1992) *Fieldwork in Educational Settings: Methods, Pitfalls and Perspectives.* London: Falmer.

Denzin, N. (1978) *The Research Act in Sociology.* London: Butterworth.

Denzin, N. (1983) Interpretive Interaction. in Morgan, G. (Ed.) *Beyond Method: Strategies for Social Research.* Beverly Hills, Ca: Sage.

Dey, I. (1993) *Qualitative Data Analysis: A User-Friendly Guide for Social Scientists.* London: Routledge.

Doling, J. (1997) *Comparative Housing Policy: Government and Housing in Advanced Industrialised Countries.* Basingstoke: Macmillan.

Dotchin, J., Davies, M. and Muhlemann, A. (1995) *An Interactive, New Media Tool for User Satisfaction Research.* Elland: Viewpoint Organisation.

Duff, P. and Hutton, N. (1999) *Criminal Justice in Scotland.* Aldershot: Ashgate.

Edgar, B., Docherty, J. and Meert, H. (2002) *Access to Housing: Homelessness and Vulnerability in Europe.* Bristol: Policy Press.

Eichler, M. (1988) *Nonsexist Research Methods: A Practical Guide.* Boston: Allen and Unwin.

Eley, S. et al. (2002) *The Glasgow Drug Court in Action: The First Six Months.* Edinburgh: The Scottish Executive.

Englander, D. and O'Day, R. (Eds.) (1995) *Retrieved Riches: Social Investigation in Britain, 1840–1914.* Buckingham: Open University Press.

Fielding, J., and Gilbert, M., (2000) *Understanding Social Statistics.* London: Sage.

Fielding, N. (1993) Qualitative Interviewing. in Gilbert, N. (Ed.) *Research Social Life.* London: Sage.

Fitzpatrick, S. (1999) *Pathways to Independence: The Experience of Young Homeless People.* Edinburgh: Scottish Homes.

Fowler, F. (1988) *Survey Research Methods.* Newbury Park, Ca: Sage.

Foyer Foundation (1998) *Foyers and Social Services: Working Together to Support Young People Leaving Care.* London: Foyer Foundation.

France, A. and Crow, I. (2001) *CTC: The Story So Far: an Interim Evaluation of Communities That Care.* York: York Publishing Services.

France, R. (2000) *Youth Researching Youth: The Triumph and Success of the Peer Research Project.* York and Leicester: Joseph Rowntree Foundation and National Youth Agency.

Gahan, C. and Hannibal, M. (1998) *Doing Qualitative Research Using QSR NUD.IST*. London: Sage.

Garland, D. (1990) *Punishment and Modern Society: A Study in Social Theory*. Oxford: Oxford University Press.

Garland, D. (2001) *The Culture of Control: Crime and Social Order in Contemporary Society*. Oxford: Oxford University Press.

Gayle, V. (2000) Descriptive Statistics. in Burton, D. *Research Training for Social Scientists*. London: Sage.

Gayle, V. (2000) Quantitative Data Analysis. in Burton, D. *Research Training for Social Scientists*. London: Sage.

Gelsthorpe, L., and Morris, A. (Eds.) (1990) *Feminist Perspectives in Criminology*. Milton Keynes: Open University Press.

Glasser, B., and Strauss, A. (1967) *The Discovery of Grounded Theory: Strategies for Qualitative Research*. New York: Aldine Publishing.

Gonzalez-Block, M. (1998) Comparative Research and Analysis for Shared Learning From Health System Reforms. *International Clearing House of Health System Reform Initiatives*. Web Site http://www.insp.mx/ichsri/ch/

Gordon, D. et al. (2003) *Poverty and Social Exclusion in Britain*. York: Joseph Rowntree Foundation.

Green, A. Maguire, M. and Canny, A. (2002) *Keeping Track: Mapping and Tracking Vulnerable Young People*. Bristol: The Policy Press.

Gupta, H. and Docherty, M. (1998) *Quality Management Auditing*. Norwich: Gupta Consultancy.

Hakim, C. (1983) Research Based on Administrative Records. *Sociological Review*. 31: 3, 489–519.

Hakim, C. (1987) *Research Design: Strategies and Choices in the Design of Social Research*. London: Allen Unwin.

Hallett, C. (1995) *Interagency Co-Ordination in Child Protection*. London: HMSO.

Hallet, C. and Hazel, N. (1998) *The Evaluation of Children's Hearings in Scotland, Volume 2, The International Context: Trends in Juvenile Justice and Child Welfare*. Edinburgh: Scottish Office Central Research Unit.

Hantrais, L. (1996) *Comparative Research Methods: Social Research Update*. Guildford: University of Surrey.

Harloe, M. and Martens, M. (1984) Comparative Housing Research. *Journal of Social Policy*, 13: 3, 255–327.

Haywood, P. and Wragg, E. (1978) *Evaluating the Literature, Ready Guide 2: Guides in Educational Research*. Nottingham: University of Nottingham, School of Education.

Heidenheimer, A. (1990) *Comparative Public Policy: The Politics of Social Choice in America, Europe, and Japan*. New York, St. Martin's Press

Heritage, J. (1984) *Garfinkel and Ethnomethodology*. Cambridge: Policy Press.

Hetherington, R. et al. (1997) *Protecting Children: Messages From Europe*. Lyme Regis: Russell House Publishing.

Hine, C. (2000) *Virtual Ethnography*. London: Sage.

Hobbs, D. (1988) *Doing the Business*. Oxford: Oxford University Press.

Holdsworth, C. and Solda, M. (2002) First Housing Moves in Spain: An Analysis of Leaving Home and First Housing Acquisition. *European Journal of Population*. 18: 1, 1–19.

Holman, B. (2000) *Kids at The Door Revisited.* Lyme Regis: Russell House Publishing.

Honville, G. et al. (1987) *Survey Research Practice.* London: Heineman.

Howard, M. (1989) *Contemporary Cultural Anthropology.* 3rd edn, London: Harper Collins.

Huff, D. (1973) *How to Lie With Statistics,* London, Penguin.

Hughes, R. (1997) Foreword. in Hetherington, R. et al. *Protecting Children: Messages From Europe.* Lyme Regis, Russell House Publishing.

Illingworth, N. (2001) The Internet Matters: Exploring The Use of The Internet as A Research Tool. *Sociological Research Online.* 6: 2. *http://www.socresonline.org.uk/6/2/illingworth.html*

James, A., Jenks, C. and Prout, A. (1998) *Theorising Childhood.* Cambridge: Polity Press.

Jones, R. (1994) The Ethics of Research in Cyberspace. *Internet Research.* 4: 3, 30–5.

Jones, S. (Ed.) (1999) *Doing Internet Research: Critical Issues and Methods for Examining The Net.* London: Sage.

Joseph Rowntree Foundation (1997) *Research and Development Programme: General Notes to Researchers.* York: Joseph Rowntree Foundation.

Joseph Rowntree Foundation (2001) *Producing Findings.* York: Joseph Rowntree Foundation.

Kemeny, J. and Lowe, S. (1998) Schools of Comparative Housing Research. From Convergence to Divergence. *Housing Studies.* 13: 2, 161–76.

Kemeny, J. (1992) *Housing and Social Theory.* London: Routledge.

Kemp, P. and Rugg, J. (2001) Young People, Housing Benefit and The Risk Society. *Social Policy and Administration.* 35: 6, 688–700.

Kemp, P., Anderson, I. and Quilgars, D. (1993) *Single Homeless People.* London: HMSO.

Kennett, P. and Marsh, A. (Ed.) (1999) *Homelessness: Exploring The New Terrain.* Bristol: The Policy Press.

Kessing, R. (1981) *Cultural Anthropology.* New York: CBS College Publishing.

Kinnear, P. and Gray, C. (1999) *SPSS for Windows Made Simple.* Hove: Psychology Press.

Kinsey, A. et al. (1948) *Sexual Behaviour in The Human Male.* Philadelphia: W.B. Saunders.

Kirby, P. (1999) *Involving Young Researchers: How to Enable Young People to Design and Conduct Research.* York: York Publishing Services for the Joseph Rowntree Foundation.

Krueger, R. (1994) *Focus Groups: A Practical Guide for Applied Research.* London: Sage.

Lacey, C. (1971) *Hightown Grammar: The School as a Social System.* Manchester: Manchester University Press.

Lindstein, T. (1996) *Working With the Children of Alcoholics.* Stockholm: University of Stockholm.

Lloyd, T. (2002) *Understanding Young Men Preparing for Work: A Report for Practitioners.* York: Joseph Rowntree Foundation and York Publishing Services.

Lodge, D. (1981) *The British Museum is Falling Down.* London: Penguin.

Lofland, J. and Lofland, L. (1984) *Analysing Social Settings: A Guide to Qualitative Observation and Analysis.* Belmont, Ca: Wadsworth.

Mack, J. and Lansley, S. (1983) *Poor Britain.* London: George Allen and Unwin.

Maginn, A. et al. (2000) *Stepping Stones: an Evaluation of Foyers and Other Schemes Serving The Housing and Labour Needs of Young People.* London: HMSO.

Maguire, M. (1994) Crime Statistics, Patterns and Trends: Changing Perceptions and Their Implications. in Maguire, M., Morgan, R. and Reiner, R. (Eds.) *The Oxford Handbook of Criminology.* Oxford: Clarendon.

Marlow, A. and Pearson, G. (Eds.) (1999) *Young People, Drugs and Community Safety.* Lyme Regis: Russell House Publishing.

Martin, C. (Ed.) (1997) *The ISTD Handbook of Community Programmes for Young Juvenile Offenders.* Winchester: Waterside Press.

Marwick, A. (1977) *Introduction to History.* (Units 3, 4 and 5 of A101, Arts Foundation Course) Buckingham: Open University.

Matza, D. (1969) *Becoming Deviant.* New Jersey: Prentice-Hall Orwell.

May, T. (1997) *Issues in Social Research: Issues, Methods and Process.* Buckingham: Open University Press.

McColgin, G., Valentine, J. and Downs, M. (2002) Concluding Narratives of a Career with Dementia: Accounts of Iris Murdoch at Her Death. *Ageing and Society.* 20: 1, 97–109.

McManus, S. (2003) *Sexual Orientation Research Phase 1: A Review of Methodology Approaches.* Scottish Executive Social Research Paper. Edinburgh: Scottish Executive.

Miles, M. and Huberman, M. (1994) *Qualitative Data Analysis.* 2nd edn. London: Sage.

Mitchell, C. (1983) Case and Situation Analysis. *Sociological Review.* 31: 2, 187–211.

Moser, C. and Kalton, G. (1983) *Survey Methods in Social Investigation.* 2nd edn. London: Heinemann.

Mukerjee, S., Beresford, B. and Sloper, P. (1999) *Unlocking Key Working: an Analysis and Evaluation of Key Worker Services for Families With Disabled Children.* Bristol: The Policy Press.

Murray, K. French Concept Inspires Confidence. *Housing Association Weekly.* 24th November.

Nachmias, C. and Nachmias, D. (1996) *Research Methods in The Social Sciences.* 5th edn. London: Arnold.

Newburn, T. (Ed.) (2003) *Handbook of Policing.* Cullompton, Devon: Willan Publishing.

O'Conner, H. and Madge, C. (2001) Cyber-Mothers: Online Synchronous Interviewing Using Conference Software. *Sociological Research Online.* 5, 4. *http://www.socresonline.org.uk/5/4/o'conner.html*

Office for National Statistics (2000) *Guide to Official Statistics: 2000 Edition.* London: The Stationery Office.

Orna, E. with Stevens, G. (1995) *Managing Information for Research.* Buckingham: Open University Press.

Pantazis, C., Townsend, P. and Gordon. D. (2000) *The Necessities of Life in Britain.* Poverty and Social Exclusion Survey of Britain Working Paper No. 1. Bristol: Townsend Centre for International Poverty Research, University of Bath.

Parsons, T. and Bales, R. (1955) *Family: Socialisation and Interaction Processes.* New York: Free Press.

Platt, J. (1981) Evidence and Proof in Documentary Research. *Sociological Review.* 29: 1, 31–66

Pretty, J. (1995) *Trainer Manual for Participatory Learning and Action.* London: International Institute for Environment and Develoment.

Prince's Trust (2003) *Breaking The Barriers: Reaching The Hardest to Reach.* London: The Prince's Trust.

Pugh, R. (2000) *Rural Social Work.* Lyme Regis: Russell House Publishing.

Ravn, I. (1991) What Should Guide Reality Construction? in Steier, F. (Ed.) *Research and Reflexivity.* London: Sage.

Rimmel, A. (1988) *Ethics and Values in Applied Social Research.* London: Sage.

Robertson, D. (1997) *People's Palaces: A History of Glasgow Community-Based Housing Associations.* Glasgow: Glasgow 1999 and The Glasgow and West of Scotland Forum of Housing Associations.

Robertson, D. and Bailey, N. (1996) *Review of the Impact of Housing Action Areas.* Edinburgh: Scottish Homes.

Robertson, D. and Rosenberry, K. (2001) *Home Ownership With Responsibility: Practical Governance Remedies for Britain's Flat Owners.* York: Joseph Rowntree Foundation.

Robertson, D. and McLauglin, P. (1996) *Looking Into Housing: A Practical Guide to Housing Research.* Coventry: Chartered Institute of Housing.

Robson, P., Begum, N. and Locke, M. (2003) *Developing User Involvement: Working Towards User-Centred Practice in Voluntary Organisations.* Abingdon: Policy Press.

Rogers, P. (1999) *Challenging Transitions: Young People's Views and Experiences of Growing Up.* London: Save The Children.

Rokach, A. and Orzeck, T. (2003) Coping With Loneliness and Drug Use in Young Adults. *Social Indicators Research.* 61: 3, 259–83.

Rosenberg, M. (1965) *Society and Adolescent Self-Image.* Princeton: Princeton University Press.

Rowntree, D. (1981) *Statistics Without Tears.* London: Penguin.

Rudgley, R. (1993) *The Alchemy of Culture: Intoxicants and Society.* London: British Museum Press.

Ruxton, S. (1996) *Children in Europe.* London: NCH-Action for Children.

Sandford, J. (1967) *Cathy Come Home.* London: Pan.

Sandford, J. (1971) *Down and Out in Britain.* London: Peter Owen.

Schuller, T. (1988) Pot-Holes, Caves and Lotus Land: Some Observations on Case Study Research. in Burgess, R. (Ed.) *Studies in Qualitative Methodology.* Vol 1, London: Jai Press.

Scottish Executive (2002) *Know The Score Drug Strategy Set Out.* Edinburgh: Scottish Executive.

Selwyn, N. and Robson, K. (1998) Using Email as A Research Tool. *Social Research Update.* 21. Guildford: University of Surrey. *http://www.Soc.Surrey.Ac.Uk/Sru/Sru2.Html*

Smith, J., Gilford, S. and O'Sullivan, A. (1998) *The Family Background of Homeless Young People.* London: Family Policy Studies Centre.

Smith, S., McGuckin, A. and Knill-Jones, R. (Eds.) (1991) *Housing for Health.* Harlow: Longman.

South, N. (Ed.) (1999) *Drugs, Cultures, Controls and Everyday Life.* London: Sage.

Spradley, J. (1979) *The Ethnographic Interview.* London: Holt, Rinehart and Wilson.

Stevens, A., Bur, A. and Young, L. (2003) People, Jobs, Rights and Power: The Roles of Participation in Combating Social Exclusion in Europe. *Community Development.* 2: 28.

Strauss, A. and Corbin, J. (Ed.) *Grounded Theory in Practice.* London: Sage.

Stroh, M. (2000) Using NUD.IST Version 4: A Hands-On Lesson. in Burton, D. (Ed.) *Research Training for Social Scientist.* London: Sage.

Sutton, C. (1987) *A Handbook of Research for The Helping Professions.* London: Routledge and Kegan Paul.

Tesch, R. (1990) *Qualitative Research: Analysis Types and Software Tools.* London: Falmer.

Townsend, P. (1979) *Poverty in The United Kingdom.* London: Allen Lane.

Turner, H. and Butler, M. (2003) Direct and Indirect Effects of Childhood Adversity on Depressive Symptoms in Young Adults. *Journal of Youth and Adolescence.* 32: 2, 89–103.

Turner, M., Brough, P. and Williams-Finlay, R. (2003) *Our Voice in Our Future: Service Users Debate The Future of The Welfare State.* York: York Publishing Services for the Joseph Rowntree Foundation.

United Nations (2000) *Human Development Report 2000.* New York: United Nations Development Program.

Valli, (1986) Quoted in Delamont, (1992) *Fieldwork in Educational Settings: Methods Pitfalls and Perspectives.* London: Falmer.

Vaughan, J. (1982) Searching The Literature: Additional Sources of Information and How to Keep Up to Date. in Hartnett, A. (Ed.) *The Social Sciences in Educational Studies: A Selective Guide to The Literature.* London: Heinemann.

Vazsonyi, A. and Pickering, L. (2003) The Importance of Family and School Domains in Adolescent Deviance: African American and Caucasian Youth. *Journal of Youth and Adolescence.* 32: 2, 115–28.

Wade, J. (2002) *Missing Out: Young Runaways in Scotland.* Stirling: Aberlour Child Care Trust.

Webster, D. (2002) Lone Parenthood: Two Views and Their Consequences. in Anderson, I. and Sim, D. *Social Exclusion and Housing: Context and Challenges.* Coventry: Chartered Institute of Housing.

Webster, F. (1995) *Theories of The Information Society.* London: Routledge.

Williamson, H. and Butler, I. (1995) No One Ever Listens to Us. in Cloke, C. and Davies, M. (Eds.) *Participation and Empowerment in Child Protection.* London: Pitman Publishing and NSPCC.

Young, I. (1991) *Justice and The Politics of Difference.* Princeton NJ: Princeton University Press.